AF434746

Important Note:

In this book there are a number of Military terms and abbreviations, both British and American, as well as French, which the casual (civilian) reader may be unfamiliar with.

To enhance the reader's understanding, there is a Glossary at the rear, and terms to be found there are marked with a subscript "g" the first time they appear in the book.

POP'S WAR

"Cy Manierre – A real soldier, a real hero, and a real gentleman I was privileged to know.

Irwin J. "Russian" Stovroff

"A very brave man who served his country as an OSS[g] Officer. He was highly respected at Stalag-Luft 1. He set an excellent example for the other POWs and the German Officers."

Roger Armstrong – Author of **USA The Hard Way**

"Great book! Pleased to be a part. I'll never forget Cy. What a great officer and person he was. God bless his soul.

Sincerely, "Gabby" F.S. Gabreski

"He was obviously a hell of a good soldier. His story was like one out of a spy novel… he was a very tough guy. "

George McCafferty

"...an extraordinary man: Major Menieres *(Manierre)*, who also fell from the sky *(parachuted)* … With the active assistance of Major Menieres, who is never so happy as when he makes a noise and demolishes something ..."

1945 French magazine: AUX ARMES !

"That should be a movie."

(From a friend)

POP'S WAR

Behind Enemy Lines with
the French Resistance in
Occupied France, 1944

Major Cyrus E. Manierre

Code name "Rupert"
Jed Team DODGE
OSS$_g$

Compiled and edited by
Carter H. Manierre

Captain Cyrus E. Manierre, Jr.
On leave in Lake Forest, 1943

This is dedicated not just to the memory of my father, whom I never had asked about his war story, but also to all those Jeds and other Special Forces who had, and have, the courage to do in real life what I have only experienced in books and movies.

A portion of the proceeds from this
book (if any) will be donated to:

VetsHelpingHeroes.org

in memory of my uncle's
Bombardier and my friend
Irwin "Russian" Stovroff.

Published by Draft2Digital in celebration of the 80th Anniversary of the liberation of Stalag-Luft 1, 4 May 1945

Copyright © 2002, 2025 by Carter H. Manierre

Contents

Legend of the Jedburghs

How Operation JEDBURGH got its name is still somewhat of a mystery. Some say it was inspired by the name of a South African town where Boers used guerrilla tactics against the British. Others claim it was based upon the name of the radio sets the teams used (Jed Sets). Still another theory states that the code name was chosen to correspond to J-Jour, the French translation of the US military term, D-Day. Or maybe "Jedburgh" was simply just the next word on a list of random code names.

One of the most popular theories, however, is that the Jeds were named after a small Scottish border town where, during the 12th Century, Scots conducted guerrilla warfare against English invaders. Legend has it that these fierce warriors wielded their Jedburgh axes with such determination that their war cry struck fear in all those who heard it. Perhaps this bit of medieval lore played a role in the selection of the OSS code name.

https://www.cia.gov/stories/story/surprise-kill-vanish-the-legend-of-the-jedburghs/

Operation Jedburgh

Operation Jedburgh was a clandestine operation during World War II in which three- man teams of operatives of the British Special Operations Executive (SOE$_g$), the US Office of Strategic Services (OSS), the Free French Bureau central de renseignements et d'action ("Central Bureau of Intelligence and Operations") and the Dutch and Belgian armies in exile were dropped by parachute into occupied France, the Netherlands and Belgium. The objective of the Jedburgh teams was to assist allied forces who invaded France on 6 June 1944 with guerrilla warfare, sabotage and leading local resistance forces in actions against the Germans.

The name of the operation was chosen at random from a Ministry of Defence code book, although several of those who took part in the operation later reflected that the name was apt as the town of Jedburgh in the Scottish Borders was notorious in the late Middle Ages for the activities of the raiders known as the Border Reivers.

Operation Jedburgh represented the first real cooperation in Europe between SOE and the Special Operations branch of OSS. By this period in the war, SOE had insufficient resources to mount the huge operation on its own; for example, it had access to only 23 Handley Page Halifax aircraft for dropping agents and stores, barely sufficient to maintain SOE's existing networks. OSS was able to augment this force with Consolidated B-24 Liberator aircraft operating from RAF Harrington (see Operation Carpetbagger$_g$).

The OSS sought to be involved since, in a single swoop, this would result in the OSS inserting more agents into northwestern Europe than it had during the entire previous period of US involvement in the war. Nevertheless, General Eisenhower, the American Supreme Commander, ensured that the French would lead the operation and on 9 June 1944 gave command of the Jedburgh teams to France.

Origins
The British Special Operations Executive (SOE) and its American counterpart, the Office of Strategic Services (OSS), came up with the concept of the Jedburghs in May 1943. The idea was that small groups of military personnel would be inserted by parachute inside territory occupied by Nazi

Germany to assist local resistance forces and to carry out military operations. Unlike SOE agents who worked in occupied Europe, the Jedburgh teams would be armed and uniformed military personnel. Fluency in the language of the European country where they would operate was required, although the language requirement was reduced for radio operators. The "Jeds" as the men on Operation Jedburgh teams were called were all volunteers. Jedburgh operations were also carried out in some Asian countries.

Jedburgh Teams

The Jedburgh teams were known by code names which usually were first names (such as "Hugh"), with some names of medicines (such as "Novocaine") and a few random names thrown in to confuse German intelligence. The teams normally consisted of three men: a commander, an executive officer, and a non-commissioned radio operator. One of the officers would be British or American while the other would originate from the country to which the team deployed. The radio operator could be of any nationality.

About 300 Jeds were selected. After about two weeks of paramilitary$_g$ training at commando training bases in the Scottish Highlands, they moved to Milton Hall near Peterborough, which was much closer to the airfields from which they were to be launched, and to London and Special Force Headquarters. At Milton Hall they received an intensive course in unarmed combat and sabotage techniques.

In addition to their personal weapons (which included an M1 carbine and a Colt automatic pistol for each member) and sabotage equipment, the teams dropped with the Type B Mark II radio, more commonly referred to as the B2 or "Jed Set", which was critical for communicating with Special Force

Headquarters in London. They were also issued pieces of silk with five hundred phrases that they were likely to use in radio traffic replaced with four-letter codes to save time in transmission, and one-time pads to encipher their messages. Each officer wore a money belt containing 100,000 francs (about 500 British pounds or 2,500 US. dollars) and 50 US. dollars. Radio operators carried only 50,000 francs. The money was to distribute to resistance fighters, called maquis in France, many of whom had families to support. Equipment and supplies were airdropped with the Jeds.

Operations in France

France was by far the most important country of Jedburgh operations. Ninety-three teams were inserted into France. The nationalities of 278 Jeds on the teams were: 89 French officers and 17 radio operators, 47 British officers and 38 radio operators, and 40 American officers and 37 radio operators. Thirteen of the Jeds undertook a second mission. The officers were lieutenants, captains, and a few majors. Radio operators were usually sergeants. The teams were parachuted into France from June to September 1944. Several of the teams inserted in August and September landed to find themselves in territory already liberated by the rapid advance of the allied armies.

The first team in, code named "Hugh", parachuted into central France near Châteauroux on 5/6 June 1944, the night before the Allied landings in Normandy, code named Operation Overlord. The Jedburgh teams normally parachuted in by night to meet a reception committee from a local Resistance or maquis group. Their main function was to provide a link between the guerrillas and the Allied command. They could provide liaison, advice, expertise and leadership, but their most powerful asset was their ability to arrange airdrops of arms and ammunition.

Like all Allied forces who operated behind Nazi lines, the Jedburghs were subject to torture and execution in the event of capture, under Hitler's notorious Commando Order. Because the teams normally operated in uniform, to apply this order to them was a war crime. However, of the Jedburgh teams dropped into France, only British Captain Victor A. Gough met that fate, being shot while a prisoner on 25 November 1944.

Maquis (World War II)

The Maquis (French pronunciation: [ma'ki]) were rural guerrilla bands of French and Belgian Resistance fighters, called maquisards, during the Nazi occupation of France in World War II. Initially, they were composed of young, mostly working-class, men who had escaped into the mountains and woods to avoid conscription into Vichy France's Service du travail obligatoire ("Compulsory Work Service" or STO) which provided forced labor for Germany. To avoid capture and deportation to Germany, they became increasingly organized into active resistance groups.

They had an estimated 25,000 to 40,000 members in autumn of 1943 and approximately 100,000 members in June 1944.

Meaning

Originally the word came from the kind of terrain in which the armed resistance groups hid, high ground in southeastern France covered with scrub growth called maquis (scrubland).

Although strictly speaking it means "thicket", maquis could be roughly translated as "the bush"; in Corsica, the saying "prendre le maquis" ('to go into the bush') is used to describe someone who leaves the village in order to live in the bush, either biding time to seek revenge, or while being pursued by others with an intent to arrest or kill. Historians have not established how this

Corsican term arrived on the mainland of France, but observe that: the Italian-derived word "maquis" is commonly used to describe woods and scrubland on the island, and evokes an all-encompassing image of woods and mountains, whereas the more limited word "garrigue" used in the south of France indicated an inhospitable terrain, and the words "bois" ('wood'), "foret" ('forest') and "montagne" ('mountain') were too bland.

The term "maquis" signified both the group of fighters and their rural location. Members of those bands were called maquisards. Their image was that of a committed and voluntary fighter, a combatant, as opposed to the previous réfractaire ("unmanageable"). The term became an honorific meaning "armed resistance fighter". The maquis came to symbolize the French Resistance and was used to describe resistance groups that fought in France before the Allied invasion of Normandy in 1944. Once the Allies had secured a foothold in France the government of Free France attempted to unite the separate groups of Maquis under the banner of the French Forces of the Interior (FFI$_g$).

The national denomination given to all maquis forces during the war is "FFI", for Forces françaises de l'intérieur. This large corp of about 400,000 active members (in 1944) is to be divided in three major sections, corresponding to three political or professional inclinations:

The Francs-Tireurs et Partisans (FTP$_g$), a para-military organism created by and for the Parti Communiste français (the French Communist Party) The Armée secrète (AS$_g$); "Secret Army" in English), most of the time led by French army officers. The Organisation de résistance de l'armée (ORA$_g$; in English: "Organisation of army resistance"), officially created in January 1943 as a more "official" and apolitical organism for the continuation of armed struggle by ex-French military personnel in the Zone libre (southern half of metropolitan France).

All three groups were deemed "terrorists" by the official French government in Vichy and by the German authorities and other neighbouring fascist regimes. Other (rare) local groups did not affiliate with these organisations.

Operations

Most maquisards operated in the remote or mountainous areas of Brittany and southern France, especially in the Alps and in Limousin. They relied on guerrilla tactics to harass the Milice and German occupation troops. The Maquis also aided the escape of downed Allied airmen, Jews and others pursued by the Vichy and German authorities. Maquisards usually relied on some degree of sympathy or cooperation from the local populace. In March 1944, the German army began a terror campaign through-out France. This included reprisals against civilians living in areas where the French resistance was active, such as the Oradour- sur-Glane, Maillé and Tulle massacres by SS troops. The Maquisards were later to take their revenge in the épuration sauvage (*wild cleansing*) that took place after the war's end.

Most of the Maquis cells—like the Maquis du Limousin or the Maquis du Vercors— took names after the area they were operating in. The size of these cells varied from tens to thousands of men and women.

(Courtesy of Wikipedia -
https://en.wikipedia.org/wiki/Maquis_(World_War_II))

Aftermath

Many of the surviving American "Jeds" later held various positions of great responsibility in the US Army or the CIA. Examples include William Colby, who became director of the CIA, Lucien Conein, who was a key CIA officer in Vietnam, General John Singlaub and Colonel Aaron Bank (first commander of United States Army Special Forces).

Among French Jedburghs were Paul Aussaresses, later founder of the SDECE's$_g$ 11e RPC$_g$, and served in French Algeria; Jean Sassi, another who later served in the 11e RPC, who pioneered conventional guerrilla commandos GCMA$_g$ with Roger Trinquier during the First Indochina War; Guy Le Borgne, commander of the 8e Choc Parachute Battalion in Indochina, the 3rd Marine Infantry Parachute Regiment in Algeria and 11th Parachute Division. Brig. General Joe Haraki SOE, Special Operations Mediterranean SO(M), special forces in Lebanon, ISF Commander Internal Security Forces.

(Courtesy of Wikipedia -
<https://en.wikipedia.org/wiki/Operation_Jedburgh>)

Pop continues his Introduction to Operation Jedburgh:

It seemed that plans for the invasion of Europe by the armies of the allies were progressing satisfactorily (D-Day lay fourteen months in the stirring, even alluring future). Included in the plans for the invasion of Europe by sea and air was a plan to organize the mass of separate and unconnected underground resistance movements on the continent these were mostly totally uncoordinated in their efforts) into a coordinated body of Allied military power which would be directed, supplied, and controlled by Allied Command headquarters (This was to be

SHAEF$_g$, under command of General Eisenhower). The redoubtable British Military Intelligence service had formulated a master plan by which one of its associated agencies was to provide personnel and a program in detail for this effort. This associated agency of British MI$_G$ was such a super-secret organization that even its own personnel were forbidden to use its name, or even to pronounce its initials, under any circumstances whether official or unofficial (now, twenty-five years later, I can refer to it by name and initials which were S.O.E. for Special Operations Executive). My interviewer, the gray-haired Captain, did not mention anything by name. Most of what I relate on this page is information which I picked up later, here and there, by rumor, by osmosis, hardly ever by formal briefing. For example, my interviewer did not indicate that the origin of the plan was British. Very likely the Captain was not aware of the details of origin of the operation which he described. He was simply the recruiting officer.

Basic element of the operating plan which had been conceived by Special Operations Executive was that teams of officers from the Allied armies would be infiltrated into the enemy occupied countries of western Europe, those countries which were considered to be of special interest to the British and American military command, France, Holland, Belgium, Denmark, and Norway (this plan did not include such occupied countries as Poland and Czechoslovakia which were considered firmly within the purview of the Russians). Each team would consist of at least one officer from the army-in-exile of the country into which the team was to be infiltrated. He would be accompanied by at least one British or American officer who was familiar with the country and who spoke its language. These would be accompanied by a radio operator, usually a high-ranking non-com from the army-in-exile of the country involved; although manpower shortage necessitated that many radio operators were American or British, and many of these spoke only English. From the operations maps in British MI headquarters areas were selected throughout all of occupied Europe into each of which would be placed one of these teams for the purpose of making contact with anti-German resistance groups there and also of maintaining regular radio contact with headquarters in London. This was called "Operation Jedburgh." Overall strategic plans would emanate from Supreme Headquarters; these plans would be reduced to specific operations orders to armies and Divisions, and further reduced to the regiments, battalions, and companies. Every element of the allied forces would have an assignment.

And the already partly organized forces of resistance inside Europe were to be given assignments also. These so-called forces ranged in degree of organization all the way from conventionally structured military units with officers and rudimentary uniforms in some of the more inaccessible mountain regions of France to single individuals operating alone and with little support who took advantage of some facet of their environment to provide assistance to the Allies. The railroad switch-man who might clumsily throw a wrong switch and delay or wreck an important train. The power company employee who might surreptitiously sabotage one or more of the generators providing power to coal mines or some strategic plant. The sub-teen age girl scout who pedaled innocently about on her bicycle acting as a courier between resistance leaders in different villages or localities and carried under her clothes compromising messages which would sign worse than a death warrant for sender and addressee - and probably for her too. In the woods and thickets and in the more inaccessible rural areas of France roamed gangs of young men, some of whom were former French soldiers who had escaped from enemy control, others of whom were teen age boys looking for excitement and escape from home while at the same time deriving the satisfaction of performing a sort of national service to the France they expected inevitably to be liberated. These gangs were called "maquis" after a thick growing, bushy Corsican thicket, in which gangs of guerrillas and outlaws have traditionally gone into hiding. Members of these resistance bands were called "maquisards", and they were proud of this name. It identified them as true outlaws and separated them from "les sedentaires", the stay-at-home resistants who committed sabotage, transmitted intelligence, or assisted in the escape of shot-down Allied airmen at the same time as they continued to live ostensibly law-abiding ways, seemingly obedient to the deeply resented regulations of their conquerors.

Loyalties among and between the maquis were generally ill-defined and as various as the many hundreds of maquis that existed. The maquis to which the British and the Free French (General de Gaulle's army-in-exile) were the closest and upon whom they relied the most was called the Armee Secret. The Armee Secret contained probably more maquis groups than any other except for the Communist maquis which called themselves the "Franc-Tireurs-Partisans". While the men in the maquis who professed orientation to the Armee Secret (there was of course no structured organization to which a maquis could "belong" or become a "member") were all distinctly partisans of General de Gaulle and of what he represented, the men who belonged to the Communist maquis were politically oriented in an opposite direction, were not favorable to General de Gaulle, and were generally hostile to the Armee Secret and to any other supporters of de Gaulle's "Free France". This hostility extended to the British and Americans and to their representatives (Allied officers and staff members infiltrated in and out of France from the earliest days of the German occupation), sometimes by parachute with exit in a light aircraft, often the round trip was made by light aircraft. Helicopters had not yet been developed to where they would have been useful. The FTP were typical Communist activists, unwilling to cooperate with any other groups.

But in each middle-sized to large town, and in each geographical area of more or less county size (how big in sq. miles?) there was usually at least one resistance leader who could be regarded as the senior in the region - the most respected, the most obeyed by the various groups and cells of resistance-minded personnel. There was no actual, structured frame or network of resistance, in France at least, there was rather a major part of the population who were hostile to the German occupiers and willing to take various degrees of risk to retard them. Nevertheless, despite this lack of anything resembling a chain of command, the members of "la resistance" were usually willing to cooperate with each other when the wiser, most respected heads among them agreed to pull together on one or another operation. This cooperation was by no means an automatic or even partly permanent thing; its existence was tenuous, strengthening or weakening depending upon the pressures of the immediate situation. For example, two or more separate maquis bands would work together in planning and pulling off such an operation as the night-time derailing of a German troop-train and guerrilla attack on the troops it carried. Such an operation required first the information of when and where the train was expected. Then the track right-of-way would have to be scouted for most advantageous places for ambush (all the time hiding from and dodging German security patrols, which were numerous).

And that is the environment into which he jumped...

Chapter 0
Before the OSS

My father, Cyrus E. Manierre, jr. graduated from the U.S. Military Academy at West Point on 29 May, 1942, and was commissioned as a 2nd Lieutenant in the U.S. Army. He wanted to be a pilot, so went to flight school. There he had an accident, cracked up a training plane, and was washed out of the program in Nov. 1942.

He was then eventually stationed at Camp Mackall, near Fort Bragg, South Carolina with the 82nd Airborne, 508th Parachute Infantry where he was posted as S3 - Operations and Training Officer, in which position he was responsible for plans, operations, and training of the 2nd Battalion.

No. 1626   TYPICAL STREET - CAMP MACKALL, N.C.

Chapter 1

In which Lt. Manierre is recruited by the
OSS and says farewell to Camp Mackall

It all started in the spring of 1943. I was in the 508th Parachute Infantry Regiment, stationed at Camp Mackall, North Carolina; we had finished our basic training and then gone off on a week's maneuvers out in the bush.

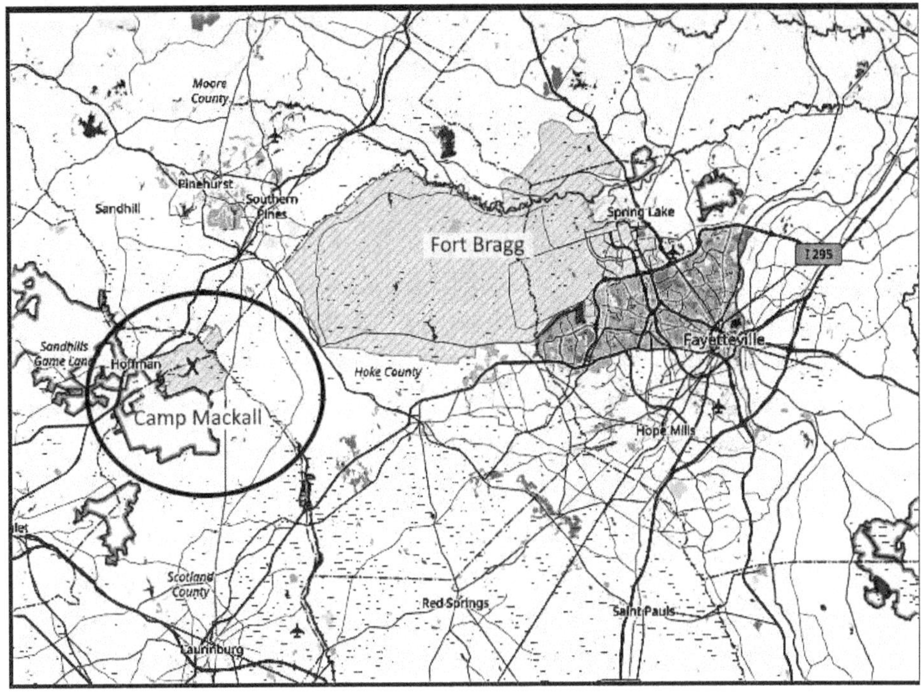

We had been maneuvering around in the pouring rain; everybody was soaking wet and uncomfortable and had marched all night, so it was a real rugged kind of a do, and at the end of the maneuvers we were very happy to get back to Camp Mackall. We had just gotten back and were washing our clothes in the sunshine and looking forward to a day or two of rest before anything else was going to happen to us. A messenger appeared at my tent while I was washing my socks and said: "Lt. Manierre, you are wanted over at Airborne Command Headquarters."

DIVISION HEADQUARTERS - CAMP MACKALL N.C.

Airborne Command was the group that commanded all airborne troops of the American Army, parachute troops, glider troops, and all that kind of thing. I've forgotten the name of the general who was in charge, but it sounded like a pretty important kind of thing to be sent for by Airborne Command. So I quickly jumped up and put on my best summer uniform and toddled over to Airborne Command Headquarters and reported. The orderly at the desk sent me into a room, sort of a waiting room where there were quite a few other Paratrooper officers, young men from different regiments. I didn't know many of them although I recognized a few from my regiment. None of us knew what we were there for. Finally I was called into the other room where there was a group of four or five officers, two of them Army officers and the others in the Marine Corps. They introduced themselves individually. The spokesman seemed to be Captain Quay of the Army. He was an older man, about my father's age, and obviously a staff officer. He wore the insignia of Staff Personnel, a branch of the Army which we used to call "Male WACS$_g$" as their duties were mostly clerical. He seemed to be keeping rather strange company with these two rugged looking Marine Corps officers with paratrooper insignia on their uniforms, but it became clear in a few minutes.

"I'm Dick Quay," he said, "and these men are my associates from the Office of Strategic Services$_g$ in Washington. You've heard of the Office of Strategic Services?"

I had to allow that I had not heard of it and didn't know who he was or what he represented, but I could feel some excitement stirring around inside me because it sounded interesting.

"The Office of Strategic Services" said he, "is the organization which has been founded by General William Donovan. You've heard of Wild Bill Donovan haven't you?"

"Yes" I said, "I have, he's the man who's been making a trip around the world on some sort of intelligence work isn't he?"

"Yes. President Roosevelt sent him off on an investigative tour and he has come back and reported directly to the President and is operating directly under the White House now as an independent agency. Let me introduce my associates here. These Marines are just back from Guadalcanal where they have been doing Marine Raider activity and they are a couple of our mainstays in this particular sort of work which the OSS$_g$ is just beginning to start. What we are trying to do is organize an operation, a military operation to be carried on in Europe behind the German lines, well in the zone of the interior, operating with the European Resistance organizations, of which there are quite a few. There are a lot of Resistance Units and Resistance Organizations, underground movements, partisan movements throughout Europe which are all very much devoted to resisting and overthrowing if possible the German control and the British Intelligence Service for years has been supplying them with arms, equipment and personnel, that's to say leadership type personnel who are British agents who are sent in by parachute.

The communication between the resistance and the intelligence service in London is quite regular and the only thing that is really lacking is that various units of resistance forces on the ground are not associated with each other. There is no real intercommunication enabling them to operate with a single objective. At the moment that fact isn't particularly important, these operations which are proceeding in different places and at different times and in different directions are all of benefit to our cause, but when the time comes for Allied invasion of Europe to take place it will be very important to have all the resistance forces in Europe operate towards a single objective - that objective being the success of our invasion. In short, as part of the invasion program it is planned that each resistance unit will be given a specific mission to perform as part of the overall Allied effort.

Now in order to do this we have to send in a lot of military personnel, American, British and other Allied nations. Men who are trained to drop by parachute, who speak the language of whatever country they drop into and who will be better off for having some acquaintance with that country, perhaps having lived there for a time before the war. These personnel will be dropped in equipped with radios and other communication devices enabling them to be in continued contact with headquarters, receive their directions from headquarters and convey the directions to the resistance forces with which they happen to be operating, so that all activity will be directed from intelligence headquarters, probably in London."

Quay went on. "The British have been carrying on this underground warfare ever since 1940 when the Germans took over the Continent, but now that the United States has gotten into the war General Donovan has begun to organize something of an intelligence service. The British who need a lot of men and a lot of material and a lot of money with which to launch this program have invited us to take part in it with them. They are going to provide the mission, the contacts on the ground and about half the personnel. The Americans will provide all the money and most of the material and approximately half of the personnel on their side, but the overall conception of this operation is the British idea. Now the personnel we drop in to go to the resistance forces will be assigned special contacts with whom they are to rendezvous on the ground and the whole matter will be arranged by radio communication beforehand. What we are to do here, that is myself and my associates from Washington, is to go through the personnel records of every paratroop regiment and pick out the names of those young junior grade officers who are said to have a foreign language qualification, meaning can speak the language of one or more European countries and also see if they have lived in any countries of Europe and have an acquaintance with them."

I at once saw how he had happened to pick my name out of the list because I had gone to school in Europe and learned to speak French pretty well there and all that was on my personnel slip for anyone to look at.

Le Rosey School

This proposal of his sounded kind of exciting and of course I accepted it immediately. I had gotten kind of tired of the way we were living anyway; the basic training was kind of dull in the regiment. We had moved from Fort Benning to Fort Bragg to Camp Mckall and the routine was the same and we were all getting pretty restless and wanted to get sent overseas and be heroes, but there didn't seem to be much of an opportunity for that and we were just hanging around the boondocks at Camp Mckall, shooting at targets and acting like GIs.

So I accepted Captain Quay's offer and he said: "Well, now, this really hasn't yet gotten off the ground, Lt. Manierre." This was something I got used to as the days went by and I served more with the OSS and later on, many years after with the CIA, this got to be sort of routine, but the first time it happened I was kind of surprised.

He continued: "We have to get approval from a lot of different sources, lots of project committees and project endorsement and appropriation of funds and that sort of thing. So the chances are it will all be called off. If it is called off, we won't be able to send you orders, you'll just have to stay down here with the regiment."

Of course I couldn't imagine anything like that happening. I was much too keen and attributed the same keenness to everyone else in the OSS in Washington, so I accepted and had all hopes of getting orders quickly. Meanwhile I was sworn to secrecy not to discuss this at all unless I had to explain to my regimental commander what I was over at Airborne Command Headquarters for, although I was allowed to discuss it with the other men who were being interviewed.

Well as soon as I got back to Regimental Headquarters the Colonel sent for me, and when I went into his office he said: "Manierre, why did they send for you over at Airborne Command Headquarters, what happened over there?" He gave me a kind of cold, suspicious look, and I felt an atmosphere of disapproval

Colonel Roy E. Linquist

emanating from him. I answered him with a good deal of excitement in my voice, thinking surely when I tell the

Colonel what a wonderful opportunity has been given me he will be very enthusiastic and shake my hand. So I told him that I had been invited by the OSS to go into this super-secret, super-colossal commando-type operation. That we were going to be parachute dropped behind the enemy lines in Europe and carry the war right into the lap of the enemy, and have all the opportunity of being a hero and all the rest of it. I expected him to pat me on the back and congratulate me.

Instead of that he said: "You'll just get lost in the shuffle. These people from Washington come out here into the field and they hire lots of officers away from their regiments and they go up there to Washington and they end up in some building somewhere, in a linen closet just shuffling papers and answering telephones and counting paper clips for the rest of the war. Did you accept this offer?"

"Yes, sir."

"Manierre, you've made a big mistake. Your assignment in this regiment is a good berth for a young officer of the regular army. We have high priority for equipment and training and personnel. Our combat assignments will be important. Your assignment as Operations and Training Officer of the 2nd Battalion was one which you shouldn't have given up just to go chasing some will o' the wisp proclaimed by this new Washington outfit. I've heard of this OSS. It's just another New Deal agency. It isn't even organized yet. They're not going to accomplish anything. They could be disbanded overnight. I'm afraid you're just going to get lost in the shuffle. You'll be a fish out of water in that bureaucratic tangle. For example, is this OSS outfit going to maintain you on jump status while you're taking training?"

"Jump status", similar to Flying Status in the Air Force, meant making at least one parachute training jump per month and receiving $100 bonus in monthly pay. (Not to be given up lightly).

I had to confess that I had not inquired about this detail. It never occurred to me.

"Well, that's just the first thing you missed. You understand that in the OSS you will not be in the Army's chain of command. Your promotions may not come through. Your efficiency reports may not be handled properly."

He enumerated several more possible disadvantages that might now accrue in my new and evidently undefinable status and then suggested that if I wished to change my mind about leaving the regiment it probably would not be difficult to "have the orders canceled." (Through what devious and influence-ridden process this would be accomplished I did not inquire). With guilty feelings and a half-hearted but unfulfilled idea that I ought to apologize I answered in the negative and at once found myself relieved of my "desirable assignment" as S-3, Second Battalion, 508th Parachute Infantry, and assigned instead to the unofficial and highly undesirable slot of Regimental Range Officer. This job, always given to junior officers under the cloud of official displeasure either because of ineptitude elsewhere or disciplinary failings of one sort or another, involved duties which made it very fitting as a penitential office for wayward or inefficient young officers.

Each day one or more companies, frequently a whole battalion, would be sent to the post rifle range to fire the official training program's prescribed schedule. Every soldier, commissioned or non-commissioned, fired his day's allotment of bullets. Targets were carefully marked, scores recorded, new targets installed (Range Officer was responsible for these items). Then a new order of riflemen would fire. The first order usually would be withdrawn from the firing line to receive training lectures or some other sedentary training until the next turn came to fire. This activity usually continued all day from breakfast to suppertime. It was the Range Officer who got himself and a few enlisted helpers out to the range in early morning well ahead of the first firing order, first having obtained all targets, markers, and other equipment needed and gotten them to the range. Targets installed, field telephone communications between target butts and firing line installed, firing rosters prepared and reviewed so that none was left out, and none should fire twice; then we were ready for the first order. The Range Officer is now equipped with a loudspeaker, or a bullhorn, and it becomes his function to command the first order to the firing line, to take position, "Ready on the right? Ready on the left? A-a-a-all ready on the Firing Line! COMMENCE FIRING"

When finished firing he retires the order in the same manner. Only then do the men come under the responsibility of their own officers; it is the Range Officer who is responsible while they are firing. It is he who must take the rocket if some careless rifleman points his weapon in the wrong direction. All matters of safety are his to enforce, as are all matters involving routine operation of the range facilities. He calls the second order to fire in the same way. And the third, and the fourth. It goes on all day. When the shooting is completed (getting on for supper time) the Range Officer dismisses the last order, which marches off to evening mess, and then settles down with his crew of loyal (or not so loyal) helpers (who are usually soldiers in bad official odor themselves and not necessarily willing subordinates) to clean up the range, dismantle communications, disassemble and store the targets, lock up the range, and proceed to his company kitchen for a late supper of leftovers and to look forward to the next day's repetition of the same stimulating activity. There was generally an assistant range officer who would have been very welcome to me, but this time, probably for punitive reasons, there was nobody in any such post. Typically, about a month had passed and no orders had come;

and I had found my duties on the Camp McCall rifle range to be more and more fatiguing.

Well, time passed and I didn't get any orders and I was getting restless. I had been relieved of my assignment with the regiment, I didn't really have anything to do and so I got on the telephone and called Washington and after a lot of delays I got in touch with Capt. Quay. He seemed surprised to hear from me.

"Oh, this has all been put on the shelf. We aren't going to be able to go ahead on this until the next time the appropriations bill comes up next year, perhaps we'll get around to it then."

And I said, "Well, what am I going to do? I've put all my eggs in one basket."

"Oh, in that case we can get orders for you, and get you up here." So I said, "Fine, I'll go up there" and I did. I got orders and went up to report in to OSS.

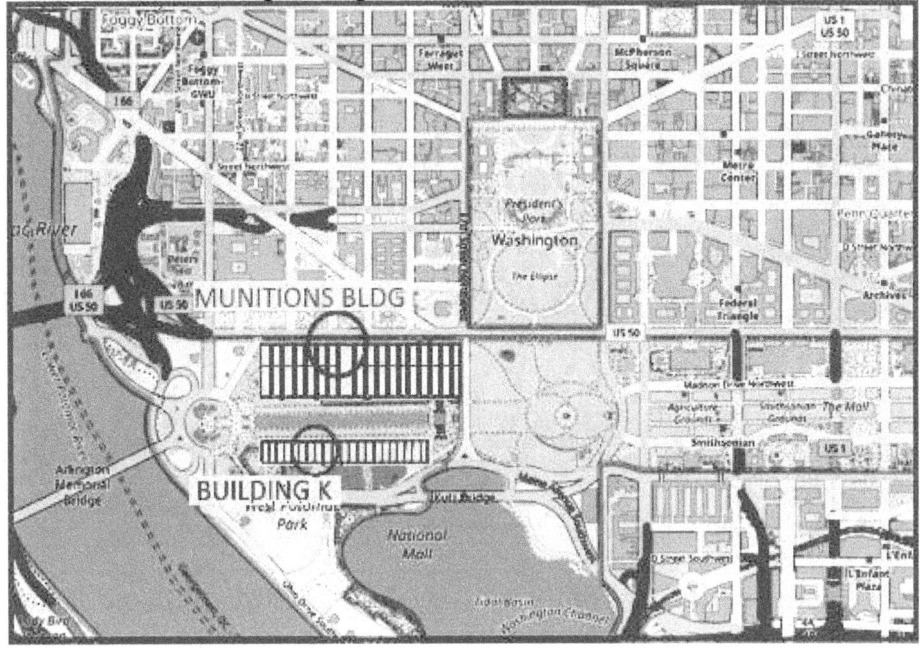

My destination in the Munitions Building turned out to be a sub-office of the Army Adjutant General's Department where my orders were duly stamped and returned to me minus one copy which was removed, evidently for the enrichment of some personnel office's inventory of interesting data.

I was informed by the friendly WAC in charge, that my ultimate destination was Temporary Building K, an unimpressive World War II Tempo$_g$ which stood at the corner of Constitution Avenue and Rock Creek Drive from 1941 until 1965, and which I surmised provided housing for Headquarters, OSS. Since it was only a few blocks down the street I availed myself of the opportunity to enjoy the pretty day and receive my first view of our our nation's capital.

Photo # 80-G-K-14433   View looking west from the Washington Monument, Washington, D.C., circa 1943-44

Reception at Temporary Building K was initiated by my being stopped at the entrance by the conventional government security guard who looked at my orders, made a short telephone call, and motioned me to have a seat. Soon, an attractive young woman, not in uniform, appeared and asked me to follow her through a labyrinth of corridors to an office where I was relieved to find myself confronted by the pleasant gray-haired civilian type of mannered Captain who had first aroused my interest in joining the OSS.

"Well, Manierre, it's nice to have you with us. Let me introduce my associates here." And sure enough all the old men in the office seemed to be executive types, typical OSS, some of them had been bankers and some lawyers, rather high-powered executive-suite sorts, in uniform, but not a bit military, smooth, polished, courtly individuals who introduced themselves. Then Dick said, "We'll just send Manierre out to Area A *(Area F)*. That's a little secret training area we've set up out in the country, where you'll be put into a training organization until we get this operation I was telling you about under way." He seemed quite optimistic about that. What he'd said over the phone made it sound as if it had been shelved for years, but now a week later he sounded as if it were all going on. I discovered this was not unusual in the organization, typical of what has gone on right up to the present. But, anyway it sounded as if this was still on the ticket and I was just going to get a little preliminary training out at Area A, whatever that might be. So in a little while he brought in a fellow whom I had known at West Point, an officer a little bit older than me whose name was Bradish J. Smith. At West Point we had called him BJ. He was a very nice chap who had come into OSS as an infantry officer and we were glad to see each other and shook hands. He was going to drive me out to Area A, so I picked up my little suitcase, everything I owned was in one little bitty suitcase and got into his car. On the way he gave me a rather interesting rundown on what OSS was like and what his impressions were on being in it.

"First of all" he said, "You want to forget all about the military life you've been leading in the Army and the military things you learned at West Point. This organization has got a lot of officers and a lot of military people in it, but they aren't really professional types, most of them are rather socially prominent people from business and other walks of life. Quite a lot of high society people mixed up in this group, I think you'll get quite a kick out of it. This is an intelligence organization and also does work in related fields such as sabotage and whatnot. The guys who are in it are prima donnas of all kinds, interesting characters, amusing persons, but not a military crowd, members of the smart set from all over the country. The Commanding Officer is none other than Lt. Col. Sergei Obolensky, a scion of the oldest and most princely house of the Czarist days."

Chapter 2

In which Lt Manierre is introduced to
the life of an OSS agent at "Area A"

A short drive out the Parkway and Massachusetts Avenue into the suburbs of Montgomery County brought us to "Area A" *(Actually "Area F"),* a training establishment very different from anything I have seen before or since. Different because, first of all it consisted of the real estate and fixed assets of the Congressional Country Club, one of Washington's more noted private places of recreation and the scene of the National Open Golf Championship in 1964.

However, as is to be expected in any luxurious establishment requisitioned for emergency wartime military use, the luxurious aspects of its amenities had disappeared, and in fact the normal conveniences of any military cantonment were minimal.

The Congressional Country Club, Training Area F, as shown in an OSS briefing board.

Now this sounds like a rather plush and luxurious place to have a training camp, but it certainly wasn't anything of the kind at that time. The whole place had been stripped of all furniture and fixtures, it was just a great big, empty building with echoing hallways and enormous deserted rooms in which as our group of personnel got larger and larger, more and more Army cots were shoved in until the whole place looked like some kind of an emergency Civil War hospital. There were beds in the halls and the basement and everywhere. The poor people who were stationed there were living out of their trunks, sleeping in the hallways of the Congressional Country Club; the amenities were at a minimum in those days. Bathroom fixtures had been removed from most of the bathrooms, and running water was available only in the kitchen and in a large public washroom which was now simply referred to as "the latrine".

I found myself given a couple of GI blankets and my choice of a bed either in one of the tents which had been pitched in rows on the sides of the club's entrance driveway or in a tiny unfurnished (except for a cot) room upstairs on one of the club's upper floors. I opted for space in a tent. Numbers of other Paratrooper officers, recruited as I had been, had begun to arrive at Area A, and they seemed to be forming a sort of field-soldier-minded community in the tent camp. Nobody seemed directly in charge on the spot. The lonely corridors and rooms of the clubhouse were empty. One rarely entered except at mealtimes, or occasionally to present either a complaint or a requisition to the administrative head of the station, a fat and inefficient Service Corps Lieutenant about forty years old who seemed to resent the presence of each of the new trainees whom it was his duty to provide with food, bedclothes, hot water, toilet paper and similar household supplies. It also was his duty to maintain grounds and property in a presentable state of cleanliness and order, and since he was clearly not supplied with anything like a staff to perform more than a fraction of this work, it was not long before he tried to talk Headquarters into letting him farm out chores among the trainee officers who were arriving daily.

This effort was not successful, but it did succeed in starting a feud between him and us. (We became about 100 strong finally), and the upper hand was clearly his. There were unexplained malfunctions in housekeeping, unexplained shortages of linen, bedclothes, electric light bulbs, even sometimes food became a burdensome bother, but to the high-spirited crowd of trainees they were all no more than minor irritations. After all, we were located no more than 30 miles from the bright lights, restaurants, and other pleasures of Washington, DC. Everybody seemed to have a car, and at duties end each day our whole crew would take off to town leaving an empty tent city and an empty dining room for evening mess. After a few weeks of this our administrator (his official title was "Commanding Officer, Training Area A", but as trainees were not under his command but only under his logistical responsibility, he really didn't command anybody but a handful of janitors and cooks), stopped serving-----

The following is from a 1945 3-part article, written by Claire Rauth, about my father's war exploits that ran in an as yet unidentified newspaper.

"COACHED BY RUSSIAN

"Although we in the paratroop units had been well-schooled, it was still necessary that I go through the training program that the OSS maintained," the Major explained, "because the OSS recruited men from all branches of service, the army, navy and Marine Corps and from foreign armies, and we all had to have a common basis of preparation."

"His training in America was under Col, 'Serge' Obolensky, one of the many celebrated men enrolled in the 0SS program. Obolensky, a. Russian prince until he became an American citizen, was long known as a member of' the glittering New York social scene. But Obolensky was not an idle and effete aristocrat.

"He was an all-around man," Manierre summed up. "He was in very good physical condition, for a man in middle age. And his background of extensive travel and wide knowledge of Europe was invaluable; he knew English, French and Russian, naturally, well." At the training school near Washington, D.C. which was in its early stage when the major entered it, the men were rigorously schooled in all the knowledge and skills which they would have to rely upon when they were sent into the enemy's stronghold to function upon their own wits and initiative."

BJ Smith took me up to Col. Obolensky's "apartment" which was about three little rooms more or less adjoining across the hall from each other. A bathroom somewhere in the vicinity was supposed to be his private bathroom. I found him a very charming character, a really nice fellow and was delighted to be serving under him, which was a new experience for me.

The program at Area A was a rather tenuous one because there weren't very many people there for long. Guys would report in on a morning with no idea of where they were supposed to be going or what they were supposed to be doing and they would join us in our training exercises and then disappear in 36 hours and nobody would have any idea where they had gone or anything like that. It was all secret and they would just go away and we would never see them again. Among these individuals was Sterling Hayden, the movie actor, who was a Lt. in the Marine Corps. He was very taciturn and unfriendly, didn't speak to anyone. He was with us a very short time, resisting all efforts of friendliness on our part, which we took to be simply because he was a Marine and we were all in the Army. Then he disappeared and we didn't hear much about him again until we learned later that he had been sent off to Yugoslavia where he was in charge of infiltration and secret small boat landing operations on the Adriatic coast in support of Yugoslavian resistance, at that the time it was the Chetniks under Mihalovitch, before Tito took over.

Here in Area A we would be summoned from our army cots usually located in the hallways or corridors of the Congressional Country Club at 6:30 in the morning and we would rush out to the golf course where the physical training exercises were usually held under the direct leadership of Col. Obolensky himself. After our physical training which involved climbing ropes and running obstacle courses, things like that, we would go in for breakfast in what I suppose is the dining room. In those days it was a big cavern of a room, full of folding tables and folding wooden chairs and we'd stand in the mess line and be given our regular GI chow. Then after breakfast we would have a lecture or some kind of a demonstration about partisan warfare or guerrilla warfare or hand-to-hand fighting, *(taught by Major "Dangerous Dan" Fairbairn")* or a talk would be given by some visiting officer of one of the Allied Armies of Occupied Europe.

"Fairbairn worked at Arisaig early in the war and then moved to the Congressional Club - if you get the chance to see any film footage of this site, *(See videos at and of book)* of which there is a section occasionally comes onto our History Channel over here, you see him in action - always finishing his lecture with 'If all else fails - kick him in the testicles, hard!" *(Tony Mills letter 26 Nov 2001)*

OSS instructor William "Dangerous Dan" Fairbairn demonstrates how to kill a man silently —almost casually—with a scalpel-thin commando dagger

A Frenchman or Belgian would tell us about conditions in his country and what needed to be done there and how important it was that we as prospective entrants into his country and participants in his country's war against the

Germans would have a familiarity with everything that was going on. Then in the middle of the morning would come a session of either running the obstacle course, which was a great collection of walls, trees that had to be climbed, and barbed wire entanglements to be crawled through, all the while blank cartridges were being fired at you and firecrackers thrown at you and noise, a simulation of crawling through an enemy barbed wire entanglement on the battlefield in a war.

Or instead of that we would have a snap shooting performance where you'd be given a pistol and stand on a target range set up over the 17th or 18th hole of the golf course, and movable targets would pop up from here and there and you would shoot at them. The more hits you registered the better, so it was a matter of pride to shoot as well as you could. Or you'd shoot on the rifle range or there was instruction in hand-to-hand fighting, judo and close combat warfare.

After lunch there would usually be what was called tactical problems, in which we would be divided up into groups of half a dozen, and each group would be put in the back of a pickup truck or maybe even a car and driven way off into the boondocks, even across the Potomac River into Virginia and then just told that you would proceed back to the Congressional Country Club as though it were a target, German headquarters of some kind, and we were a small partisan warfare unit which was to proceed through enemy territory and attack the Club and destroy the military headquarters inside it. Naturally this kind of thing being done in broad daylight in the suburban area outside of Washington, DC, attracted a little attention. We all wore our fatigue uniforms, there were some Marines and a couple of Britishers and the rest of us Army officers and it wasn't long before our activities became rather conspicuous in the surrounding country. Housewives got so they wouldn't even wave at us when they saw us crawling on our bellies through their front lawns, rushing in leaps and bounds across the ditch on the other side of the woods, past the Burning Tree Golf Club and on back to where our target was.   One of our group was very anxious to put on a parachute demonstration for the rest to impress them with how wonderful the paratroopers were. He thought the best thing to do would be to go down to Bolling Field and get permission from the commanding officer and have an airplane fly over the Congressional Country Club with half a dozen or so of us in it, and do a parachute jumping demonstration for those chaps who had never been in on that kind of thing, it would be educational and a good training exercise for everybody. So we went to Bolling Field and the operations officer was very sympathetic to our suggestion. The unfortunate thing was that he didn't have a transport plane of the kind that was used, no DC- 3s or C-47s, the old-fashioned Douglas two-engine plane. It happened that he had a Piper

Cub, a little observation plane that could only carry the pilot and two other men, so we decided to have a demonstration with only two paratroopers instead of a whole stick of six or ten. Myself and one of my friends got into the plane and took off, our audience was waiting for us, sitting on the golf course and the plane got down nice and low, 300 feet or so, the pilot cut back his engine and we were gliding and my turn was to go out first. As I got to the door of the plane I realized that I wasn't going to be able to get my parachute out of the door. When I got into the plane I didn't have my chute on, I just crawled through the door and put it on while I was inside, as had my companion.

As I started to go out the door my chute caught on it and held me there and I couldn't go through. By this time we had gone past the point where I was to jump out so I signaled to the pilot who was looking at me kind of anxiously. He turned around and came back and as we flew over the jump area I turned around backwards and crammed the chute through the door with my buttocks and was carried out head over heels backwards and pulled the rip cord much too soon.

Anyway the parachute opened and I found myself floating along nicely, but unfortunately the wind caught me and blew me way off from where I was supposed to come down on the golf course. I came down in the middle of a housing development some ways off, children were running up and down, pointing at me and worried housewives looking out of windows and waving brooms got a good deal more excitement and more information out of that parachute jump than our associates who were left to sit on the empty golf course.

In the words of Robert Kehoe, radio Operator of Jed Team Frederick: "We then traveled to "Area F," our temporary base on the grounds of the Congressional Country Club just outside Washington. It was a beautiful spot, and the tents scattered about added a note of romantic intensity in the lovely fall weather. We lived in the tents, but activities and meals were centered in the former clubhouse. It was here that I became acquainted with the men who were to be my close comrades for many months. We lived, trained, and worked together but, because of the unique team nature of the Jedburgh mission, we did not fight together. We were but a small percentage of those in Area F, where there were representatives of all parts of OSS. They were a fascinating collection, possessing a wide range of language and specialized skills. There were, for example, members of the Operational Groups, whose training emphasized weapons and demolitions. They impressed us as being fierce people ready to throw the Germans out of occupied Europe on their own. They were not quite so forbidding on closer acquaintance; like most of us, they were big on talk but more cautious in action."

Chapter 3

In which the budding saboteur learns
the pleasures of blowing things up

There was another training area we used to go to. This was called Area B and was in Prince William County, Virginia, across the Potomac and on the other side of Washington from where Area A was. It was a public recreational area, sort of a forest preserve of untouched woodland with a collection of small log cabins set way back from the road, which was Route 1, so that we were really in a primeval, pioneer type settlement. This aspect was heightened by the fact that there was no running water or other facilities; the whole place was strictly a basic shelter situation with a roof and not much more over our heads. The cooking facilities were very primitive and we didn't have a cook attached to our unit, in fact we weren't a

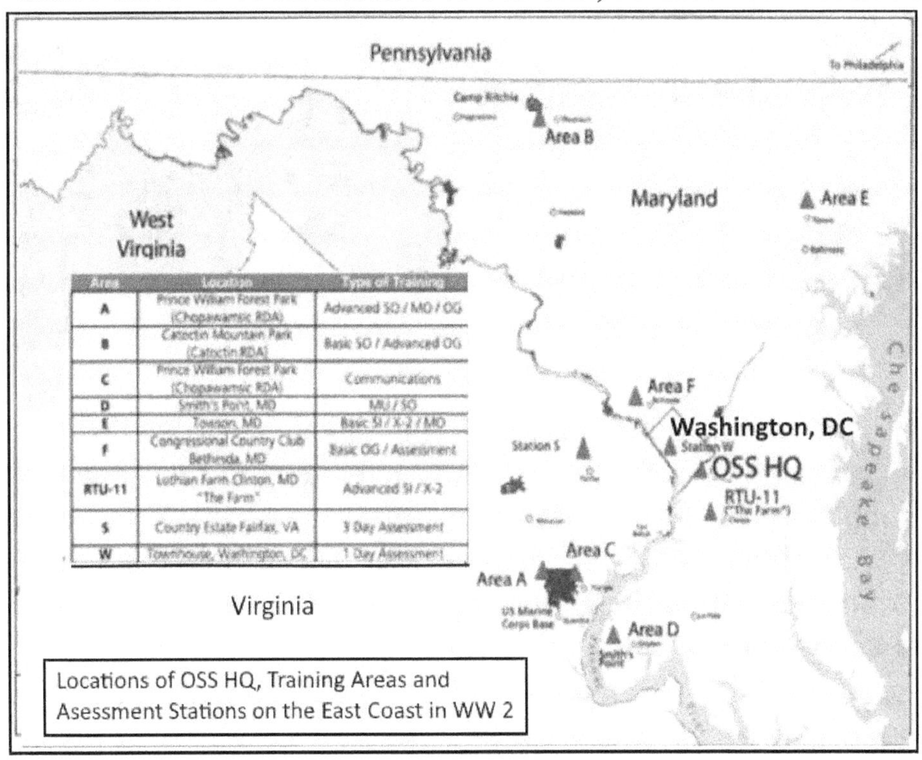

Area	Location	Type of Training
A	Prince William Forest Park (Chopawamsic RDA)	Advanced SO / MO / OG
B	Catoctin Mountain Park (Catoctin RDA)	Basic SO / Advanced OG
C	Prince William Forest Park (Chopawamsic RDA)	Communications
D	Smith's Point, MD	MU / SO
E	Towson, MD	Basic SI / X-2 / MO
F	Congressional Country Club Bethesda, MD	Basic OG / Assessment
RTU-11	Lothian Farm Clinton, MD "The Farm"	Advanced SI / X-2
S	Country Estate Fairfax, VA	3 Day Assessment
W	Townhouse, Washington, DC	1 Day Assessment

Locations of OSS HQ, Training Areas and Asessment Stations on the East Coast in WW 2 unit in any sense of the word, we were just a group of casual officers assigned to OSS for training and later assignment and the OSS hadn't any logistical capabilities, no cooks or bakers or medical services, so we had to scrounge our rations from the U. S Army Engineer School at Fort Belvoir down the road. We'd drive there in an Army pick up truck, carrying our requisition and introduce ourselves as assigned to the OSS. This didn't mean anything to the supply sergeant at Fort Belvoir, who gave us a very suspicious look. When eventually, more because we looked hungry than because we had any conformity to Army regulations behind us, he would release the rations and we would take them back to camp and try to cook them ourselves.

Training in Area B was limited by the fact that this little public park wasn't very big. We were supposed to be having problems in jungle warfare and survival technique, but there wasn't very much room, and we were never more than a mile from our camp throughout the whole thing. So it became necessary for us to get permission from the commanding officer of the adjoining military reservation which happened to be the Marine Corps School at Quantico.

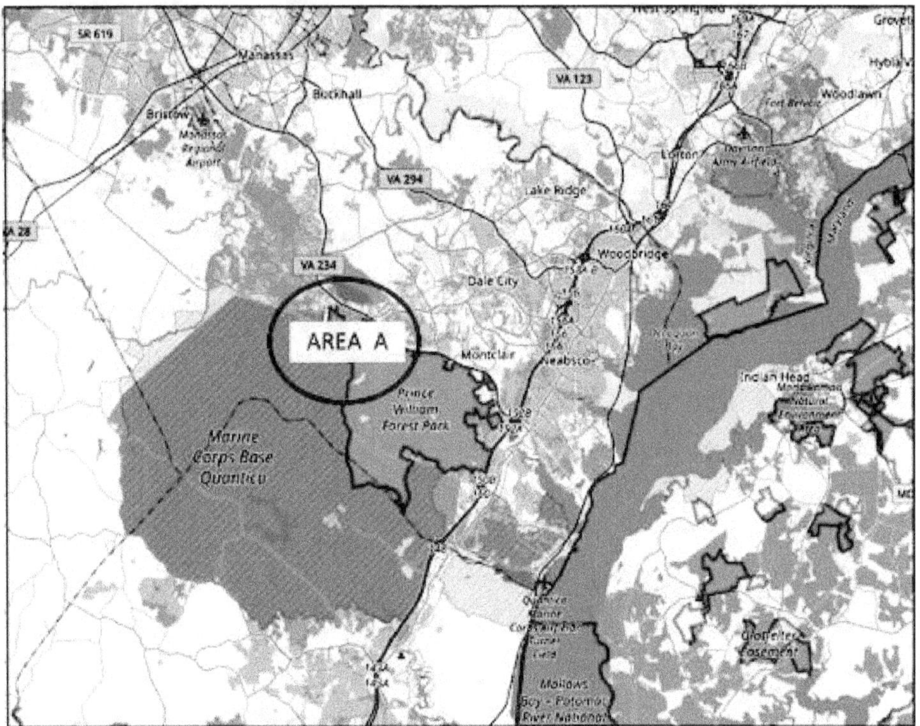

The Operations and Training Officer at Marine Corps Schools wasn't at all pleased about our presence next door to his area and he wasn't at all enthusiastic about our wanting to carry out operations in his area. Eventually through higher headquarters and somewhere General Donovan himself might have been mixed up in it, the Marine Corps finally bowed to the authority of the President, I suppose, and they gave permission for this small OSS detachment to have its training exercises on the area of the Marine Corps School.

Some of our exercises consisted of long marches, we would hike all day with packs and weapons and field rations, and as we would march down the roads of the Marine Corps Reservation large trucks of Marines would drive by on their way to their own exercise and each time they would yell "Bow wow wow" when they saw us dog faces going along.

Our welcome at Quantico, which was a qualified welcome at best, we soon wore out by what I suppose was the casual way that we treated explosives and had demolition exercises on this training area. The Marine Corps Reservation had a lot of old farmhouses and empty buildings and things scattered about which used to be homesteads and now are useful as sort of tactical points of reference for use in training as targets or shelters or objectives to be assaulted as attack problems. When we devised the idea that one of them would be an excellent target to surround and attack and destroy by blowing it up with demolitions, this suited us fine, but after it had happened to the accompaniment of loud explosions,

in a very short time a collection of Military Police vehicles drove out to where we were, way out in the middle of the boondocks. We didn't even think anyone would hear the explosions, but what had happened was that somebody in the Marine Corps headquarters had heard them and realizing that they weren't having any explosions of their own they wanted to find out what it was all about and sent out a whole mass of Military Police.

They found us milling about, congratulating ourselves on the swell operation we had just had and the great job we had done. We were called up before the Operations and Training Officer of the Marine Corps Schools and given a very severe chewing out about the whole thing, and told we were no longer welcome on the reservation. Again our friend in higher headquarters arranged for us to stay and we just had to behave ourselves and not destroy any more Marine Corps property.

Chapter 4
Ready to Go

At these training areas the life was enlivened a bit by our weekend activities. Every Friday afternoon, upon completion of duty, whether we were in Area A or B we'd rush back to our quarters and change into our best uniforms and

shave and cover ourselves with paratrooper badges and dress the part of our commando motivation and drive into Washington where headquarters always was the Mayflower Hotel. We'd go into the Palm Lounge where there was plenty of opportunity for encounter and resemblement (*rassemblement$_g$ – Fr.*) of one sort or another and it was a good starting point for what usually was a very active and gay weekend for all concerned and we'd all come stumbling back to our training headquarters at 2 o'clock Monday morning to snatch a couple of hours sleep before getting up for the day's activities.

More and more people kept coming into Area A all the time, they were mostly Army paratrooper lieutenants and captains. We were getting a very large collection of men there and in October of 1943 we'd been there for months with no real tangible target or goal at which to aim. We'd been recruited for an underground, unconventional warfare operation in Occupied Europe, but nobody had ever told us specifically about it except generally what it was supposed to be for and what it was supposed to do. The only thing we did know for sure was that it had not been finally approved and was indeed subject to being disapproved or shelved or forgotten about, in which case we all would have been a bunch of zombies sitting there at the Congressional Country Club with no assignment of any kind, everybody eager and straining at the bit, ready to go and be a hero. We were the opposite of the kind of guy who doesn't want to go to war. Everybody was just crazy to go, get into the action, to be a paratrooper, kill the enemy and generally blood and guts. Consequently our morale hadn't been so good, we were always saying, "When are we going to go? When are we going to get orders? What's going to happen?" Finally that October an officer from headquarters came out to Area A, we were called together into a large assembly hall and he told us that we were being subdivided, lists were made up subdividing us into groups and these groups were going to be sent to England very shortly and we would continue our training in England preparatory to the operation which was definitely going to take place.

Well, you can imagine that the official announcement that the operation was really on, and that we were all going to be sent overseas in a matter of weeks caused a great deal of pleasure and excitement in our organization. Of course our pleasure was heightened by the fact that everybody got ten days leave before being sent overseas and our morale hit a new high. Our various elements were to be sent from different ports and on different ships and not connected with each other in any way. I suppose this was to preserve some kind of secrecy, although actually the secrecy of our operation didn't seem to be anything so important. We all talked about it among ourselves and were never warned not to do so and I believe that the security our outfit was supposed to have had rather low priority.

Psych Assessment and Evaluation

Back in World War II, the United States was woefully prepared to enter the war, especially in the field of intelligence operations where they didn't have a national, professional intelligence service. But that would change very quickly. After President Franklin Delano Roosevelt appointed General William "Wild Bill" Donovan to head up the fledgling Office of Strategic Services (OSS), he quickly used his British contacts with getting the Americans the training and experience they would need in the coming months.

After OSS grew from their original COI (Coordinator of Information$_g$) roots, the U.S. copied the British program of psychological/psychiatric assessment similar to that in the English War Office Selection Boards (WOSBs). OSS was searching for what the personal makeup would be for assessing the perfect applicant for paramilitary$_g$ operations (Guerrilla warfare, sabotage, and assassination), intelligence operations (espionage), propaganda operations and select skills such as radio operators. They were starting from scratch. No one really knew what would make a perfect candidate for any of those.

So Donovan and his staff assembled a team of psychologists headed up by Dr. Henry Murray, a Harvard-trained psychologist who was a pioneer in personality assessment. He would head up the Assessment and Selection committee. They would screen nearly 5400 candidates to weed out the unfit for the dangerous job of being involved in the U.S.' first foray into the intelligence and Special Operations business.

The candidates, military and civilian, men and women would be brought to Station S. (Schools and Training) at the prior Willard Estate in Fairfax, Virginia. The initial problem that arose was that there were no job descriptions for the candidates and therefore the psychologists had a difficult time in assessing candidates because they didn't know what they were actually assessing for.

But what the Training School cadre of doctors came up with is a basic tool that is still used today, not only in Selection and Assessment for Special Operations Forces but in the civilian world in assessing managers.

Candidates would be required to build and maintain as completely as possible a cover story for himself, claiming to have been born somewhere he wasn't, to have gone to school and educated in an institution other than those he had attended, to have been engaged in work or profession different to his own, and to live now in a place that was not his true residence. The cover story was to be maintained with staff and students alike at all times except under when speaking to cadre members for the purposes of assessment. The candidates could reveal anything about themselves except their names and true identities.

During the assessment cycle, this was the first test of what would become the real world test of living undercover abroad in a foreign country that may be under enemy control. The candidates were rated on several key factors which included: Motivation, Practical Intelligence, Emotional, Stability, Social Relations, Leadership, Physical Ability,

Observation and Reporting, Propaganda Skills, and Maintaining Cover.

Each factor was rated on a six-point scale: Very Inferior, Inferior, Low Average, High Average, Superior, Very Superior.

(https://sofrep.com/specialoperations/how-oss-operatives-were-assessed-and-selected/)

*(There is a very entertaining book by Roger Hall called **YOU'RE STEPPING ON MY CLOAK AND DAGGER** that covers this activity, well worth reading.)*

Chapter 5
In which the newly trained Jeds board
a freighter and sail to Bonny Scotland

Going to Europe wasn't quite like going on a trans-Atlantic luxury liner. I and a few others were assigned to a funny little American freighter called the "SS Marina", the property of the Bull Line and there were only a few of us soldiers on board, vastly outnumbered by the Navy gun crew, on the ship for anti-submarine work, and the crew of the ship itself.

The SS Marina was a C1-A class Cargo ship –
like the one above.

(During wartime, the Bull Lines operated Victory ships and Liberty ships. The ship was run by its Bull Line crew and the US Navy supplied United States Navy Armed Guards to

man the deck guns and radio. The most common armament mounted on these merchant ships were the MK II 20mm Oerlikon autocannon and the 3"/50, 4"/50, and 5"/38 deck guns. Of the ships operated by the Bull Lines 19 ships were lost to German U-Boats, beginning with the loss of the SS Major Wheeler with all hands (35) on February 6, 1942. Bull Lines had lost 14 ships to U-boats by the end of the summer of 1942, and lost its last ship, the SS Delisle in October 1943. Over 275 crew were lost during the war aboard Bull Line ships.)
(https://en.wikipedia.org/wiki/A._H._Bull_Steamship_Company)

Both of these took a dim view of us, as they took an equally dim view of each other, and as we took of both of them. The only affinity that the Navy gun crew had with the professional civilian crew was they all liked to shoot dice. As it happened the ship's crew being typical lifetime seafaring men were better at shooting dice than the young teenage type Navy recruits, who were just kids in uniform and always taken for a terrible beating whenever they shot craps with the Merchant Marine crew. There was only one Navy officer in charge of the gun crew and we noticed that he was ostracized by the ship's officers, he ate at a little table all by himself and none of the ship's officers had anything to do with him, so we invited him to come and sit and eat with us, which he did. He turned out to be a good fellow and we all got together famously, this was Bonner Bowring. The ship's officers were just a bunch of meat balls and Bowring was a gentleman and here he was stuck on this little boat with all these mugs and living the life of a hermit in Times Square.

We passengers were all mustered into anti-submarine duty as soon as we got on board and divided into watches and every one of us had to do four-hour watch every night. On for two hours, then back to your cabin to sleep for awhile and then some guy would wake you up and do another two hours of watch at some out of the way place on the boat like the bow's end or on a corner of the bridge somewhere or stuck out on a gun platform, right over the water and you'd sit there for two hours and this was in October in the North Atlantic and it wasn't any too warm. You'd just sit there, you couldn't smoke and looking out into the jet-black darkness, hoping that you'd see a submarine, if there were any about. Nobody every saw one on our ship although there were some scares and destroyers ran around shooting off depth charges. It took us about ten days to cross the Atlantic and none of us knew just when or where we were to arrive. We expected that we were going to England and were not surprised therefore to wake up one morning and find that our ship had anchored in a little bay with a rocky, steep, forbidding looking coast ahead of us and nothing but a small fishing village tucked away at the bottom of the cove and a few little boats came out from shore and were paddling around us with the occupants waving.

I remember leaning over the rail and calling to one of the chaps on the boat who was a funny looking old man and saying. "Well, I'm glad to be in England, finally."

"Och, lad, you're no in England, you're in Scotland," was the reply.

As it happened we had proceeded to a place called EWE on the east *(west)* coast of Scotland. We didn't know if we were going to unload there or just what was going to happen, we thought it would be carrying security to an unreasonable degree to unload us all at Ewe and send us ashore secretly and lock us up in some kind of a closed training area, and we had unpleasant visions of being kept in seclusion for training purposes for months, sort of like we'd been doing outside of Washington, never knowing where we were going to go or when or what was going to happen next. So we breathed a sigh of relief when the convoy took off again and left Ewe in its wake and sailed on for another day and finally came into the harbor of Edinburgh.

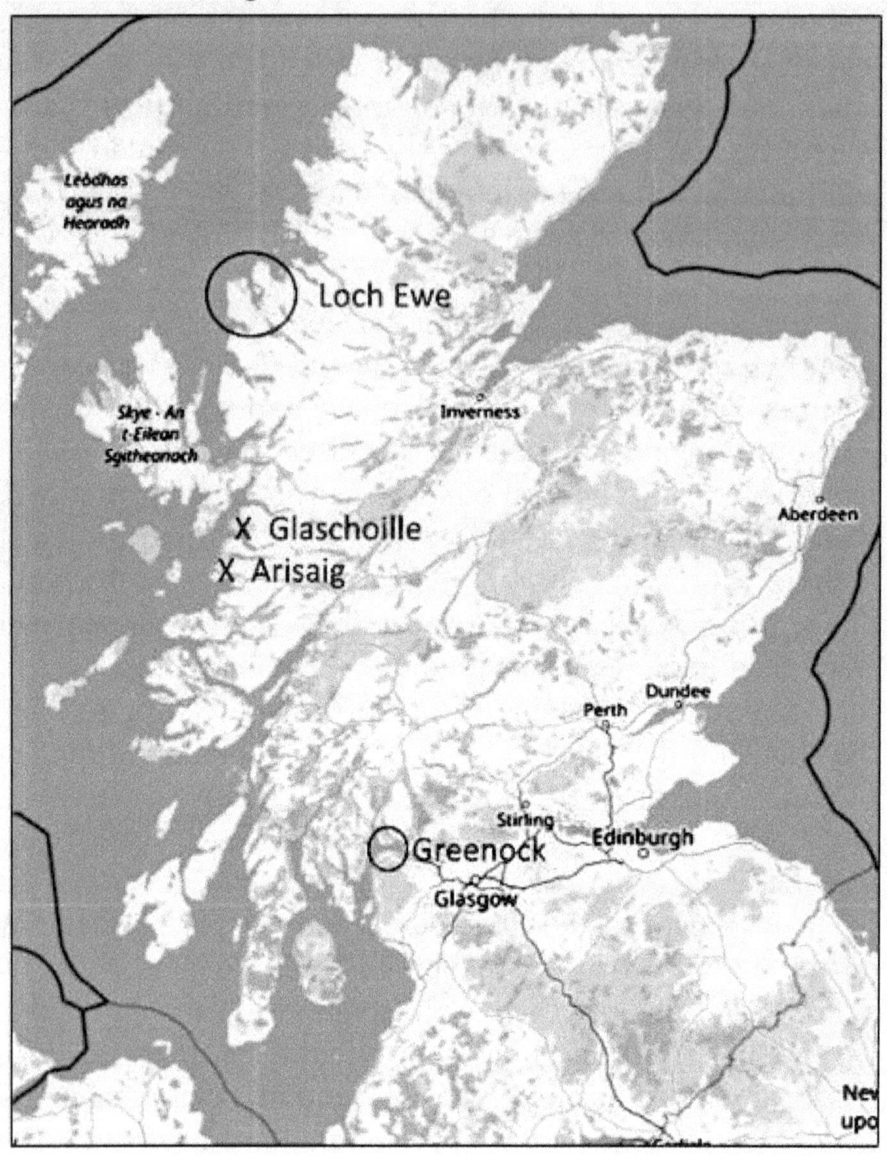

Here began a series of conflicts between the rules and regulations laid down by the military commander of the British Isles and the customs which had become explicit in our behavior. For example, we were told that in order to be unloaded off the boat we were going to have to put on full

42

combat uniform: field dress, field helmet, carry our side arms and gas masks. Finally we were taken off the boat in lighters and taken over to a dock where there were some railroad trains pulled up. We made ourselves as comfortable as we could in third class railway carriages which were filled to capacity. We didn't know where we were going, but jammed into the carriages, really dressed for war, uncomfortable and unable to stretch out in any way and it was getting dark and the train started and we shortly learned we were headed for London.

We presumed that we would then go to headquarters and get instructions to our ultimate destinations. It never occurred to me that we wouldn't be sent to a training area somewhere, but instead of being sent directly from the dock, the OSS method was to send us to London in full combat gear and give us our orders when we got there.

So the train went banging along across Scotland and the North of England and the Midlands and finally down into London and we arrived in the morning and got off. A few of the wise guys in our group who were a little closer to the top than we were had learned just where we were going and who they were to meet and as soon as they got off the train these older men, who had been to London before, and were "Oh So Social" types who knew London well, so they just took their guns and walked off the platform and got into taxi cabs and drove off to Piccadilly or the apartment of a friend or took hotel rooms to wash up and change out of their combat dress and put on some more civilized sort of clothing and went down to headquarters after having a rest and a bit of breakfast. I was not one of these favored few, so I stayed with the majority on the platform, looking around for somebody to tell us what to do, and it turned out that the officer who was in charge of us was one of those who had disappeared and taken a taxi off to Claridge's$_g$, with our orders.

In time some intrepid soul managed by telephoning

different headquarters and places to get in touch with OSS headquarters to announce that we were on the platform of Euston Station and Colonel so and so had disappeared, so what do we do? (That was Col. Charlie Neave who had been very quick to wave farewell to us and dash into the taxi and disappear. His last words being, "Goodbye boys, see you down at OSS headquarters," although we didn't know where that was or how to get there or anything else).

Well, as I say, with an airy wave of his newly acquired swagger stick, Charlie Neave was off to Claridge's for a bath, a rest and change of clothes before meeting his cohorts, meaning us, at OSS headquarters. The railroad station was full of Military Police and one of our group went over to the Provost Marshal and informed him of our situation and it wasn't long before a jaunty well-dressed officer came into the waiting room and said that he had brought transportation for us. So we went and climbed into regular Army trucks, in our combat gear, carrying our little suitcases in our hands, and were driven through the heart of fashionable West End London to 70 Grosvenor Street, just down from the American Embassy, which was the headquarters we would come to know so well.

There we shook hands with people who were meant to be in charge of us, among them was John Tyson, a Major, who said he had picked out several of us for duty as instructors, to run a sort of training program for newly acquired personnel. None of us wanted to be instructors, but unfortunately my name was on the list, so five or six of us were separated from the rest of the group and told that after having a few days to adjust ourselves here in the theatre of operations that we would be sent to Scotland to take some commando type British training in unconventional warfare which would be given us by the British Intelligence Service, the SOE_g, and the Special Air Service. The Special Operations Executive which worked with the SAS_g ran a lot of very worthwhile and important unconventional operations on the continent and had been doing this ever since the fall of France in 1940.

In a few days our little group received orders and got on a train in London, a nice overnight train with sleeping cars and Pullman accommodations, each of us in a little private bedroom and we really were enjoying life riding this comfortable train up to Glasgow, Scotland. On the way we noticed there were five or six younger officers of the British Army in the same car, one in Highland dress and others in battle dress, wearing the insignia of rather noted British regiments and as typical Englishmen they were not the least bit friendly and just ignored us, so we didn't try to start up an acquaintance with them either. When one of us would nod to one of them as we passed in the aisle he would walk on by as if he hadn't seen us, an attitude we were to become familiar with, of course.

Chapter 6
In which training is continued at
Glaschoille House in Scotland

When we got to Glasgow the next morning we were met by a British officer who came looking for us and it turned out that the five supercilious, unfriendly Englishmen were also part of our group, and we were lumped together and climbed into the back of a truck and driven from the station away out into the sticks, up the coast, to a funny little fishing town on one of the deep lochs, and there got into a couple of motor boats. You can imagine how bewildering all this was to us, just come from London after a rather peculiar trip from Scotland to London and then back to Scotland. We were transported by boat about an hour's journey across a choppy estuary to a funny little island. This turned out to be one of the training establishments of the Special Operations Executive. The island had an odd little house on it, icy cold and unheated. Probably before the war it had been a weekend fishing lodge belonging to some landowner or sportsman, the name of this was Glaschoille House.

We arrived just in time for tea, so we put our suitcases upstairs where we were later to be assigned rooms and hastened down to an extremely cold room heated only by a small, guttering handful of coals, smoldering in the fireplace. Here we had our tea and began vaguely to get acquainted with the Brits who were part of our training group, but continued to ignore us in precisely the same way as they had on the train.

I remember sitting at a table beside a little English Jew and I turned to him and said "Well, Lieutenant, I'm Captain Manierre of the American Army." He gave me a look with a tenuous smile and nodded and said, "Oh, is that so?" He didn't

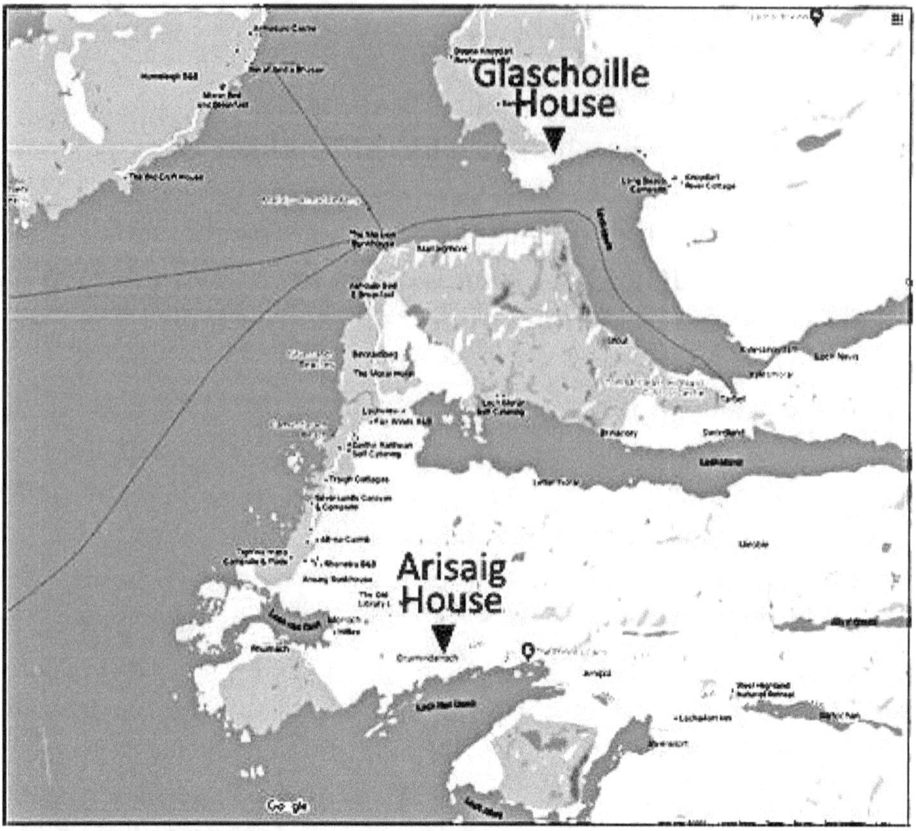

Glaschoille House
Arisaig House
Glaschoille House

shake hands or introduce himself, so things got off to a nice cozy start. We took our baggage to the rooms, there were four or five, sometimes six in a room and the beds were double-decker bunks without mattresses, just plain wooden benches set on top of each other and the mattresses were made of straw and there were no sheets or anything, so the idea was to put a blanket on top of the mattress and crawl under that, keeping on your socks and underwear and often not even unbuttoning your shirt. In the morning a British sergeant would rap on the door and wake us up and immediately behind him would be a private carrying a tray with steaming cups of tea. We'd drink our tea, dress, and then have to go outside for Physical Training. At this time in late October and early November it was getting pretty cold up there in the Highlands.

A very good-natured and friendly Scots sergeant would put us through our paces, running around, doing push ups and exercises of that sort for 25 minutes, followed by a nice little instruction in hand to hand combat, judo, jujitsu and various types of holds which would have been more interesting to learn about on a full stomach in a warmer atmosphere.

Then it was time for breakfast, which was not the type we were accustomed to in the American Army, but consisted of nothing but a bowl of oatmeal and all the coffee you wanted, which wasn't very good, and plenty of toast and margarine and jam. No eggs, no fruit, nothing like that, but we managed to get along on this.

After breakfast we would have a lecture about demolitions and be shown how to blow up things, or instruction in various kinds of weapons and occasionally we'd be taken out for practice firing at the target range or maybe for a tactical problem where we would be divided up into small groups and then have to maneuver around, crossing the wet Highlands on our bellies, most of the time, to attack houses and installations which were supposed to represent enemy

targets. This went on for about two weeks and then I received a call from London to come right back, there was something important that they wanted me to do. Just me, not the others, so I was very excited and took off for London. It took a long time to arrange for a boat to carry me from the island to the shore and then it was a drawn out and inconvenient thing to get official transportation to carry me to the railroad station in Glasgow and there I had to buy my own ticket as no arrangement had been made for me to be sent officially. I finally reported in at headquarters in London and was told by John Tyson, "Cy, we've got a large shipment of personnel coming in; officers and men who have been recruited into 'Operation Jedburgh' and who are on their way over from the United States now, having been at Area A. They are landing at Greenock tomorrow and we want you to be in charge of going out to the ship and getting them off and over to the training area."

The only advantage of this trip to London was that at least I got to spend the night there with nothing to do but enjoy myself, and since there were all kinds of nightclubs and little honky-tonk places where one could have fun, and since I had friends there anyway. I looked forward to a pretty good evening before heading up for Glasgow the next day.

Chapter 7
In which he shepherds the newly arrived
Jeds from Greenock to Arisaig House

So after an amusing evening in London I presented myself at headquarters the next morning at the appointed time and was more fortunate as they gave me Pullman tickets and orders, so I got back on a nice comfortable train and went back to Glasgow again.

There it turned out that the "Queen Elizabeth" was not arriving that day, but two days later, so I had to be quartered in the city for two nights. I managed to get a billet in transient officers quarters, which was nothing but a warehouse with a lot of cots in it and a bathroom at one end. I made myself reasonably comfortable and then went on an unguided tour of the bars and pubs and amusement places which turned out to be interesting for a transient officer. I made arrangements for a couple of American Army quartermaster trucks to meet me in the morning at the warehouse and drive to the dock and wait for me to bring the men and get them on the trucks and to where we were going. Of course I woke up in the morning and the quartermaster and the trucks hadn't arrived, so I went down to the end of the warehouse where the sucker was still in bed and snoring. I had to shake him awake and he got all confused and excited and got on the phone and luckily the trucks were waiting for him to call so it all turned out all right.

We drove to the dock at Greenock and the "Queen Elizabeth" was anchored out in the river in her gray war paint. It was a cold drizzly day and a dismal scene. I managed to get on a little launch to take me out to the Queen, and having orders and official status, they gave me an armband so I could get on board and started to scout around for my party.

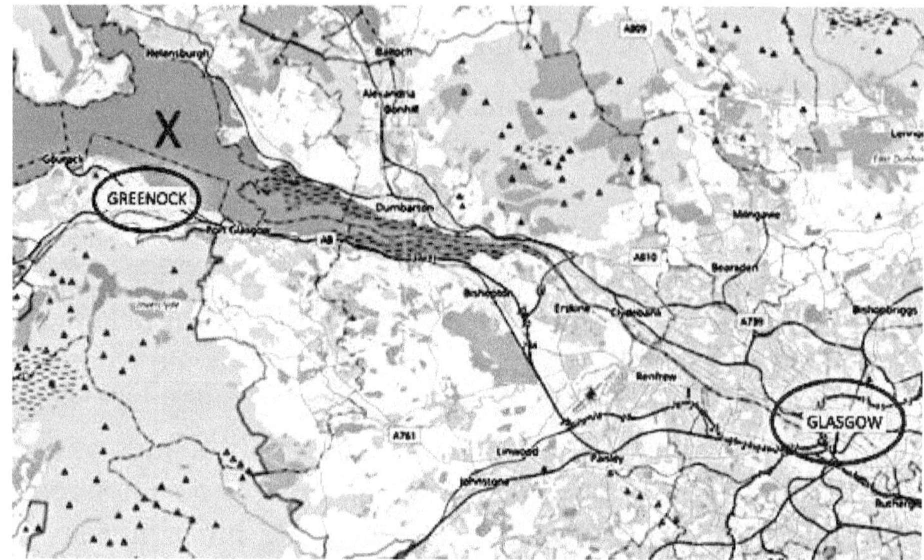

It was kind of eerie to walk around the "Queen Elizabeth" at this point as I remember what she had been like in peacetime, a luxury liner, beautifully decked out - inside and out.

In the words of Robert Kehoe again: "On 23 December, we boarded the Queen Mary for a rough but rapid journey across the North Atlantic. That ship and its crew were among the heroes of World War II. I do not know how many times it crossed the Atlantic without escort. With its stabilizer removed, it sailed at high speed on a zigzag course, thus reducing the chance of accurate U-boat targeting. Icebergs were another danger; we spotted a number of them. On this voyage, the ship carried about 15,000 men. In good weather, using bunks on deck, the total was more than 17,000--the manpower of an entire division!"

I got on board before any of her passengers were unloaded; there was a whole division of troops plus casual detachments like the one I was to pick up. It was just like getting into a big Army barracks, everything was GI and there were thousands of men walking about, and cigarette butts all over the place.

I was looking for my party when I heard a French voice scream "Cyrus, Cyrus, everything is snafu$_g$, everything is snafu." I turned around and sure enough there was my friend, Le Capitan Gerard Lambert, one of the French officers who had done training with us in Area A. He had stayed there when I was sent off to Scotland and was to come later, and here he was with two or three other French officers and they were part of the group I was to meet. It was no surprise to see him wringing his hands and complaining that everything was snafu. Gerard then introduced me to the officer who was in command of our little detachment and this turned out to be a tall, slim, pleasant, but severe looking Marine Major, Horace Fuller.

Hod had come back from the fighting on Guadalcanal and had been wounded and somehow recruited into the OSS because he'd had a great deal of experience handling small boats, and they were getting some Marines into that operation that was being run off Yugoslavia, getting boats across the Adriatic Sea. That was what he had originally come in for, but because he could speak French and had lived part of his life in France he drifted into our Continental operation.

Hod was in charge of this group and he gave me a resigned look and said things were pretty much mixed up and the morale was not very good because nobody knew where they were going or what they were supposed to do. They didn't have the equipment, they'd really been "lost in the shuffle" to use the words of my commanding officer when I left to join the OSS. Hod was comforted, however, to see that the representative who had been sent to meet them, myself, was wearing paratrooper uniform and seemed to be more of a field soldier than the types who had sent them overseas.

We got unloaded and to the dock and sure enough the trucks were still there. I'd gotten a little worried as I had been on the ship for a matter of a few hours, so they took us back to the Bachelors Officers Quarters where I had spent the last few nights. I had to say to the men. "Well, fellows, here we are. This is where we're going to stay for awhile."

I got on the telephone right away and was told that these men and I were being sent to another training area in Scotland, not far away, a place called Arisaig. After a rather unhappy night in the warehouse, we were armed with orders, taken to the railroad station, and loaded on the train for Arisaig.

"The paramilitary schools were based at ten shooting lodges in the Arisaig and Morar areas of Invernesshire, with the SOE staff headquarters in Scotland based at Arisaig House.

The courses lasted at first for three weeks but were later increased to five weeks. They included physical training, silent killing, weapons handling, demolition, map reading, compass work, field craft, elementary Morse, and raid tactics.

"The agents being trained came from a range of nationalities, and each group was housed in separate schools, as security protocol dictated that they should not mix. This policy was applied right up to the final briefing.

"The training began with a hard slog over the unwelcoming terrain of Invernesshire. Both men and women had to complete the course, and they would be equally tired, aching and covered in cuts and bruises having crawled on their bellies and trekked up mountains.

"Their weapons training and unarmed combat equipped agents for close combat only. William Fairbairn and Eric Anthony Sykes - two ex-Shanghai municipal police officers - taught unarmed combat, or silent killing. The pair gave their name to the FS fighting knife - a small knife used mainly by the Commandos - and their Fairbairn Fighting System was subsequently taught to members of the FBI and CIA.

"Weapons training introduced the students to the Colt .45 and .38, and to the Sten$_g$ gun, which was considered unreliable by some. The students were taught to fire by 'pointing' the gun, tucking their firing arm into their hip, rather than by the more orthodox method of taking aim, and they always fired two shots to be certain of their target. This system was known as the Double Tap system and it was specific to SOE agents. One of the props used to help the students with target practice was a life-sized figure on a winch, set to come at the agents at speed.

"Demolition and explosives training was essential, as sabotage was high on SOE's remit. Using dummy explosives, rail sabotage was carried out with the cooperation of the West Highland Line, who also supplied the school with a train. From a letter from Tony Mills: "The basic commando training for SOE was from the STS$_g$ at Arisaig House. I have included a section from a map – notice the tunnel on the railway line, this was used by the Jedburghs as they trained in Railroad Sabotage, charges and fog signals, then walk away and hide." We stayed there for about two months doing the kind of training I have already described, spending Christmas and New Years there too.

Rail bridge at Arisaig, also used for demolition training

The staff at Arisaig were all soldiers from Scottish regiments and the instructors were also. I was one of the few non-Scots instructors and these men were delighted to be hosts to the Americans at a Scottish New Years Eve party.

This was an affair that consisted mostly of the playing of bagpipes, drinking whiskey, and climaxed by wild dancing of a very roughhousing type at which everybody got quite drunk. I remember the bagpiper was so plastered he couldn't play his pipes, the Americans yelling "Wahoo", and clicking their heels and jumping around making a lot of noise and turning it into a kind of barn dance. But everything was done in good form, and it was there I learned words to the song ***"The Ball of Keirrimuir"***, which is of course a Scots song, and a very dirty one.

(See Appendix for words of this song)

Chapter 8
Wherein the Jeds arrive at Milton Hall
for the last of their training

After New Years in Arisaig we went down to London where I got orders as one of the instructors to go to a new and final training area. It was one which had been acquired and put into operation especially for us, as others in Scotland were simply borrowed, they had made room for us as we didn't have any other place to go. This was Milton Hall outside of Peterborough, the seat of Earl FitzWilliam, a renowned Master of Foxhounds.

It had been requisitioned by the Army and turned over to SOE for the training, but the big estate was still farmed and the manager, who was a very nice gentleman, was living in his house down the road, where he used to have some of us in for dinner occasionally. The kennels of the FitzWilliam Foxhunt were still operating, full of foxhounds, and three days a week the huntsman and the whippers-in, dressed in their scarlet hunting coats, would take the hounds out and go hunting, usually there were not many out with them, but they went out just the same.

There was a story that during one of the German air raids in the neighborhood, this pack of hounds and the huntsmen had been strafed by German fighters and had to gallop away to escape. I don't know how true this was, but it sounded very colorful.

At Milton Hall our training became a bit more crystallized and we followed a more regular program and in time after we got set up our fellow trainees began to arrive in groups. Our group consisted of over 100 people; several hundred perhaps, of whom approximately half were officers of Continental Armies of Occupied countries. Most of these were French, but a good number were Belgian, Dutch, Norwegian and Danish, and the other half was made up in equal part of British and Americans. There were a bunch of radio operators who were sergeants who trained along with us.

Robert Kehoe adds: "At the beginning of February, our contingent moved north to what was to be our main training base at Milton Hall near Peterborough, in eastern England.

"This was a great English estate with a rambling old mansion from the 1700s. It could have been the setting for a Thackeray novel. One easily imagined supporters of the Stuart pretender roving secretly through the dark corridors within. The main house was used for administration, recreation rooms, and a lecture hall.

"The latter had been the mansion's grand hall; its walls were covered with portraits and paintings--family treasures from another era. The mansion was surrounded by several hundred acres of fields, woods, and gardens. These were soon covered with our men, competing for space with the sheep who dotted the fields here as throughout Britain. A number of temporaries were erected near the main building as living quarters, classrooms, and eating facilities. They were spacious and well located in these pleasant surroundings."

"There were communications men and the idea was that Jedburgh teams were to consist of one Continental officer, one either British or American officer and one radio operator, whether American or a citizen of the country where the operation was taking place. As these people began to arrive, some from London and some from other places where they had been kept "on ice" before being sent to Peterborough, they arrived in various stages of morale. Some of the Europeans had been in British employ undergoing training and some had been in operations with the British and were veterans at this sort of thing. Their morale was high as they had gotten accustomed to the way the intelligence service seemed to operate which was a very vague and tenuous way of doing.

"Most of the British personnel seemed to have come straight from the Army, right out of regiments and military organizations, recruited by the British counterpart of the OSS, the same way we'd been recruited and their morale was pretty good, but the morale of the Americans was about the worst, due entirely to the fact that they had been treated so casually by the OSS. For example, the group that I had left up in Arisaig, that were taken off the "Queen Elizabeth", were finally sent down to Milton Hall, when they came they were all frowns and looked mad and sat down in the dining room where the rest of us were having our meal, and one of them, a large, tall, red-headed fellow named Bazaltoff, jumped up on a chair and said. "Boys, let's give a cheer." And all the ones who had come in with this group cried, "Forty-eight, forty-nine, fifty, some shit."

As things went on at Milton Hall the training was nothing much more than a repetition of what we had already had before, and the morale got lower and everyone was disgusted. I remember Bill Peach (*Pietsch*) wrote a big sign on the blackboard saying: "NEVER HAS SO LITTLE BEEN

DONE BY SO MANY." Fights would break out among these guys.

Jedburgh officers at the bar in Milton Hall on Bastille Day

There was a little bar set up and in the evenings after duty we'd put on our Class A uniforms and have a drink at the bar before going to the mess hall for dinner. One guy, Conrad Dillow had gotten drunk and he started walking around insulting the English-men, saying "These sons of bitches, English," and making himself very unpleasant indeed, and they just ignored him as only the English can, so Dillow started to pick on me. "You lousy West Point so and so, you son of a bitch." I obliged Dillow by grabbing him by the front of his coat and shaking him and then giving him a light backhanded, mutton chop blow across the face. Of course he retaliated and in a minute we were in a swinging affair. It

63

didn't last long, however, as all the others dove in on us and stopped the fight, but I was actually in danger of being kicked out of the operation because of that, and Dillow did get kicked out. I was perfectly happy with this as I didn't have a bit of sympathy for him. I suppose if I had taken his part I could have prevented it, but I didn't feel like doing that.

Robert Kehoe continues: "It was here that the name Jedburgh was introduced: it is the name of a small town on the Scottish border. (In this area, Scots conducted guerrilla warfare against English invaders during the 12th century.) Traveling through the region many years later, I came across a plaque noting that men of Jedburgh were to be found on many battlefields, wielding the Jedburgh ax and staff to such purpose that their war cry struck terror. I suspect that this bit of medieval legend played a role in the selection."

On the weekends we'd be given time off Friday night, Saturday and Sunday to enjoy ourselves and we'd usually go to London, going in trucks to the station in Peterborough and get on the train, always the same one every weekend and take two and a half hours to get to London. There was always a good deal of curiosity displayed by bystanders as this mass of officers in foreign uniforms, all wearing parachute insignia, would jump out of the trucks and go to the ticket seller and stampede aboard the train. This way of life went on until sometime in March or April then the mission began to become more clear. We'd been divided into Jedburgh teams, each of us knew his partners and some of the teams had been assigned to specific areas in Europe where they were to operate and they were getting briefed on who was there, what was going on and in general what to expect and how to conduct themselves when they got on the ground. My team consisted of myself, a French officer and a radio operator who had not yet been selected and we were to go somewhere in Southern France. Of the many Jedburgh teams which were being created there must have been twenty which would be dropped there and it was decided to send us down to complete our training in North Africa and to fly into France from there as the flight from England would be too long.

The Real Thing
(From Robert Kehoe, to give the "color" of the times)

"We were getting anxious. Everyone knew an invasion was being planned but did not know when or where it would occur. The Jed teams were supposed to be dropped into France well before the landings. The teams were ready, but the problem of how to get them into France remained unsolved. During the spring months, the Germans had carried out a number of roundups of Resistance units. Of particular concern for our operations, the Germans also had uncovered and destroyed many of the clandestine radio links that had maintained contact between France and England.

"Our leadership had planned on the help of these radio contacts in arranging receptions for Jed teams. The alternative was to drop "blind," which meant parachuting to a location with no guidance available to the pilot or to the team. This was dangerous for the pilot and for those making the drop. The pilot, lacking guidance from the ground, found it difficult to determine location and altitude, thus increasing the risk of injury for the parachutist. If the drop was successful, the parachutist had to rely on his speed, skill, and knowledge of the area. Accurate information on ground conditions was not current. There is no doubt that the German counterintelligence actions during the winter and spring of 1944 dealt a serious setback to early exploitation of the Resistance in support of the landings.

"In late May, most of the Jed teams were dispersed around the countryside in a large-scale, two-week exercise. Our team was working at the simulated headquarters when we received instructions to report to Milton Hall. It was a Friday morning. On returning to Milton Hall that afternoon, we and the members of one other team were told to gather our equipment and prepare to join in an exercise with the Special Air Service (SAS), a British paramilitary force. The exercise was planned to last about five days but could go on longer. We were to prepare ourselves and our equipment as if for a combat operation and be ready to leave for London on Sunday morning. We and our equipment were checked thoroughly on Saturday. Captain Wise and I both suspected that this was a cover story—it seemed too realistic to be another exercise. Agueric *(S/Lt Paul Bloch-Auroch, (Paul Agueric) – French, Jed Team Frederick, second)*, having experienced so many false alarms over the years, was more skeptical."

Chapter 9
On the way to Blida in Algeria

From unidentified newspaper: "He still knew nothing of the exact mission which would be assigned him. These details were handled by the high staff, and the men who were to carry them out were being given general training until the last minute before setting out for France, the Balkans. or Italy.

"As the invasion of France drew nearer, the leaders of the OSS planned their campaign of undercover work on the continent in conjunction with the army general staff. And in April. 1944, 25 men were sent from London to train at Algiers for missions in the south of France.

So our little collection of about 20 Jedburgh teams loaded up onto a train for Liverpool where we boarded a very handsome and pleasantly appointed liner of the Union Castle Line, the **"SS Capetown Castle"**. It turned out that we were nicely quartered with comfortable staterooms and good food

in the dining room. The companionship was improved by the fact that almost half of the passengers were women, representatives of different British Auxiliary uniform services. They were friendly and we all hit it off very well.

The military band of the Grenadier Guards was on board and they would have a concert every afternoon on the back deck and several times the musicians would treat us to a little dance music and we'd have a dance in the evening after supper down in the dining room. We were really going first class.

The Special Services Officer on the boat acted as a sort of purser or amusement steward, the idea being to keep up morale by organizing deck sports and games and activities for everybody, and athletics were certainly pursued. We had with us a little Irish sergeant major who was in charge of physical training, that being his specific job in the British Army. He was Sergeant Major Fernandes, I say he was Irish for that's what he told me. Fernandez was not an Irish name and his appearance was extremely Spanish. He had black hair, black eyes and eyebrows, rather dark skin, a lean aquiline face, a beaky nose and looked like a Spanish mountaineer of the old days.

I said to him, "Sergeant Major, were you born and raised in Ireland?"

"Oh, yes sir, I'm Irish."

"Well, surely your family must be descendants of shipwrecked sailors of the Spanish Armada."

He shook his head, "I don't know anything about that, sure and I'm Irish and that's all there is to it."

He was our Special Services Officer as well as physical training teacher and he decided that nothing would do but that the ship would organize a boxing tournament, and he worked out a nice little program whereby the American, French and English officers and everybody in our group would sign up as participants in this. We were told that we were just going to box among ourselves. We did a little boxing anyway as part of our daily physical training plan, so the idea was to box with each other in front of spectators, and after it was over we'd all shake hands, just a nice friendly little boxing match done for the amusement of all concerned.

The Capetown Castle arrived in Algeria in mid-May, 1944, and the Jedburgh personnel prepared to be dropped for their missions into France. The drops were to be made by either the US 15th Air Force, 885th Squadron, flying B-24 bombers, or RAF 624 Squadron from – both based at Blida.

OSS Headquarters in Algeria, Villa Magnol

Aïn Benian
Bologhine
Alger ⴰⵣⵣ.ⵉⴰ◎
الجزائر
Staoueli
Belouizdada
Bordj El Kiffan
El Achour
Bachdjarah
Dar El-Beïda
Zeralda
Souidania
Alger الجزائر
Rahmania الرحمانية
Khraïcia
Hamme
Fouka
Les Eucalyptus
الكاليتوس
Koléa القليعة
isti
Birtouta
Sidi Moussa
Meftah
Boufarik
Chebli
Larbaa
Oued El Alleug
Bougara
Beni Tamou
Bouinan
Blida البليدة
BLIDA ⵀ⵰ⵣⵀⵉⵜⵠ.
Daira Bougara
zala
البليدة
Parc National
de Chréa
الحظيرة
الوطنية
الشريعة

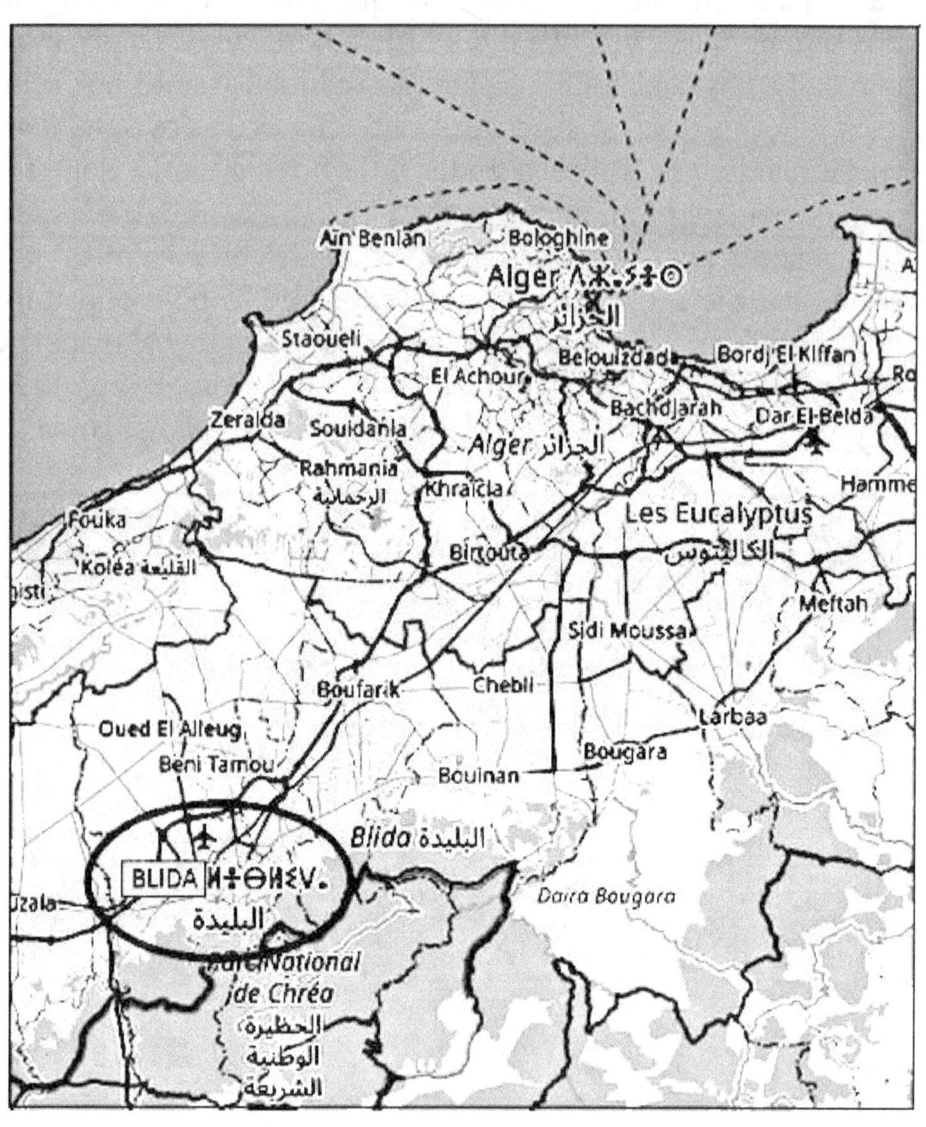

70

Photo from scrapbook – Pop, Lt Gennerich, Lt McIntosh

Letter from Tony Mills: "Many many thanks for sending the photographs, they are very much appreciated. Yes I can identify the two other guys in the picture.

Team Dodge - <u>Major C E Manierre</u> (US)
Sgt. L T Durocher (Canadian)

"Inserted 24th June 1944. An SOE Massingham_g team, to harass German communications on the left bank of the Rhone and roads and railway transport, Lyon/Vienne area. Replacing Team Veganin, Sgt Gardner (Jess) killed on drop, and Maj N. Marten, upset by his wireless operators death and returned to Algiers where he took overall charge of the Jedburghs at the SOE base at Massingham.

Team Chloroform - Capt. J Martin (Fr)
Lt. Henry D McIntosh (US). Served in Team Hyena in China
Lt. J Sassi (Fr)

Inserted 29th June 1944. Another SOE Massingham mission, to re-establish resistance in the Drome$_g$ and Haute Alpes$_g$ region, after the recent attack on the Vercors$_g$ area resistance. McIntosh became a doctor (Heart Surgery) after the war and treated President Johnson.

Team Novocaine **Lt. Charles J Gennerich** (US) Served in Team Gorilla, China
Lt. J. Y. Pronst (Fr)
Sgt W. (Bill) Thompson (US) Served in Team Alpaca in China

"Inserted 6th August 1944. Massingham mission, to stimulate guerrilla activity in the Hautes Alpes$_g$ region, contacting Jockey circuits. Bill Thompson became a Red Cross executive after the war.

"It must have been taken shortly after the Jedburghs landed in Algiers. They left Milton Hall early April and sailed on Capetown Castle as the records show, from Glasgow on 2nd May." *(Note: Pop reports having sailed from Liverpool)*

May 1944, arrived in Algiers for staging to be inserted into France by the 885th Squadron 15th Air Force.

Below is a photo of RAF Blida, some miles south-west of Algiers -

"At the time of the 15th Special Group (Prov) organization, its component squadrons, the 885th Bombardment Squadron (Heavy) (Special) and the 859th Bombardment Squadron (Heavy), were already relative veterans in the developing field of air force special operations. The 885th, formerly the 122nd Bombardment Squadron (Heavy) and before that the 122nd Liaison Squadron, had been supplying the French resistance from Blida and Maison Blanche, Algeria since November 1943. Initially, as the 122nd Liaison Squadron, it conducted special operations under 334 Wing (RAF). In April 1944 it was redesignated the 122nd Bombardment Squadron under Col. MacCloskey. This change formalized its special operations status and organization and increased its compliment from ten aircraft, including seven B-25 medium bombers, to fifteen heavy bombers (B-17s and B-24s) modified for special operations. It was once more redesignated on 15 June, 1944, as the 885th Bombardment Squadron (Heavy) (Special) at Blida under the 15th AAF. In September 1944, with the support of the French Resistance no longer a pressing requirement, the unit relocated to Brindisi, Italy and continued operations in support of Italian partisans.

"Similarly, in the summer of 1944 the 859th, attached to the 801st/492nd Bombardment Group of the 8th AAF, operated out of Harrington, England as part of **Operation Carpetbagger**$_g$, also in support of the resistance in Western Europe. The 859th had been organized as the 788th Bombardment Squadron (Heavy) which originally operated as a conventional heavy bombardment squadron."

"In June, the final preparations were made and Manierre boarded a plane with a French Canadian named Durocher as his radio operator. The French had been informed of their coming by the secret channels of communication, code radio and underground agents, and the lone plane left Africa bound for the secret rendezvous point, a field near the small village of Beaurepaire, 50 miles south of the city of Lyon along the valley of the River Rhone which flows down southeast France past Switzerland and Italy.

Chapter 10
Lucien Durocher - "Oswald"
Lt. Lucien Joseph Durocher (1920-1985)
Royal Canadian Corps of Signals – SOE

"Born on 26 June,1920 in Casselman (Ontario), Lucien Durocher received his schooling in Embrun, L'Orignal and Ottawa (LaSalle Academy and Ottawa Technical). He joined the Royal Canadian Corps of Signals on 3 September 1939. Shortly after, Lucien was sent to Barriefield Camp, near Kingston, where he was trained as an operator in wireless telegraphy. In early December, three months after he had enlisted, he was on his way to England as a member of the advance units of the First Canadian Division. Durocher was also with the Canadian brigade sent to Spitzbergen in August 1941 — from June 1943 to early 1944 he was a wireless operator with battalion and headquarters in Sicily and Italy. From there, he was recruited by the UK's Strategic Operations Executive (SOE) and sent to Algeria for accelerated training. Having received the rank of sergeant a few weeks prior, Durocher left for Algiers in North Africa in

April 1944. There he received specific training for specialized work behind enemy lines.

"Close to midnight on June 23, 1944, a solitary British plane winged its way over a quiet countryside somewhere in southern France. Suddenly, a light blinked feebly but clearly from below. Without hesitation, two men jumped from the plane and, their parachutes billowing in the inky blackness, floated slowly to earth.

"A thousand yards away was a German military camp, but if the Germans heard the plane or suspected anything out of the ordinary that night, they did nothing about it. It was not wise for German soldiers, except in very large numbers, to venture forth into a lonely countryside in those days of the Nazi occupation.

"One of the men who dropped that night into a life of constant danger and excitement was an American captain. The other was a fair-haired French- Canadian sergeant - Lucien Joseph Durocher of Ottawa.

"The two men belonged to what was called the Special Force Unit. They had been specially trained in North Africa and flown from there to France to help organize the Maquis and to send news of enemy troop concentrations and guns positions to the Allies. Lucien Durocher - then a sergeant, now a lieutenant - is one of an undisclosed number of Canadians selected for this hazardous work. He is one of few who survived. He is at present back in Canada, his job in France having been successfully completed, enjoying a well-earned leave.

Enlisted in 1939

"He had completed his third year, was just about to return for his fourth when war broke out. On Sept 4, 1939, he enlisted as a signalman in the Royal Canadian Signals Corps. He had been a member of the Non-Permanent Active Militia for two years previous. He admits that, while patriotism had something to do with his joining up, the main impulse which prompted him to do so was a craving for adventure.

"England was something new to the young French-Canadian who, although born in Ontario, had not had much intimate contact with English-speaking people. He found the English strange and distant at first but gradually came to like them. Of his English-speaking comrades in the army, he says they were all "one happy family".

"I think from my own army experience that, if French and English Canadians would mix more together, they come to like each other," the young lieutenant says. "The trouble is we didn't know each other."

Many dull months of routine battle training passed until one day in August, 1941, Lucien and some of his comrades were given new equipment and put on a train for a Scottish port, from which they sailed for the Norwegian island of Spitzbergen.

"The purpose of the trip was to destroy the weather forecasting equipment on the German-occupied island. It took about three days to get there. The expedition arrived at Longyear Byen at noon, and after the Norwegian flag had been hoisted as a signal, Lucien and seven others landed, meeting no opposition. The others followed.

"A week later, after destroying the vital weather equipment and setting fire to coal mine shafts and huge piles of coal, the expedition left the devastated island for Britain - still completely unmolested by the Nazis - bringing with them the 1,500 Norwegians and two Germans who had resided at Longyear Byen.

Operation Gauntlet
"Operation Gauntlet was an Allied Combined Operation from 25 August until 3 September 1941, during the Second

World War. Canadian, British and Free Norwegian Forces landed on the Norwegian island of Spitsbergen in the Svalbard Archipelago, 650 mi (1,050 km) south of the North Pole. Coalmines on the islands were owned and operated by Norway at Longyearbyen and by the Soviet Union at Barentsburg; both governments agreed to their destruction and the evacuation of their nationals. The objective of Gauntlet was to deny Germany the coal, mining and shipping infrastructure, equipment and stores on Spitsbergen and suppress the wireless stations on the archipelago, to prevent the Germans receiving weather reports.

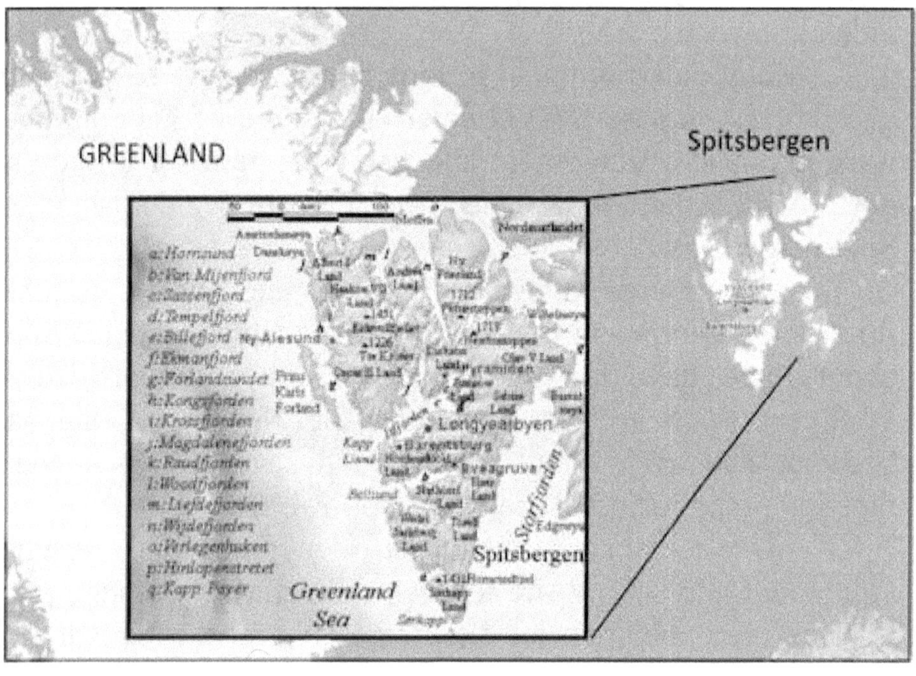

"The expedition sailed from the River Clyde on 19 August in **Empress of Canada** and rendezvoused with Force A (Vian) with the cruisers Nigeria, Aurora and the destroyers HMS Anthony, Antelope and Icarus. The ships put in at

Hvalfjörður in Iceland to refuel and departed on the evening of 21 August. Late on 22 August, the destination of the force was revealed to the troops. Force A met the oiler Oligarch and its trawler escorts on the evening of 24 August, west of Spitsbergen and as the force approached, an aircraft made a reconnaissance flight over Isfjorden, the large inlet on the western coast of Spitsbergen island, the most populated area of the archipelago. At 4:30 AM Icarus landed a signal party at the Kap Linne wireless station at the entrance to the fjord, where they were welcomed by the Norwegian operators. The big ships entered Isfjorden, steamed on to Grønfjorden at 8:00 AM and anchored off the Soviet mining township of Barentsburg. Potts went ashore to confer with the Soviet authorities about the embarkation of the population and its delivery to Archangelsk as the Canadians occupied other Soviet and Norwegian settlements along Isfjord.

"The evacuation proceeded slower than planned because the Soviet Consul wanted machinery and stores loaded on Empress of Canada as well as personal effects. The Empress of Canada set out for Archangelsk at midnight on the night of 26/27 August, escorted by Nigeria and the destroyers.

"Aurora stayed behind to guard the landing parties and assist in the embarkations from the remoter settlements. The Canadian engineers set fire to about 450,000 long tons (457,221 t) of coal dumped at the mines, fuel oil was poured into the sea or burned and mining equipment was removed or sabotaged, during which, Barentsburg was mysteriously burned down. On the evening of 1 September, the Empress of Canada and its escorts returned from Archangelsk to Green Bay.

"Normal business was kept up at the wireless station by the Norwegian Military Governor Designate, Lieutenant Ragnvald Tamber except for bogus reports of fog, to deter Luftwaffe air reconnaissance. Three colliers sent from the mainland were hijacked along with a whaler, icebreaker, tug and two fishing boats. On 2 September, about 800 Norwegians boarded Empress as did 186 French prisoners of war, who had escaped from German captivity and been interned in the USSR until the German invasion. Force A sailed for home at 10:30 PM on 3 September, with 800 Norwegian civilians and the prizes, after a ten days' occupation, having never been in darkness. Anders Halvorssen preferred not to join the Norwegian army-in-exile, hid and remained on the island. The final wireless message was transmitted on the evening of 3 September and the sets at Barentsburg, Longyearbyen, Kap Linné and Grønfjord were destroyed; as Force A made its return journey, a German station was heard calling Spitsbergen. The spurious weather reports had led to the cancellation of Luftwaffe weather reconnaissance flights by the Wettererkundungsstaffel.

"Gauntlet was a success; the Germans had not known of or had been able to challenge the expedition. The raiders had suffered no casualties, the local civilians were repatriated, several ships were taken as prizes and one German warship was sunk on the return journey. After the operation, the British expected the Germans to occupy Svalbard as a base for attacks on Arctic convoys but the Germans were more interested in meteorological data, the Arctic being the origin of much of the weather over western Europe.

"More battle training followed in England until June, 1943, when, attached to the Princess Patricia's Canadian Light Infantry, he left for the Mediterranean theatre of war. On July 10, he landed in Sicily, one of the first wave of infantry to reach the shore in the island's invasion.

"The invasion of Italy followed, and Lucien was in the front lines until after the battle of Ortona, one of the fiercest of the Italian war. But by this time, not having suffered even a scratch, he was finding the throes of battle somewhat monotonous. When a British officer asked for volunteers to do liaison work with the French resistance movement in German-occupied France, he volunteered. "Sicily and Italy had not satisfied me," he says.

"Made a sergeant only a few weeks before, Durocher left for North Africa in April, 1944. There he was specially trained for work in an enemy-occupied land. Finally, just when everybody believed that the recruitment phase must surely now be over, Sergeant LJ Durocher of the Canadian Army (he was French-Canadian) was found in Algiers and, being fully qualified, quickly recruited by SOE as a Jedburgh W/T_g operator - about whom, more later.

"By mid-1944, many mixed teams were being sent into France; Americans, Canadians, Free French, and British. Some were commando units, others sabotage teams. At the end of June, he and an American captain were furtively dropped from an airplane in southern France. They were met by the local leaders of the Maquis whom, until the invasion of southern

France in August, they trained in guerrilla warfare and themselves helped to fight the enemy.

"Four teams were sent in during June, one of them the two-man team named DODGE, led by Captain C.E. Manierre (US) accompanied by Sergeant Durocher.

"On 5 August, Manierre was captured at Valence, Drome and ended his war in Stalag Luft$_g$ I in the Baltic. The day after Manierre's capture, Durocher was made up in the field to commissioned rank and took charge of the operation."

17th October, 1944

To: Lt. Colonel D.L.C.   From: Major Champion.
     Carleton-Smith.

83

Sgt. DUROCHER

The above-named was parachuted into the LYONS area on the night of the 26th June, 1944, to act as wireless operator to Major C.E. Manierre, U.S. Army.

During the period until over-run by Allied forces, his work was exemplary. The area to which he was sent was one of the most difficult, and he carried out his duties with extreme devotion, particularly after the capture on Major Manierre by the Gestapo.

I can thoroughly recommend him for a commission.

Major.

1/Attach wo/1/3 (DAAG(L))
10/Durooher L.J./1

29 Nov 44
O i/c Records, CMHQ.
O.C 1 Cdn N.E.T.D

Lieut. L.J Duroher.

1.   The m/n officer (formerly C.3524 A/Sgt.
Duroher, L.J.) has been granted an immediate
commission in the Cdn. Army (Gen List) effective
6 Aug 44 and this appointment is appearing in
Supplement to Overseas RO 5295.

2.   This appointment has been authorized for
the period that this officer is speoially employed
with NO 1 (SP). He hving oeased to be specially
employed arrangenents are being made for his return
to Canadian control and he will, therefore, be s.o.s
"Q" List v.e.f. 3 Dec 44 and t.o.s.1 Cdn N.E.T.D.
4 Dec 44, where arrangements will be made for his
return to Canada. He will report to the Adjt,
1 Cdn H.£.T.D., Tweedemuir Camp, Thursley, Surrey
on 4 Dec 44.

                              (A.B. MacLaren) Major

DAAG(L

                              for (C.S. Booth) Brigadier
                              Deputy Adjutant-General
                              Canadian Military Headquarters.

Copy to:
No 1 (SP) War Office.
DAAG, AG 1 (Offrs N) War Office
C.P.M.
C.T.C.
Lieut. L.J. Durooher.
A.G..2a.

"Many are the tales which Lieutenant Durocher tells, once he can be persuaded to talk of secret missions, of blowing up German troop trains, of attacking the enemy along lonely roads in the night. One of the lieutenant's tales concerns a shoe factory, where there were hundreds of pairs of boots which the Nazis planned to seize and ship off to Germany. In a daring raid, Durocher and his French companions drove up to the factory, filled their truck to capacity with boots. Back in their hideout, they counted the boots - 1,500 pairs.

"In July 1944, after the invasion of Normandy but with the Allies still far away, Lucien was with a group of some 15,000 resistance forces who had liberated 10 square miles east of Grenoble in the Alps at a point close to the Swiss frontier.

"The Germans decided on a major attack. The French commandant ordered the Canadian sergeant to leave the area. He managed to escape through the Nazi lines on a bicycle. Some days later he returned, following the German attack. He says the scene was one he will never forget. There was complete devastation, with hundreds of civilians killed and bodies of months-old children lying scattered about.

"Durocher has no kind words for the Germans. He recalls finding the body of a Maquis who had been tortured with steel wires being turned on his wrists until his hands dropped off. The man's eyes had been gouged out, but still he would not talk and had finally been killed.

"He says the Maquis were a wonderful people - "brave, young and real patriots." He says it was a great pleasure to work with them.

"Lucien and his group finally made contact with the conquering Allied troops on September 4 last. This meant that his work was finished. He remained in France until October 14, visited Paris and was transferred back to London. There the young sergeant found that he been made a first lieutenant on August 6. Durocher, a tall, lanky young man who spoke fluent French and who was a skillful and experienced wireless operator, was unique among the Canadian volunteers with SOE in Europe; he was not commissioned as he had the rank of sergeant; and he was part of an OSS (Office of Strategic Services — precursor to the CIA) mission. By mid-1944, many mixed teams were being sent into France; Americans, Canadians, Free French, and British. Some were commando units, others sabotage teams.

"American Major Cyrus Manierre who headed the small DODGE team was full of praise in his letter of commendation for Lucien Durocher. He was recommended for a Silver Star by my father, and while this decoration was not awarded, the recommendation alone shows the respect and appreciation he garnered."

APO 413
14 June 1945

<u>Recommendation for Award to Sgt - Durocher, R.C.C.S.</u>

Sgt Durocher parachuted into France with me on 24 June 1944. He was immediately successful in establishing radio contact with Algiers, and for over eight weeks he acted as a secret radio operator behind the enemy lines in enemy occupied territory. Sgt Durocher was required to make long trips in civilian clothes through a German occupied region, and he carried his radio on each of these trips. His accomplishments as a radio operator behind enemy lines were completely successful due to his courage, foresight, and endurance in the face of enemy obstacles and hazards as well as his high professional ability.

Sgt Durocher has not already received an award similar to the one recommended.

CYRUS E. MANIERRE JR.,
Major, U.S.Army.

"Sgt Durocher parachuted into France with me on 24 June 1944. He was immediately successful in establishing radio contact with Algiers, and for over eight weeks he acted as a secret radio operator behind enemy lines in enemy occupied territory. Sgt Durocher was required to make long trips in civilian clothes though a German occupied region and he carried his radio on each of these trips.

"His accomplishments as a radio operator behind enemy

lines were completely successful due to his courage, foresight, and endurance in the face of enemy obstacles and hazards as well as his high professional ability."

Lucien Durocher was awarded the following medals:
a) 1939 -1945 Star,
b) Italy Star,
c) France and Germany Star,
d) Defence Medal,
e) Canadian Volunteer Service medal with clasp, and f) War Medal 1939-1945 with Mention in Dispatches.

MS/1510   30th June, 1945.   A.2.

To: Miss R.D. Viner,   From: AD/B.
    Jedburgh Section (through AD/E)

Sgt. DUROCHER, L.J., R.C.C.S.

Your DRJ/1068 of 27th June.

A recommendation for a Mention in Despatches has, as you are aware, already been forwarded. That recommendation precludes any other citation or recommendation for the same work.

As the attached draft recommendation from Major Manierre, U.S. Army, covers the same period and work, it is regretted that it cannot be entertained.

PB
fn AD/B

Lucien Durocher's armlet worn while behind enemy lines in Occupied France (1944)

"When Lucien Durocher returned from Europe to Ottawa in February 1945, he was featured in a number of Ottawa newspapers in which he describes his experiences. In an article in the Ottawa Journal on 15 February 1945, he recalls that, since he was a tall blond-haired man, he stood out as a non-native in southern France — in Lucien's words: "My French commandant finally succeeded in getting me to cut my hair in a brush-cut style — like a German's. After that, the Maquis started shooting at me!"

"After Major Manierre was captured, Lucien worked with Team Veganin - (see Veganin report.) I*n the last page of Pop's Jedburgh Activity Report he wrote:* "I recommend Sgt Durocher of the Canadian Corps of Signals for the Silver Star in recognition of his courage, fortitude, and standfast devotion to duty as well as his willingness to don mufti whenever he was asked to."

Here follows an example of the type of duties Sgt. Durocher performed:

"SUMMARY

The basic weapon furnished the Maquis was the English Sten gun. The simplicity of construction, the ease with which it would be dismantled and carried in small packages, the fact that it used 9mm parabellum$_g$ ammunition, the most common calibre of German ammunition – all these made the choice for delivery both to secret groups and to Maquis. As the open guerrilla warfare period of resistance developed, more English Enfields$_g$ and American carbines were sent in.

     "For heavier weapons the British Bren$_g$ was
the principal automatic weapon although many
American Brownings were also dropped. The British
two inch mortar and Piat (anti-tank weapon) and
the American Bazooka were in great demand by the
Maquis. Grenades, both fragmentation and
phosphorous, were part of most deliveries.

     "But to these basic weapons for Maquis
warfare must be added a list running into
hundreds of special items to supply the sabotage
agents and teams. Plastic and detonators,
portable radios and spare parts, medical
supplies, shoes and blankets, special clothes,
maps, cash and false papers, instruction
pamphlets on sabotage - these were but part of
the many items that made up the contents of
containers and packages.

     "A brief outline of the system for securing
a parachutage of supplies would be as follows:

     a. Some agent who knew the requirements on
the sizes and security of a field selected a
suitable dropping ground and organized a group of
local resistance personnel to serve as a
reception committee for the field.

     b. The coordinates and description of the
field were sent to London by radio, carrier
pigeon, or courier together with details of the
type of arms and explosives needed.

     c. London accepted the field and notified
the agent as to what special BBC message would
mean delivery on that field.

     d. The agent hearing the message such as
"The donkey wears a blue hat" which perhaps meant
"expect two planes tonight" notified the
reception committee to assemble on the field.

     e. When planes were heard, either by means
of bonfires in special patterns or by means of
special radio the committee indicated that all
was safe for the delivery of supplies or
personnel.

f. The containers and parachutes were picked up and either hidden in camouflaged pits or taken away on farm carts to safe houses for storage and eventual distribution.

"This with certain variations such as the actual landing of Lysander and Dakota planes or daylight operations was roughly the way that all supplies and personnel were sent to France by plane. There were also some deliveries from motor torpedo boats or light destroyers but the volume by these methods was relatively small.

"Quite understandably some of the supplies fell into German hands. In some cases the Germans surprised the reception committees while they were trying to collect the containers; in others, raids were made on Maquis storage depots. In certain sections losses were nil to but 5 per cent; in others, especially before D-day, losses were estimated to have run as high as 50 per cent to 60 per cent. Since the bulk of deliveries were made after D-day and sent to fairly secure areas, an over-all loss figure of 15 per cent to 20 per cent would seem to be reasonable.

"Communications between those in the field and home offices were maintained for the most part by radio telegraph. With each agent or mission there was dispatched a highly trained radio operator who had with him anywhere from one to six or eight separate radio sets complete with special apparatus for recharging batteries. One of the chief concerns of any organizer or agent was the protection of his operator. Whenever possible an operator would have a number of sets in different houses at a good cycling distance from each other.

"By moving from house to house after a certain number of transmissions, the operator ran less risk of being picked up by German radio DF squads.

"In addition to his work of coding,
decoding, and actual communication schedules, the
operator would listen to the regular BBC
broadcasts for special messages either referring
to parachutages for the local reception fields or
giving the signal for action in accordance with
the broad sabotage or guerrilla warfare plans. In
the United Kingdom there were two large base
stations operating on twenty-four hour a day
schedules and Algiers operated another large
base.

"American personnel who worked behind enemy
lines directly in support of French resistance
were of these three classes. The smallest but by
far the most important group was that of the 77
Americans who volunteered to work, for the most
part in civilian clothes, as organizers of secret
networks or as radio operators or as arms and
explosive instructors. Thirty- three of this
group were active in France before D-day (6 June
1944)."

D/CE. AMX.   DUROCHER LUCIEN JOSEPH
21126

P.T.C.   4.5.44. (M.I.5. & C.R. only)
N.T.   9.5.44.
Nationality   Canadian.
Born   27.6.1920. Casselman, Ontario.
Occupation   Radio Operator.

4.5.44.	P.T.C. with a view to possible employment as an Agent in the Field.
15.5.44.	D/CE.2. advised: 21126 has been employed as an Agent in the Field with Massingham Mission. (See life history with D/CE Q.)
6.12.44.	D/AG advised: 21126 granted an immediate Commission in the Canadian Army (General List) and to be Lieut. w.e.f. 6.8.1944.
18.12.44.	Signed off. Posted to Canadian Army.

Chapter 11
Going In

Robert Kehoe again: "On the evening of 9 June, we lined up, parachutes attached, ready to board one of the converted Stirling bombers for the flight to our secret destination in France. The large bomb bay of the Stirling reduced the risk of hitting one's head while exiting the plane; this occasionally occurred with the circular opening of the Lancaster *(and Halifax)* bombers. Three planes were designated for our area and each was packed with the crew, a dispatcher, some 15 parachutists, and a number of heavy steel containers bulging with weapons and equipment. The departure was at a late hour because the June days were long and the distance not great. There was some cloud cover; if it increased, it could reduce the moonlight available and possibly abort the mission. We were nearing the end of the moon phase suitable for such drops, making delay very undesirable.

Stirling - Interior

"The pilot followed a prescribed route out of southern England, which was one vast airbase with thousands of planes coming and going in support of the operations in Normandy as well as the continual bombing of targets across the Continent. Once over the Channel, the pilot had to dodge antiaircraft fire by using different routes and altitude changes. He then had to locate the drop zone from map readings and by observation of ground reception, hopefully lighted by fires and with a prearranged flashlight signal in Morse code. He had to fly low, a dangerous move with these heavy planes over the rough and irregular terrain. Nearing the drop zone, he throttled down the plane to about 110 mph. This improved the chance of locating the drop zone and reduced the likelihood of physical injury to the parachutists, but it also made the plane and the men more

94

vulnerable to enemy ground fire.

"The success rate of these flights was impressive, but there were exceptions. Planes sometimes had to turn back, which was hard on the morale of those planning to drop as well as those on the ground. There were cases of discharge of men and cargo into enemy hands, such as a series of drops in Holland in 1942 that severely damaged the Dutch Resistance. These, however, were not the result of pilot error but of effective German counterintelligence aided by mistakes in London.

"Once in the air, we heard only the sound of the motors and the passing wind. It was a pleasant night, with the half moon low in the sky. Suddenly, the quiet within our plane was broken by the moans and mumblings of one of our SAS colleagues who had probably had too much to drink. We had been flying for not much over an hour when the dispatcher gave the alert signal. The plane circled the drop zone and then, on a second pass, we were ready to go. By this time, any fear of jumping had disappeared because my fear was concentrated on what was below. Would it be rifle or machine gun fire? Or silence? If silence, did it mean the enemy was waiting to pick us up? Here we were, armed, in uniform, with bundles of valuable equipment. Our orders were to avoid capture at all cost, and I now wondered just how to do this. To come up shooting might injure those venturing to help us. There was, of course, a chance that things might just go as planned. All this was not a careful analysis but rather a series of flashes rushing through my head faster than we were flying. What remnants of religion still with me came forward, with repetition of the 23rd Psalm taking precedence over any rational thoughts about the present and future.

"Action soon displaced contemplation and pushed fear into the background. We readied ourselves for the jump, with all senses attuned to the dispatcher and the actions of our comrades. I was the fourth to jump. The discharge was without incident; the chute opened properly, but the ground appeared very quickly. I believe we dropped from lower than 500 feet, which made for a fast ride and a severe jolt on landing. Although concentrating on landing safely, I was alarmed on hearing some strange sounds - sort of "put-puts" - while I was still in the air. I wondered if it might be pistol fire but, completely immersed in the task at hand, I paid little attention."

Chapter 12
Jedburgh Activity Report

I was ordered to make my drop into the Drome, France, on 14 May 1944. However, the weather being bad on this date the mission was scrubbed. It was scrubbed again for the next ten days, and it was only on Saturday, 24 May, that my radio operator, Sgt. Durocher and myself received our final briefing from Major James Champion of the British Army, and got into the plane to make our drop.

RAF 624 Sqn - Halifax JN888 (F/Sgt. J L Paulden)

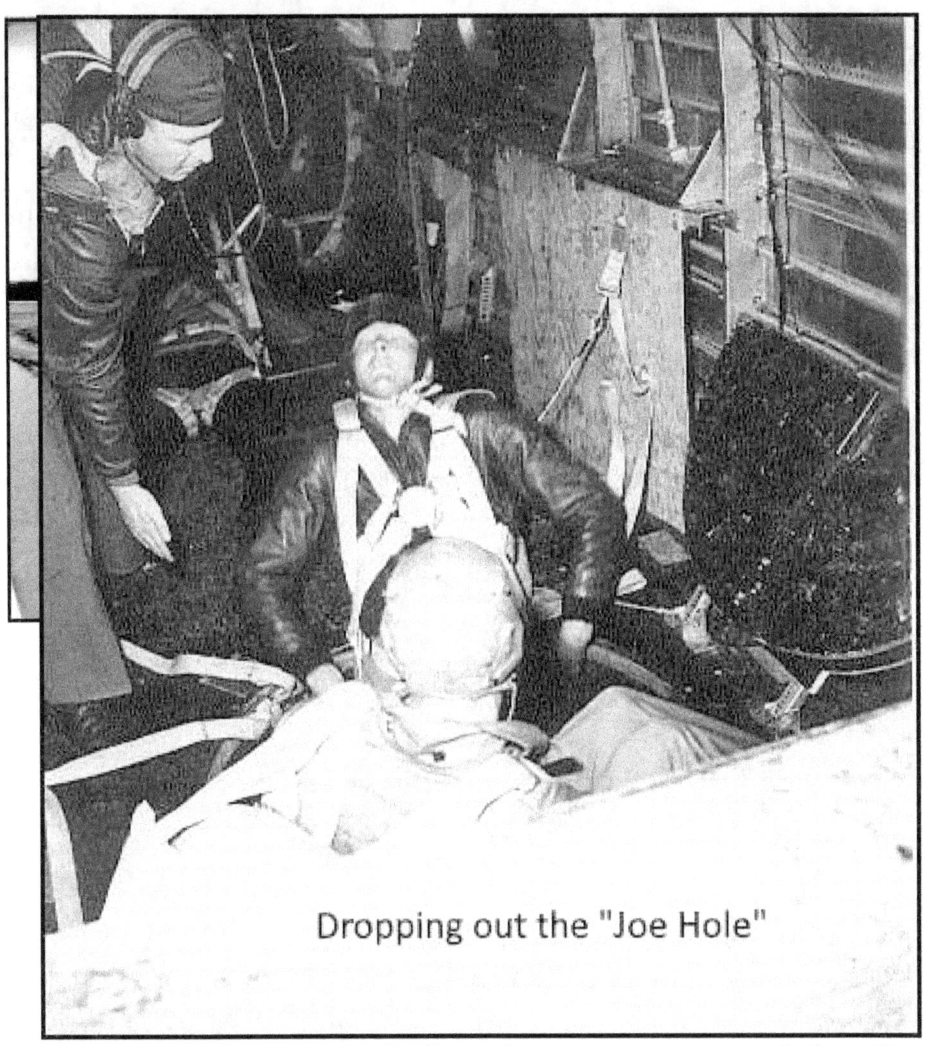

Ensminger, who verified that they <u>were</u> inserted by 624 Squadron)

"The team was dropped at a drop zone, code named "Tarsis" near the village of Pact (Isère), near Beaurepaire d'Isère. This Drop Zone was connected to the groups operating in the Drôme department. It is very difficult to check these drop zone codes because they are either missing or badly printed in the wartime documents.

"The nearest large city near the DZ is Vienne, south of Lyon. The village of Pact is about 13 miles SE of Vienne, near the town of Beaurepaire. The 'one month' error is not uncommon in wartime reports, when they were made a long time after the operation. The 'one week' error is quite common. I have checked all the official information I have

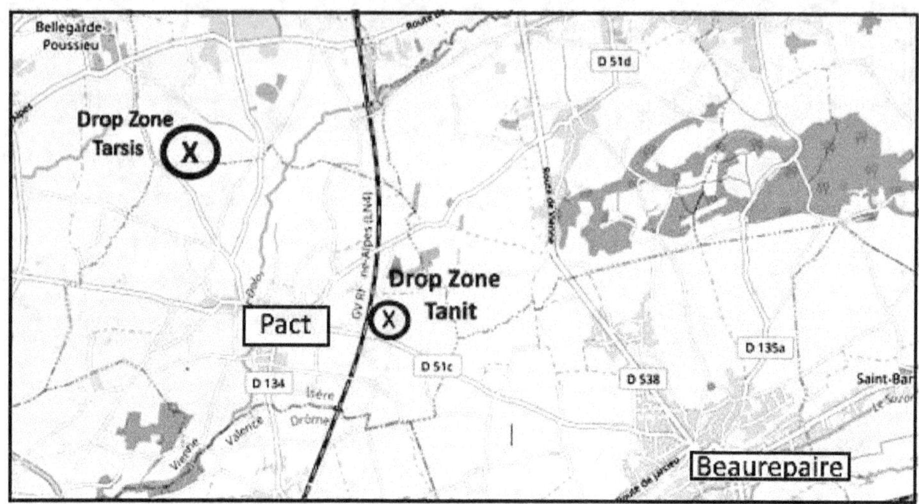

about your father's mission and I can confirm he was dropped in the night of 24-25 JUNE, 1944, at 00.30 hrs (12.30 was impossible, as day missions did not begin until the area was liberated). No confusion is possible."

"They had been given the password; a phrase which Manierre said he has now forgotten, and he had been briefed in the general nature of his task, with authority to alter it in particular details as might be necessary according to changing conditions after he landed.

"The landing was made at night. The French were waiting at a small field outside the city where lights had been placed to guide the plane in. With some anxiety, Manierre and his sergeant waited the command to jump, for the Germans had frequently learned of these landings and several British agents had been captured recently by the Germans who had taken the fields and were in waiting.

"But their concern was dispelled as they landed and as Major Manierre loosened himself from his chute which caught in a tree, he identified himself to the underground men and prepared to begin his task. He landed eight days after the Allies had poured out of the beachhead at Normandy, and more than two months before the Allies were to land on the coast of southern France. His assignment was to cut the communications of any German troops which might be sent against our troops in the north, and to harass the Germans so that they might not oppose the planned invasion to the Mediterranean coast. *(From undated, unidentified newspaper article written by Claire Rauth)*

Back to Pop:

We were dropped in at 1230 hours on 25 May, 1944 *(0030 hrs, 24/25 June)* at Beaurepaire de l'Isere *(**Drop Zone "Tarsis"**, near the village of Pact, near Beaurepaire)* and were met by a reception committee of about 30 men. Our briefing had been substantially that we were to meet Major Neil Marten and Major Noir, a Jedburgh team previously sent in. We were told that Major Marten would be on the ground to meet us. Further details of the briefing were vague, and we were told that we would receive further instructions in France.

On the ground we found that Major Marten was about 60 miles away, that Major Noir was not present, and nobody knew where he was, that the radio operator of his team had been killed making his parachute jump, and that the reception committee on the ground had not been expecting anybody to drop, but had been expecting only supplies. The leader of the reception committee was M. Brazier of Beaurepaire, who received us very well and took us to the house of M. Rochat, where we spent the rest of the night. The following day we were taken to the Maquis, where we contacted Mabou, a well-known FFI$_G$ figure in that region. Mabou was not expecting us, but he put us up for the night. At about 3 o'clock the next morning Major Noir appeared in the barn where we were sleeping. He woke us up, welcomed us and told us to come with him. We went with him to another Maquis, which was led by Bocambo (***Bozambo***). I spent three days with this Maquis, doing very little, simply consulting my maps, getting a certain amount of orientation data from the French, and attempting to contact Algiers.

Major Noir explained to us that Commandant Hermine was the French FFI leader in the region. He said that Hermine had ordered that all Maquis and all would-be soldiers of the FFI were to come to the Vercors, that Hermine was planning a large operation requiring up to 10,000 troops, and that the

Maquis of the region were preparing to leave their own special areas and go to the Vercors. At this time we were at La Cote St. Andre, about 50 miles from the Vercors. It was most desirable from our standpoint that Hermine be prevailed upon to change his order. If all the Maquis were to obey Hermine's order it would have stripped the countryside of all resistance, and would have made our mission practically impossible. We therefore decided to go to the Vercors ourselves. We told our Maquis to stay behind, and we contacted the other Maquis of the immediate area and told them to stay where they were until they received orders from us. They willingly agreed to do this. We then set out on foot for the Vercors, which is an extremely steep range of mountains, with practically no foothills.

"Manierre began the long trek to the headquarters of this leader, a former general in the French army who had escaped to England and had later been parachuted into his native land to organize the resistance groups. Under his direct command, he had 2,000 men, dug into the mountain spur of the Vercors which they held as a fortress against the enemy until finally routed by superior numbers.

"The trip to the headquarters was like the adventures of Roberto in "For Whom the Bell Tolls." Manierre had to elude German patrols, and submit to the search of the French again and again, for they were naturally suspicious of anyone seeking to enter their lines."

We received fire from a French roadblock and were forced to give ourselves up to the Maquis with our hands up, and we had a little difficulty in identifying ourselves.

Nevertheless, we succeeded in being taken to the headquarters of General Joseph (at that time Lt. Colonel Joseph of the French Army), who was recognized as the legal commander of all troops in the Vercors. General Joseph treated us extremely well, and invited us to attend a conference in which he was discussing with Hermine the pros and cons of stripping the countryside of resistance, and centering all resistance in the Vercors.

Col. Joseph (left) Hermine

It was while attending this conference that I met Major Neil Marten, in the company of Roger, who had been helpful to me when I first landed, and learned from him that he was planning to return to Algiers on what was presumably a secret mission. He therefore told me that I was to take his place on the Jedburgh team. This was what I had already done in fact. At the conference we succeeded in convincing General Joseph that Hermine's order could not be carried out without prejudicing the position not only of the FFI units but also the security of all loyal French families in the region surrounding the Vercors.

General Joseph therefore rescinded the order, notified Hermine of his decision, and instructed us that we were to organize as much as possible and direct the operations of all the Maquis surrounding the region in which we had been dropped. We took his order to mean that we were to organize and direct all the Maquis in the Drome that were not directly under his control in the Vercors.

General Joseph then explained to us that he wanted us to cooperate with his Maquis insofar as our cooperation would not interfere with our own orders from Algiers. We agreed. He also explained to us his purpose in fortifying the Vercors. This was to make it a nucleus of all resistance for that entire section of France, to which French partisans could retire in order to get weapons, supplies and so forth, and which would be virtually impregnable to all but the most determined German attack and which, since it straddled an important line of supply and communication running from Marseille to Germany, might be expected to play an important role in hindering German evacuation.

GETS HIS ASSIGNMENT *(Claire Rauth interview)*

"After meeting the general, Manierre conferred with him, brought him the latest information on Allied plans, and used his radio to send out messages which the general had.

From the general, Manierre received his next assignment, which fitted in with the orders he had received from his own officers in North Africa.

"He was to travel south to take over direction of French opposition forces in the department of the Drome. There, he was to weld together these groups of often disagreeing fighters into a functioning unit. As an American army officer he would have the advantages of being a fresh man, untarred with the local feuds, to whom they might rally; but most important, he would have control in the issue of any Allied equipment which would be flown in, guns; which everyone needed badly.

"On the other hand, he was to be in strange territory, faced with the overwhelming problem of reconciling fierce fighters and uniting men who had been accustomed to months of solitary guerrilla fighting."

The next day Major Noir left the Vercors in a car. Since there was no room for me in the car, I followed him on foot with a guide. Major Marten and Roger requested that we leave our radio operator in the Vercors, since they had important use for him, and since their priority at Algiers was higher than ours. They explained to us that anything we wanted we could ask them for, and that due to their higher priority we would receive it faster through them. I returned to La Cote St. Andre, where I met Major Noir. This was on approximately 1 June. *(1 July)*

Major Noir and I set up our standard procedure on the following day: Major Noir was to travel throughout the entire Drome, day and night, contacting all Maquis leaders, soliciting their cooperation and tempting them with offers of supplies

and money. I was to follow Major Noir and do the actual   organizing of the individual Maquis into a military unit, instruct them in weapons, explosives and military procedure, and lead the individual Maquis on whatever operations on which I thought my presence might be of assistance. It took about two and a half weeks to get this performed. Meanwhile Major Noir had taken off his uniform and was wearing civilian clothes. He advised me to do the same whenever I moved across the country in the daytime.

"In addition, he was to face the numerous German patrols with their superior equipment, their tanks and cannon, and planes. The mission required executive ability and a frontiersman's versatility, and Major Manierre accomplished it.

"As he set out for the Drome, Manierre was on the first leg of an assignment which had far-reaching benefits in the liberation of France and the defeat of Germany. Ahead of him lay two months of bloody, secret fighting before his capture by French collaborationists and his imprisonment in the sprawling prison camp in northern Germany.

"Traveling by night and hiding out by day, Major Manierre slowly made the 50 mile trip to the section of France in which he was to lead underground French forces in a two month battle against the enemy.

"After special training in OSS schools, he was ready for the vitally important mission of hamstringing German resistance in France so that our invasion forces would not meet the full power of the German army. His duty was to prevent the Nazis from rushing reinforcements to the north where the Allies had landed in Normandy and to prevent the Germans from organizing defense against the Allied invasion which was to hit the south coast of France in August, 1944.

"From the general, who was entrenched in a mountain spur called the Vercors, he had received an assignment to weld together the Maquis, the underground French, in the relatively unorganized section of the Drome. The general was firmly lodged in the mountainous region. similar to much of the terrain of the land below the Alps. From his fortress, the leader waged war against the Germans, and held out in much the manner of the Spanish troops which Hemingway described in "For Whom the Bell Tolls."

"Not until Aug 24, 1944 were the French driven out of this mountain retreat, and then it was only by the force of the superior German numbers and equipment. Serving with the French was a company of OSS paratroopers.

"One of the American officers, who was invalided with an appendectomy, provided one of the rare examples in which the Germans failed to commit an atrocity in this bitter and bloody fight against the French underground," Manierre said.

"Manierre had known the officer, Lt. Chester Meyers, in America, but had not known Meyers was on duty so near him. Meyers was recovering from his operation in a cave when two infantry divisions and one armored division of Germans moved to wipe the French out in late August.

BLOODY ATROCITIES

"As the Germans advanced they committed the worst atrocities, and the French retaliated," Manierre said. "It was pretty bloody."

"But although Meyers was captured by the SS and then handed over to the Gestapo$_g$, he was not maltreated or killed. Manierre, too, when he was captured, was fortunate enough to escape the torture and death which these German forces dealt out so generously to their prisoners.

"But the retreat of the French was two months in the future as Manierre left them early in June. When he set out on his three-day trip of the 50 mile route, he was on his own, on a mission that almost required him to forge his own army against the might of the German military machine.

"When he arrived in the Drome, he began the herculean task; he set up headquarters and sent out messengers to the leaders of the small groups of French who were isolated in their resistance. He had the credentials to assume leadership; but papers and orders were only as good as he might make them with the force of his personality, his command, and most importantly, he said, his control of American weapons and munitions.

A MOTLEY ARMY

"As was to be expected in such a force as the Maquis which sprang up locally and had no central organization as in a national army, control was split up in the persons of local chieftains; some were Communists, some were conservative peasants, some were merely pro-French and anti-German. But added to these differences of ideas were the local hatreds and feuds.

Maquis Bozambo at St. Christophe et le Laris

"We had pow wows," Manierre said as he explained how he whipped the factions into a strong line; we'd talk, and that usually brought them into line. For I had the power of deciding who was to get the guns and ammunition which the Americans were flying in.

"From his headquarters Manierre managed the campaign of attack against the Germans - he directed the plans, and talked with representatives of the local groups who were stationed with him.

les Granges farm –
Headquarters of the Maquis Bozambo,
near Saint Christophe et le Laris

WORKS IN DISGUISE

"He rode about the countryside, visiting the leaders and surveying the region in which he served as commander. For this work, he was forced to discard his American uniform and put on the clothing of the peasant. In the strange American uniform, he might have been shot by the French by mistake, and would certainly have been shot by the Germans with no mistake. As an American officer in civilian clothes, of course, he was liable to punishment as a spy; but he was forced to take that risk and trust the luck which did not desert him when he was finally captured."

At "les Granges" farm

(Chapters 15 and 16 contain further info about the activities of Teams Veganin and Dodge)

Chapter 13
Resistance Leaders – "Jockey Network"

Francis Cammaerts

Alias "Roger"
Civil status
Age in 1940: 24 years
Profession in 1940: French
teacher
Domicile in 1940: London
Resistance places of action:
Drôme
Resistance Organization:
SOE Buckmaster Network

Francis Charles Albert Cammaerts, DSO$_g$ (16 June 1916 – 3 July 2006), code named "Roger", was an agent of the United Kingdom's clandestine Special Operations Executive (SOE) during World War II. The purpose of SOE was to conduct espionage, sabotage and reconnaissance in occupied Europe and Asia against the Axis powers, especially Nazi Germany. In France, SOE agents allied themselves with French Resistance groups and supplied them with weapons and equipment parachuted in from England. Cammaerts was the creator and the organiser (leader) of the Jockey network (or circuit) in south-eastern France in 1943 and 1944.

At the beginning of World War II in 1939, Cammaerts declared himself a conscientious objector, but in 1942 he joined the SOE. He recruited and supplied with arms and training a large number of resistance networks and cells over an extensive area east of the Rhone River extending to the border with Italy and north from the Mediterranean Sea to the city of Grenoble. Despite being very careful in his work, Cammaerts was captured by the Germans in August 1944, but saved from execution by his courier, Christine Granville.

Of the more than 450 SOE agents who worked in France during World War II, Michael R.D. Foot$_g$, the official historian of the SOE, named Cammaerts as one of the half-dozen best male agents. He was one of only three SOE agents to be promoted to the rank of Lt. Colonel, along with George Starr and Richard Heslop.

Early Life

Cammaerts was born in London and raised in Radlett in Hertfordshire, the son of Professor Emile Cammaerts, a Belgian poet, and Tita Brand, a successful actress. He was educated at Mill Hill School, where he was a contemporary of Francis Crick and Patrick Troughton. He became a pacifist in the 1930s while at Cambridge, where he read English and history at St Catharine's and also won a hockey Blue. After university he briefly began a teaching career. He taught in Belfast before moving on to Beckenham and Penge County School for Boys, near London, where he taught with his close friend from university, Harry Rée who also joined the SOE.

In 1940 Cammaerts was refused registration as a conscientious objector by his Local Tribunal, but it was granted by the Appellate Tribunal, conditional upon him taking up agricultural work. He joined a farm training project at Holton cum Beckering, Lincolnshire. During this period he met Nancy Findlay (Nan), and they married on 15 March

1941. After the death of his brother Pieter while serving in the Royal Air Force, Cammaerts believed he could no longer stand aside from participation in the war, and, as a French speaker, he succumbed to the urging of Harry Rée to join SOE.

A Frightening Beginning

Cammaerts began extensive training with SOE in October 1942. Training included fieldwork experience in the New Forest, Scotland and Manchester. Cammaerts was considered by some of his training officers to be lacking in physical skills, and was 'more intellectual than practical'. Nevertheless he was considered to be above average in all areas. He was given the rank of captain and the code name Roger, and flown into occupied northern France in March 1943. More than a dozen SOE circuits were active in France at that time. Cammaerts was assigned to the Donkeyman network or circuit, then operating in the upper Rhône Valley, but his reception party from Donkeyman and the Carte network drove him first to Paris, with a dangerous disregard for security that alerted him to the risks of such behaviour. Cammaerts concern was heightened by his appearance. He was 193 cm (six feet, four inches) tall with feet so large his nickname in France was "Big Feet." He spoke French with a noticeable Belgian accent. Cammaert's worries about security were confirmed one day after he arrived in Paris when Carte leader, André Marsac, was arrested by the Germans. Cammaerts fled Paris by train to Annecy.

Near Annecy in the village of Saint Jorioz he met with Odette Sansom, Adolphe "Alex" Rabinovitch, and Auguste Floiras of the Spindle network. Once again his antenna warned him of the poor security of Spindle and he departed after two or three days for Cannes.

Rabinovitch declined to work with Cammaerts because his "appearance was too English" and he spoke French with an "atrocious" accent, but gave him the address of a safe house in Cannes. Floiras would soon join Cammaerts and become his best friend and wireless operator; Sansom and several other members of the Spindle network were arrested and imprisoned shortly after Cammaerts departed Saint Jorioz. He spent a month in Cannes establishing his cover story as a teacher recovering from jaundice.

Security

Cammaerts worked primarily in rural areas. SOE networks were more secure in rural areas which had a much smaller presence of German soldiers and milice$_g$, the pro-German French militia, than large urban areas.

In the words of the official historian of the SOE Michael R.D. Foot, impeccable security, the hallmark of the best SOE agents, characterized Cammaert's survival as an SOE agent for two tours totaling fifteen months, far longer than the average agent served or survived in France. Cammaerts never stayed in the same house for more than three or four nights, he avoided hotels as their registers were checked by German and French police, and he also avoided large train stations which frequently had check points. He never told anybody his plans, nor made appointments nor visited unknown addresses without careful reconnoitering. He did not communicate in writing or by telephone, nor did he know the real names of the people he worked with, only their field names. He had a squad of seven or eight men who followed and investigated potential recruits before they were contacted and he divided his recruits and associates into cells of no more than 15 persons each and discouraged contact between cells. Cammaerts told his agents to always have a credible reason for being where they were if stopped by a German patrol.

While seeking air-tight security, Cammaerts said that he always informed the families in the places he spent nights, usually rural farmhouses or in villages, that he was English and left them no doubt of the danger they were in by hosting him. He was always received, he said, with "open arms." As in the case of others who operated in enemy-held territory for prolonged periods, he gave a great deal of credit to the ordinary French citizens who had provided him and his colleagues with safety and comfort. In the BBC TV series Secret Agent, broadcast in 2000, Cammaerts said, "The most important element was the French housewife who fed us, clothed us and kept us cheerful."

Jockey Network

Disillusioned with what he had seen of the Carte Organization and the Spindle network, Cammaerts organised his own circuit (Jockey). He worked initially in the area of Montélimar. His first associate was wireless operator Auguste Fioras, a man as cautious as Cammaerts himself. The first message the pair sent to London was on 27 May 1943. Fioras would late transmit 416 wireless messages to London during 1943 and 1944, a record for SOE wireless operators.

In the latter part of 1943 Cammaerts established several small semi-autonomous groups of resisters to the German occupation. They were located along the left bank of the Rhône between Vienne and Arles and eastwards through the hinterland and into the Alps. He traveled around on a motorbike visiting each group. By the end of 1943 Cammaerts had ensured that his Jockey circuit was ready to play its part in any sabotage that might be required. In November 1943 he was recalled to London for debriefing, and, while there, he raised the problems among the SOE agents working in France, often at cross-purposes, some under the command of General

Charles de Gaulle's headquarters and others, many of them French citizens, under the command of SOE's French section.

On his return to France in February 1944, Cammaerts' aircraft crashed on landing, although he was unhurt. He went on to check that his Jockey circuit was operational and later visited the 3,000+ group of Maquisards (young Frenchmen who had fled to the Vercors plateau to avoid being sent for forced labour in Germany). In April 1944 he informed SOE's London headquarters that the Vercors had a finely organised army, but they needed long-distance and anti-tank weapons. Cammaerts' Jockey circuit played its part following the

Normandy Landings: they and the other SOE circuits cut railway lines and helped to severely hinder German troop and machinery movements. Cammaerts was appointed head of Allied missions in southeastern France. By this time he had built up an organisation of more than 10,000 people.

The situation in the area of the Vercors plateau did not fare so well, with London having refused Cammaerts' and others' requests to provide the Resistance with heavy weapons. Allied High Command felt, based on the Yugoslav experience, that guerrillas were not trained to stand and fight. Cammaerts understood and was even sympathetic to this view, but he had no control over the belief by French Resistance leaders that, with Allied landings taking place in the north, the war was coming to an end and the Germans were fatally weakened. In fact, Vercors was attacked by two German divisions complete with air support, and German reprisals were ruthless. It was a rout and the surviving Maquisards fled to whatever hiding places they could find, with an estimated 600-plus maquisards and civilians slaughtered.

Arrest and Release
Despite his meticulous care for security, on 13 August 1944, two days before the Allied Operation Dragoon landings in southern France, Cammaerts, Xan Fielding, an SOE agent who had previously operated in Crete, and a French officer, Christian Sorensen, were arrested at a roadblock by the Gestapo at Digne-les-Bains. Cammaerts had received a large amount of money for operations which he divided among the three of them, an action that would prove a mistake. Entering Digne by automobile, they came upon a German checkpoint. Under questioning, Fielding denied knowing the other two, but a young German civilian examining their forged identity papers noticed that the serial numbers of the money each of them carried was in the same series, thus indicating a

connection among them. The three were taken to Digne prison and roughly interrogated. They claimed they were involved in black marketing to account for the money. The Germans apparently did not know they had captured Cammaerts, the most important SOE agent in southeastern France, but decided to execute the three suspecting they were associated with the French resistance.

On August 17, Krystyna Skarbek, a.k.a. Christine Granville, a Polish-born SOE operative and Cammaerts' lover managed to get Cammaerts and the others released. She confronted two collaborators, Albert Schenck, a French liaison officer to the Gestapo, and Max Waem, a Belgian interpreter for the Gestapo, telling them that American troops would arrive within hours and that if they did not co-operate she would ensure the pair were handed over to an avenging mob of French citizenry. The collaborators agreed to the release of Cammaerts, Fielding and their French colleague, on condition of the payment of a two million franc ransom, which Skarbek obtained by an airdrop from London. The three SOE agents were to be executed on the evening of the day that Skarbek negotiated their release. The rescue of Cammaerts is fictionalized in the last episode of the British television show Wish Me Luck.

Helping the Allies

Digne was liberated by the American army two days after Cammaerts was released from prison. The maquis had cleared the way for the Americans and there was little opposition. On August 20, Cammaerts and Granville met the American commander, Brigadier General Frederic B. Butler, at Sisteron who dismissed them as "bandits." Leaving the American army behind, the two proceeded to Gap where the Maquis had captured the German garrison. Several hundred Polish soldiers, soldiers in the German army, were among the captured Germans. Granville addressed the Poles with a megaphone and secured their agreement to join the Allied forces, provided that they shed their German uniforms. The Poles stripped off their uniforms. General Butler arrived and disapproved of the proceedings, threatening Cammaerts and Granville with arrest and court martial if they didn't leave. Author Arthur Funk said, "The historian can only wonder at Butler's short-sightedness in ignoring a British officer who knew a great deal about the terrain and the people in it." Later, Cammaerts and Granville received a better reception from Butler's superior officer, General Alexander Patch, who appointed them as the liaison for the Americans with the maquis. The couple continued northward to Lyon and Paris.

Cammaerts' time in occupied France ended in September 1944. He was promoted to lieutenant-colonel, awarded the Distinguished Service Order and the Legion d'honneur, Croix de Guerre and the American Medal of Freedom for his work in south-eastern France.

SAARF$_g$ and Immediately Post-war

In March 1945, when the Allies had crossed the Rhine, Cammaerts was asked to join the Special Allied Airborne Reconnaissance Force (SAARF). Many of the personnel were SOE or OSS agents. Their main objective was to help in the reconstruction work in Germany after the fall of Hitler. For Cammaerts it primarily meant dealing with the appalling aftermath of the newly liberated concentration camps. Cammaerts visited Dachau, Belsen and Ravensbruck. He was appalled and felt impotent in the face of what he found. He later said 'the SAARF period was blank and grey and one of those certain areas in my life when I didn't know what I was doing'. SAARF was disbanded in July 1945.

Cammaerts wanted to be transferred to work in the diplomatic world, but despite his extraordinary war record the

Foreign Office considered Cammaerts to be a foreigner, as his father was Belgian, and so unable to work at the Foreign Office. In 1946 he was offered work in Brussels with the Inter-Allied Reparations Agency, and he was able to move with his family to Belgium for 18 months. In 1948 a daughter, Christine (named after Christine Granville), was born with multiple disabilities. For the remainder of her short life, Christine's circumstances played a large part in the decisions made by the Cammaerts' about their own lives.

Education Work and Retirement

In 1948 Cammaerts became the first Director of the Central Bureau for Educational Visits and Exchanges, which was a UNESCO agency and enabled him to undertake international trips including to the USA. In 1952 Cammaerts returned to teaching, with the encouragement of John Newsom and Ronald Gould. He later became the headmaster of Alleyne's Grammar School in Stevenage for nine years, at a time when Stevenage New Town was growing rapidly. Cammaerts was keen to implement the Labour Government's move towards comprehensive education, encouraged by Newsom. Alleynes enrollment increased from 170 to roughly 600 boys during Cammaert's tenure, and new classroom blocks were added.

Cammaerts did not forget his wartime lover, Christine Granville. Following her murder in 1952, he became part of a group of men dedicated to ensuring that her name not be "sullied and succeeded in stopping several press reports and two books" to protect her from stories of her active and diverse sex life.

He was the subject of "This Is Your Life" in 1958 when he was surprised by Eamonn Andrews at the BBC Television Theatre. In 1959 he appeared for the defence in the notorious trial of Penguin Books over the publication of D.H.

Lawrence's Lady Chatterley's Lover. The trial, at the Old Bailey was front-page news and Cammaerts statement under cross-examination that he had let members of his 6th Form read the book and they did not appear to have been corrupted or become depraved, was widely reported. The publisher won the case.

He was Principal of the Leicester Teacher Training college in Scraptoft, between 1961 and 1966, overseeing a liberalising of the training methods used. He then moved to Kenya to help with the development of the country's education system in the immediate post-colonial period. Cammaerts became Professor of Education in Nairobi from 1966-72. He later returned to England, to become head of Rolle College, a teacher training college at Exmouth, which later became part of University of Plymouth. In 1981, aged 65, he came out of retirement to start a teacher training college in Botswana. He had a major impact on the development of education on all levels in the country, which had the most advanced policies on the African continent. Cammaerts finally retired in 1987, returning to live in the south of France until his death in 2006.

Cammaerts' nephew, children's author Michael Morpurgo, in his novel, In the Mouth of the Wolf, wrote about Cammaerts' time in the Resistance.

<https://en.wikipedia.org/wiki/Francis_Cammaerts>

I was fortunate to have been able to correspond with Mr. Cammaerts several times and send him a copy of POP'S WAR. One of his replies is reproduced below:

CAMMAERTS WEY

MAISON DES IRIS, 20 RUE DES CAVES, 34230 LE POUGET, FRANCE

Téléphone : 04 67 88 73 06 • e.mail : jwey@cario.fr

23 · 1 · 05

Dear Carlos. I must write & thank you before I finish the reading — I am slow but I have got to page 100 + I have come to recognise your Pop. We met & shared gatherings — if you ever feel capable of coming this far I would happily give you a day to explain many of the difficulties of identifying the truth about life in France in 1944. It was too complex for a card or even a multi page letter, there were at least a dozen organisations all kept apart from each other but all designed to get the German occupation out — Para military British — French — Polish. Belgian — Escape routes — information gathering etc but from May 1st 1944 Para military was supposed to be F.F.I. & if Communist Party dragged their feet you have to look back to the Hitler/Stalin agreement which set it all off. You have done a very conscientious & worthwhile job. Arthur Funk is the best American sources but Victor — not very unreliable.

Best wishes Frances

("Dear Carter, I must write and thank you before I finish the reading – I am slow but I have got to page 100 and I have come to recognize your Pop, we met and shared (gatherings?) gastric sup(?). If you ever feel capable of coming this far I would happily give you a day to explain many of the difficulties of identifying the truth about life in France in 1944, It was too complex for a card or even a multi page letter. There were at least a dozen organisations all kept apart from each other but all designed to get the German occupation out - Paramilitary British - French -Polish. Belgian - Escape routes - information gathering, etc. But from May 10, 1944 para- military was supposed to be F.F.I. & if Communist Party dragged their feet you have to look back at the Hitler/ Stalin agreement which set it all off.

You have done a very conscientious and worthwhile job. Arthur Funk is the best American Source, but Vuchot - Noir very unreliable. Best Wishes, Frances")

Gaston Claude Vuchot (Major Noir)
(JEDBURGH)

Contexte historique:

 Saint-Cyrien of the Joffre promotion, Gaston Claude Vuchot comes from a Jura family. In his first assignment, he joined, in 1932, the 71st Alpine Fortress Battalion in Modane where his corps commander noted him as

Captain Gaston Vuchot
French (Major Noir)

"embodying the perfect type of the French officer". In June 1939, a senior officer presented him as: "the pearl of the French army". The war found him a lieutenant. He was then assigned to the 57th Senegalese Mixed Tirailleurs$_g$ Regiment and took part with this unit in the hard fighting of May and June 1940.

Seriously wounded in Versigny, on June 12, he is cited to the order of the army: "Vuchot Gaston Claude, lieutenant in the 57th Senegalese Mixed Colonial Infantry Regiment, officer with high morale, admirable courage and composure, was seriously wounded on June 12, 1940 by two bullets at the time when he himself directed, under heavy fire, the fire of his mortars, most of whose servants had just been put out of action".

Evacuated to Bordeaux and then to Castelnaudary, he recovered after a long stay in hospitals. He suffered physically, but the forced inaction imposed on him by his wounds caused him much greater moral suffering. Patriot, devoted to his country, he did not accept defeat. After his convalescence, he was assigned to the 13th Battalion of Alpine Hunters. Not enjoying himself in the armistice army, he asked and obtained his departure to Africa with the Sudan regiment in Kali, near Bamako. Promoted to captain in November 1942, he served as an instructor at the Boulhaut camp. Pursuing his goal: to help liberate his native soil, he took many steps to go to England. He succeeded, joined the French Fighting Forces in which he would follow an intensive training in the paratrooper commandos. Captain Vuchot joined Milton Hall Castle, 7 km from Peterborough in Northamptonshire, in February 1944, just as the training of Jedburgh volunteers began.

Gaston Claude Vuchot, who according to the sister of the person concerned chose the pseudonym of "Black Commander" because it corresponded to a surname very widespread in the Jura, was parachuted in an alpine hunter's outfit with the Veganine team. The team, commanded by British Major Neil Marten (Team Leader), included Vuchot and British Radio Sergeant Denis Gardener (who was killed during the parachuting on June 9, 1944 at 2:15 AM, on the "Tanit" field between Sonnay and Beaurepaire). The parachuting was poorly carried out: the drop altitude between 600 and 700 meters lead to a wide dispersion on the ground, several containers were not found and, to make matters worse, the two radio packages were found very damaged, the quartz preset frequencies broken. The mission assigned to the Veganine team consisted mainly in harassing as much as possible German communications on the left bank of the Rhône (RN 7_g and railway lines from Lyon to Marseille) and, possibly, along the railway lines from Lyon to Grenoble and from Grenoble to Valence, then to trigger guerrilla actions between Valence and Vienna. The first of the Jedburgh missions for the Drôme, Veganine was to be talked about for its effectiveness.

On June 12, he was led by Georges Berruyer to the Bozambo Maquis where he contacted René Fanget, head of the northern zone, who recounted this interview: "We had not been warned of the arrival of this mission. So we were taken aback when the "Black Commander" made us aware of a mission order signed by De Gaulle. This text enjoined the FFI troops (French Forces of the Interior) of the sector to line up with the direct orders of the "Black Commander", with a view to intensifying the Green Plan; the operation being ordered to help the Resistance between Valencia and Vienna and to encourage and support the action of the guerrillas in the area of the main lines of communication, on the left bank of the Rhône.

On June 15, the Germans invaded Saint-Donat-sur-L'Herbasse and behaved like vandals; Descour asked René Piron to move his company from the region of Saint-Donat to the Vercors and "L'Hermine" ordered Fanget to transfer his units from Nord-Drôme to Combovin or Léoncel in advanced defense of the Vercors. As this would strip the Rhone Valley, "Black", whose mission was not to defend the Vercors, but to practice and support guerrilla warfare in the Rhone Valley, opposed this order. The chiefs of the region and the Vercors decided on a compromise: two companies from Nord-Drôme, Piron and Sabatier, would reinforce the western flanks of the Vercors; Fanget and Simon were to set up their PC in Léoncel; the units that remained in the northern zone passed under the command of "Black" who, attached to the region, would not depend on the head of the Drôme, nor that of the Vercors. Prophetic, Gaston Vuchot confided to Marcel Desgranges ("Lieutenant Marcel"), his deputy: "On the roads that lead to the Vercors, the cars touch each other... If it is not already done, the German snitch will soon spot them. They'll drop a company of paratroopers on Vassieux and it is over for the Vercors."

In his area of responsibility, in just two weeks, by the conviction and authority with which he began his mission of activation of the Green and Turtle Plans, he restored the confidence of the inhabitants through the multiplicity of his contacts and earned the esteem of his men whom he trained with care while training his groups and engaging them in incessant and effective guerrilla actions. Henri Brunel ("Ravel") recalls: "Day after day, I knew his admirable activity, his precise sense of reality, his contempt for danger, his inexhaustible goodness, his subtle clairvoyance. It is to him alone and to his clever military tactics that the city of Tain must have been spared the horrors and destruction." Allied officers, such as Major Neil Marten of the British Army and US Major Cyrus E. Maniere Jr. were complimentary of "the remarkable things he did in the Maquis," and testified to their memory full of admiration for "a wonderful soldier whose exceptional qualities as a leader traced our line of conduct and his hard work and his tireless efforts during our mission were an example of what is most lacking in the world today."

When Colonel Paul Adams, commander of the 143rd U.S. Infantry Regiment, arrived in Romans, Gaston Vuchot came to talk to him: "I asked him if he could not approach the Rhone, and he replied that he had instructions and that he was going to attack Valence. I pointed out to him that it might not have been very useful to take Valence, Tain or other cities on the RN 7, that the Germans could still concentrate enough manpower to force a passage, but that it would be very useful to deploy a few ambush tanks hidden among the hills with the RN 7 in sight. This would certainly produce quite different results from what we ourselves could achieve with our small arms, and would force the Germans to use secondary roads."

At the end of 1944, Gaston Vuchot could have stopped fighting: it was offered to appoint him battalion chief if he agreed to serve on the staff in Paris. But he wanted to serve until the total liberation of his country; for him, the place of an officer is in combat until the war is over. He was then assigned to the 1st Parachute Fighter Regiment (1er RCP).

Charged with leading an attack on Colmar on February 1, 1945, he received the order to seize the southern agglomeration of Jebsheim. His chief of Corps, Lieutenant-Colonel Faure, commander 1st RCP$_g$, appreciated the mission "which he carried out brilliantly since with a minimum of losses, he made very many prisoners and left on the ground many enemy corpses. This operation that he led was crucial and allowed the crossing of the Colmar Canal. The regiment was charged, that same night, to take the village of Windensolen. It was there that after the fighting and during a violent reaction of the enemy artillery, he was seriously wounded."

The text of his last citation with the award of the Croix de Guerre with Palm and having accompanied his appointment to the rank of Knight in the National Order of the Legion of Honor reads: "Vuchot Gaston Claude, captain in the 1st regiment of Parachute Hunters, magnificent officer, combining exceptional courage and composure with a high conception of duty. In charge of the attack on the southern sector of Jebsheim, by the speed and method of the establishment of its means, defeated on January 29, 1945 a very strong enemy counter-attack. On February 1, 1945, was seriously wounded while coming under heavy artillery fire at the height of the advanced elements of the battalion during the attack on the village of Windensolen."

If it remains that Vuchot's relations with Huet, commander of the Vercors, and with De Lassus, commander of the FFI of the Drôme remained somewhat ambiguous, it is certain that Gaston Vuchot has taken place in history alongside the purest heroes. The municipality of Tain-l'Hermitage wanted to give him an eminent testimony of gratitude by deciding to give the name of "Black Commander" to one of the streets of the city.

(Auteurs : Pierre Balliot
Sources : Report on Jed Teams Veganine and Dodge. Étude de Bertrand Souquet publiée dans le bulletin n°191 de Symboles & Traditions. Pour l'amour de la France, Fédération des unités combattantes de la Résistance et des FFI de la Drôme, Valence -Peuple Libre 1989. Archives Madame Chapell) *(Translated from the French)*

Bozambo:

Charles-André Lahmery (pseudonym "Bozambo") was born in 1921 in Lyon. On the departure of Geyer, who took command of the Vercors maquis in December 1943,

"Bozambo" became the leader of the Chambaran maquis, installed near Saint-Christophe-et-le-Laris. The action of this maquis was very important in the north of the Drôme - a number of actions of recovery of equipment, guerrilla, and various sabotages. His maquis, which became the backbone of the AS and then the FFI in Drôme-Nord, acquired great popularity among the population. In June 1944, he came under the command of Vuchot (Noir). The maquis "Bozambo" actively participated in the fighting for the liberation of the Drôme department before September 1, 1944, the liberation of Beaurepaire and Vienne. After this date, he belonged to the 2nd Alpine demi-brigade, was directed to the Italian border, then to Alsace where he joined the army of De Lattre de Tassigny.

Few people seem to know the name of Captain Charles-André LAHMERY, but as soon as one pronounces the word "BOZAMBO", everything changes; and yet it is indeed the same man, emblematic figure of the Resistance in Vercors. Born in LYON in 1921, he enlisted for the duration of the war in the 110 Cuirassiers Regiment, whose Standard is the only emblem of the French army to bear the inscription "VERCORS 1943-1944" in its folds.

*(Photo above - **Captain Charles Lahmery**, known as Bozambo (center) and **Colonel Cammaerts** (left) during the inauguration of the stele erected to the victims who were from the Bozambo resistance network.)*

"Bozambo", Officer of the Legion of Honor, was one of the founders of the Federation of Combat Units and FFI of the Drôme of which he was the president. He died on April 13, 2001.

L' Hermine:

Jean Drouot, known as "l'Hermine", architect of the liberation of Gap and Briançon.

Born on 15 September 1907 in Luxeuil-les-Bains (Haute-Saône)

Military career: Coming from the Air School, he fought the Luftwaffe during the Battle of France in 1940.

Demobilized on September 25, 1940, he tried in vain, from October 1940 to March 1941, to leave for England. Appointed in 1941 director of the Dauphiné- Savoie executive school, he took advantage of this privileged situation to, under the cover of an official body, start a propaganda action against the occupier and his collaborators. At the same time, Drouot organized, in Lons-le-Saunier, a channel to cross the line of demarcation, in both directions, mainly for escaped prisoners. The organization provided them with false documents. In 1942 his action continued and gained momentum because of the persecutions against the Jews. From January 1943, he participated in the organization of the Resistance in the department of Drôme. He received the first southern airdrop and participated in all actions, notably the shutdown of the Carbone-Lorraine factory, the only factory in France and Germany manufacturing DCA searchlight electrodes, used to make the intense light of the searchlights. At night, he entered the factory in full activity and placed the explosive in the transformer. Twenty minutes later, everything was blown up.

At the end of November 1943, he was called to the command of the FFI of the Drôme and organized many sabotages and destructions (twenty factories, railway networks, electrical installations). In the Drôme from 1 December 1943 to 6 June 1944, the FFI - under the command of Battalion Chief Jean Drouot, known as "L'Hermine", was directly responsible for 108 attacks on rail traffic, the decommissioning of 107 locomotives, longer or shorter stops in about 20 factories, the destruction of 57 high-voltage lines and the reception of parachutes of 67 aircraft. At the same time, about 500 Germans were killed and a thousand wounded by the Drôme FFI.

In February 1944, L'Hermine received as deputy commander "Legrand", nom de guerre of Jean-Pierre de Lassus Saint-Geniès. On the morning of June 6, 1944, 4,000 armed men, organized into three battalions of 28 companies, were in combat. Constituted as a regiment, the maquisards were to see their strength increase from 4,000 to 7,500 men between June 6 and August 30. After the Normandy landings and during the short period (24 days) during which he commanded the Drôme regiment, Commander Drouot-l'Hermine protected the western advance of the Vercors, at the cost of hard fighting.

At the beginning of July 1944, the FTP$_g$ and the departmental liberation committee lobbied for the dismissal of L'Hermine. Colonel Zeller then appointed him lieutenant-colonel and gave him a regional command in the central Alps. He organized the struggle in the Champsaur (commandos of L'Hermine). He freed Gap on August 20, 1944, making 1,200 German prisoners, and went back to Grenoble, opening the road from Sisteron to Grenoble to the 36th American Division. He then participated in the revival of Briançon. With his men, Lieutenant-Colonel Drouot was incorporated into the 4th RTM$_g$ of the 2nd DIM$_g$. His units fought in front of Héricourt,

Belfort; Drouot was shot on 22 November 1944 in front of Bischwiller. Its formation lost in combat 80% of its personnel, killed or wounded.

Lt. Henry McIntosh, of Jedburgh Team Chloroform, entering Gap on August 2, 1944, with local *maquisards*, before the Allied landings.

Post-war career

He left the army for a second career. Engineer, director of companies, he was also a municipal councillor of Paris and general councillor of the Seine in 1952 and 1953. He was elected, in November 1958, deputy of the 7th constituency of Seine-et-Oise (Poissy) and re-elected in 1962. A member of the UNR$_g$ group and a member of the National Defence Committee, he was also Vice- President of the Democratic Union (UNR) and of the Legal Affairs Committee in the European Parliament.

Jean Drouot died on May 23, 1969 in a car accident.
Distinctions: Commander of the Legion of Honor; Companion of the Liberation (decree of 17 November 1945); Croix de guerre 1939-45 (six citations); Medal of the Resistance;

Rescue Medal; Distinguished Service Order (United Kingdom)

(Author: Colonel Pierre Ba Sources: Chancellery of the Order of the Liberation; Alban Vistel, La nuit sans ombre, Paris, Fayard, 1970) *(Translated from the French)*

Henri Zeller:

Henri Zeller, alias Ménard, Joseph, Faisceau. Born March 18, 1896 - Besançon, Doubs.

Died April 16, 1971 - Paris (Hôpital du Val de Grâce).

He participated in the First World War and continued his military career. In 1939, he was assigned to the general headquarters. After the defeat, he joined the resistance and became a member of the Army Resistance Organization (ORA$_g$). He was the head of the ORA for the Southern Zone (December 4, 1942 - April 30, 1944), and commander of the FFI in the Alpine Region R1 and R2 (April 30 - August 30, 1944).

In the Vercors at the time of the attack, Zeller and his group managed to cross the German lines and reached Saint-Nazaire-le-Désert on July 22. Arriving in Algiers on August 3,

1944, he was received the same day by General de Gaulle, to whom he explained his plan for an offensive towards the north, mainly by the Route Napoleon, after the Provence landing. Convinced, de Gaulle sent him to Naples to meet General Patch, the commander of the landings, on 6 August, to have the plans modified. The plans were approved and Grenoble was reached on D+7 instead of D+90 as initially planned, which allowed the troops landing in Normandy to join forces in the heart of Burgundy on September 12.

Chief of Staff, military delegate for the southern zone (August 21 - September 28, 1944), then commander of the 16th military region in Montpellier (September 1944 - end of 1945), he became General de Lattre's Chief of Staff in 1946, major general of the army in 1948 and finally military governor of Paris from 1953 to 1957. General of the Army (January 1956), he died in Paris on April 16, 1971.

He was awarded the Grand Cross of the Legion of Honor (February 1, 1958), the Croix de Guerre 14-18 and 39-45, and the Rosette de la Résistance. Although he is not well known, the role of General Henri Zeller was of considerable importance in the liberation of France. Curiously, Henri Zeller was not made a Companion of the Liberation.

(Translated from the French)

Collines-du-nord-de-la-Drome

This region was favorable to the installation of outlaws and maquis who found shelter and refuge in the woods and food in the numerous farms. It was in this region that Charles Lahmery's maquis (**"Bozambo"**) and Narcisse Geyer (**"Thivollet$_g$"**) found refuge. *(Translated from French)*

Chapter 14
The Legend of Bozambo
(Translated from the 1945 French magazine "AUX ARMES!")

We have recently published an article on the Maquis of the Drome, necessarily over-simplified and incomplete, since it is still too early to make the definitive history of the Maquis. Also the history of the Maquis is no longer separate from the legend, and in certain cases as in the one to which our story relates, it is good that it is so, because the legend was, from the first moments, the inseparable auxiliary of the history.

The day after the Army was disbanded, Lieutenant Geyer, who was to become Major Thivollet, founded a Maquis at the Grand Serre. At the beginning of 1944, he was called to take over the command of the Vercors from Commandant Rouvier (Le Ray) and left some elements at the Grand Serre under the direction of Bozambo.

We returned with Bozambo to the site of this Maquis, which is most likely to have been the first Maquis in France. In the hills, between the Grand Serre and the Laris, we saw the huts of branches that the wood-cutters had not yet destroyed, the pantry and a few traces of fireplaces - vestiges of a past so far away - so close to our hearts.

About forty Maquisards were there under the direct command of Lieutenant Roure, an admirable figure of a young Syrian from Lyon, who was to be killed later in the Vercors.

Continuing through the thicket, we found three graves: those of Private Cronidas, Sub-lieutenant Viboud, and Lieutenant Mabboux.

They had been brought back to the Maquis, to their

Maqus, when it was impossible to bury them elsewhere. They remained there. Nothing is more moving than this eternal rest in places where some of the first who wanted to fight gathered. Bozambo looked at the graves of his comrades for a long time, and then he said simply: "They wanted to live in the woods. They must be happy now."

Les tombes en plein bois:
Lieutenant Mabboux, tue a Serves, le 14 aout 44.
Sous-lientenant Viboud, tue au Creux de la Tine, le 12 sept. 1944.
Soldat Cronidas, tue au meme androir.

We have extracted the following account from the book currently being published, by an English writer, Charles de

142

Richter, who lived through the occupation in the martyred village of Saint-Donat-sur-l'Herbasse. Numerous testimonies confirm what he tells.

Basically, I think it was his name that caught my attention. It reminded me of one of my favorites from the screen and the novel. You know the admirable negro (*"Bosambo$_g$"*) that we find in **"Sanders$_g$"**, one of the most successful creations of Edgar Vallace…

Of course, I suspected that it could not be this Bozambo, but in my imagination I formed an image of a thick-lipped boxer, with an imposing build and fists that could knock out an ox. I didn't see him quite black, but very dark.

The unfortunate thing is that while everyone was talking about Bozambo, it was almost impossible to see him. This devil of a man was everywhere at once. He was reported in Romans, and the next day he was in Grenoble. You might as well have wanted to catch a wildfire.

It was a time when the Maquis was on the move and the quiet little streets of Saint-Donat were bustling with the incessant passage of cars and motorcycles.

A small black car would whiz by and, as a hand waved at the door, someone would kindly inform you: "That's Bozambo passing by. That's little Lily". Only, when you looked up, Bozambo had disappeared. He was already far away, either to other missions or, more often than not, to some fender-bender.

What was consoling was that the Germans found him just as elusive and that, when by chance, they made contact with him or with his men, they had only one regret: that of not having been on another coast that day.

And the legend grew day by day. The confidence too. When the worst happened, we knew we could count on him. In case of trouble, the first word was: "Where is Bozambo? The second, which allayed any fears: "Bozambo will be there". For there was no example that he was ever called upon unnecessarily. Just as there was no example that he had ever caused any danger to the people.

And I don't mind saying that not all the leaders of the Maquis had the same wisdom. What can I say, they were young. They had been held in check for a whole winter and were looking forward to the glory they had been promised. Put yourself in their place!

The (Normandy) Landing and liberation had come, and each step sees the name and reputation of the man grow. Wherever the enemy is, he attacks. His Maquis has only one path, that of honor.

I think there was only one person who never managed to see him, me, and I was beginning to get used to it when, one morning, Dr. Andre Levy, entering my humble store that had been transformed into a house, said to me from the doorway: "I bring you Captain Bozambo!"

There are announcements that take you by surprise. I stood up abruptly.

My negro was a tall, young, friendly boy with a fresh, smiling face. Elegant with that and race to the point of making female admiration understood. With that, not the slightest bluff, not the slightest pose. Clean and pure features; a supple and nervous neck, used to the hard life of the Maquis, but which has lost none of its charm.

He sat down without fuss, once the presentations were done, and, pulling out a cigarette, started to chat. Something struck me then: the softness of his voice, but also his firmness. He was dressed in khaki, short pants and white stockings. On his beret, three tiny gold lines. The same discreet elegance in his attire as in his person.

I wanted to know his story and he simply told it to me, without trying to pose as a hero, without insisting on the features that could have put him in the spotlight. If, at times during his story, he emphasized certain points, it was when it was a question of magnifying the effort of his men. When he talked about them, he lost his composure. Sometimes his voice would become veiled: that's when he talked about the dead. Those whom he had seen fall by his side.

The Pontiffs three graves assure that the habit of fighting hardens the heart of the man. Let them come and talk for five minutes with Bozambo and then give me their opinion.

His real name? Well, I didn't ask him and he didn't tell me. I only know that his nickname was given to him by his regimental comrades, probable admirers of **"Sander of the River**ɡ**"**.

He was unaware of the existence of my negro and I must say that I was very careful not to tell him about it.

At the armistice, he was a sub-officer in the ll Cuirassiers in Lyon. The Regiment's pennant has three fleurs-de-lis and the tradition is to salute it when entering the mess. Guye and Bozambo took the pennant and the tradition to the Maquis and this made them very angry at the suspicions of the brave F.T.P. They saw it as a royalist maneuver! Fortunately, with Bozambo such mistakes are not long- lasting.

So he was in Lyon, getting over his boredom and regretting every day not to have been able to join General de Gaulle's forces. In order not to waste his time, he formed with some friends a Gaulist cell.

And there it was that one fine day, in 1942, Mr. Hitler suppressed "his" French army. Just like that. As a result, Bozambo no longer hesitated, his path was finally marked out, he would act.

With the help of an officer of the same II Cuirassiers, Lieutenant Geyer, he recruited men. His first Maquis is at Grand Serre but the beginnings are rough. It is necessary to fight with the distrust of the population. Let's not blame them, the insidious propaganda of Vichy had done its work. By dint of talking to a hundred brains of terrorists and murderers, one ends up hammering this nail into a few.

We are at the beginning of '43 and Bozambo is training his men. They are all fired up, but what is lacking is weapons. All in all, they had eight machine guns, a few French muskets and little ammunition. It is impossible, as we can see, to waste powder on sparrows... and on Germans.

In the spring, fortunately, things will improve. A coup de main took place against a German fuel and supplies depot.

Bozambo, who had been in the drop, attacked the Italian-run Brezin airfield. Again, everything worked out well, and the big prize was a radio car that the 2nd Bureau estimated at two million francs. A pretty good sum as you can see.

Un detachement du maquis Bozambo descend des collines
du Larris vers le terrain de parachutage de Miribel

Unfortunately, the Germans were furious and the alerts multiplied, and the maquis had to be evacuated from time to time; too often, in fact; almost every two weeks, and the morale of the men was affected. The lack of equipment was again felt, not to mention the lack of supplies. In addition, the staff is insufficient. For every hundred men that this maquis now comprises, we count as leaders Lieutenant Thivollet, Second Lieutenant Roure, Lieutenant Bozambo and Sergeant Capadero.

In early October, a serious incident occurred. The maquis is sold out and the Germans operating at the Grand Serre descend in force. The command post and the village were surrounded by the enemy. In the morning, at 7:30 a.m., they burst into the liaison center, seized part of the equipment and took 20 hostages from the population of Grand Serre. These hostages, despite all the questions and threats, did not speak, and the maquis, which had been able to escape in time, would not have suffered too much if two liaison officers who were coming back from Lyon by bus had not been stopped by a Gestapo checkpoint at Peage-de- Roussillon.

Bozambo, for his part, barely escaped. The Germans burst into the hotel he was staying in and rushed to his room, showering his bed with machine-gun fire. They're paying for it. Bozambo, who was alerted in time, had been able to evade their search. An adventure in which our hero almost lost his life a few days earlier probably explains this sudden interest by the Germans in the region.

Being in Lyon, Bozambo was arrested by the Gestapo. Searched and stripped of his papers, he was judged to be an excellent catch, whereupon he was ordered to march. There could be no doubt as to his fate. It was Montluc[g] first, then death. Any other man would have flinched and accepted his fate.

We played and we lost. Too bad. We shrug our shoulders and go home. Bozambo is not of this type. He was in the middle of Lyon, rue Vendome, and five armed men were surrounding him.

He quietly set off, waited for the right moment, then leaping forward he took flight. Shocked by this maneuver which they had so little expected, the Germans opened fire. For fifty meters. Bozambo is showered with bullets that all miss him. Finally, a turn of the street hides him and he can quietly finish his walk... hygienic.

L'ouverture des containers à côte du terrain.

The unfortunate thing is that the Germans had his papers, and among them, a map of the Drome. They knew where one of the patriots' nests was located. These famous patriots of whom they have not finished hearing about.

So Bozambo and his men were once again forced to take off. At Christmas 1943, Thivollet went up to the Vercors, while Bozambo stayed in the Drome.

He spent the winter reorganizing his maquis. The funds are what he lacked most, but he sacrifices everything he has been able to put aside in the happy days before the war. Don't worry, it's not much.

If
In the service of Austria
The military is not rich.

The French military, in this report, can give him a hand.

Thanks to Dr. Andre Levy, whom I mentioned earlier and who, for some months now, has been taking care of his wounded, he has established a connection with Saint-Donat, which is one of the main centers of the A.S. The Bozambo maquis, for its part, belongs to the "Free France". Even if we work and fight under different labels, we quickly reach an agreement when the ideal is the same. This is what happens here. Under certain conditions, the fusion takes place with captain Rene and, from that day, Saint-Donat becomes one of the rallying points of Bozambo.

The winter of 43 was spent in incessantly attacking the Rhone Valley railways. Vichy and Philippe Henriot loudly denounced the terrorists, and the Germans took action. Nothing worked. March, April, May see the attacks - and the success – intensify.

It is that now the maquis is not alone in the game. The Americans have understood its importance and especially its usefulness. The idea of the army of the Resistance takes shape.

One attends then in Algiers this thing which seems a tall story: a school of the maquis intended to prepare the American officers to the hard life which awaits them after their parachuting. In short, the perfect art of the maquisard in 15 lessons. There are tents, papier-mâché Germans, a Gestapo representation. It's as Hollywood as it gets, and the real maquis laughs out loud at the news.

Needless to say, there is about as much similarity between this ersatz and the real thing as between a movie gangster and a real Chicago killer.

But the main point is that we think about the maquis.

At the beginning of July, the first airdrop takes place. A little later, a Franco-British commission will land at the Grand Serre. It will include an English colonel and a French officer and will have for its mission, among others, to film the maquis. Bozambo, for his part, will have the honor of commanding his men before it.

Other airdrops follow and here are men who will be called to play a great role in the history of the maquis: first, Major Noir with Major Martin (June 1944), then, fifteen days later, Major Meniere (sic) with the Canadian Staff Sergeant Durocher, known as Fil-de-fer…

All these distant friends arrived full of energy and, perhaps more importantly, with weapons and equipment.

Le major parachute Menieres qui, plus tard,
devait etre pris et abattu par les miliciens.

In June 1944, the long-awaited order for the general insurrection of the Drome was given. The entire maquis caught fire and descended on the towns. It seems that the Germans no longer exist or are a hundred miles away. A company commanded by Lieutenant Monnot, from Saint-Sorlin, attacked Saint-Rambert, but failed. A company of AS and another of F.T.P. occupied Saint-Donat, almost officially breaking with Vichy.

Bozambo, for his part, remained in Laris and continued to harass the Germans in the Rhone valley. The enemy is overflowing everywhere. Every day there are some clashes. A scuffle between advancing elements of the maquis and the Germans of Romans occurred, and its consequences, unfortunately, were to be serious. It will be the day of June 15 when Saint-Donat was to undergo a terrible ordeal.

The Maquis, fortunately, was warned in time that the 2nd Company had been able to withdraw. This withdrawal saved the village and the lives of many of its inhabitants. One shot was fired and it could have been a replay of the Oradour-sur-Glane massacre.

The engagement will take place however. It will take place at Saint- Andeol and will result in the tactical, but not strategic failure of the Maquis. The courage of the men must be put aside; only the lack of equipment and ammunition can be considered as responsible.

What remains of the 2nd Company joins Bozambo in Laris. We need its enthusiasm and its flame. It is also necessary to put some discipline in the ranks. The arrival of Captain Noir fortunately changes the situation. Weapons and ammunition fall from the sky without stopping. We can equip ourselves. It is obviously not yet the war in lace - it will never be - but it is no longer in rags.

Bozambo resumes his attacks on the Rhone valley. The Germans are harassed, overwhelmed. Ah! that terrorist, if they would hold them! M. Henriot is getting more and more vituperative, but he is at the end of his career, a few bullets will get the better of him.

At the end of June, Rene and the First Battalion returned to the Boche-free Vercors and declared the zone free.

Bozambo remained alone with his company to occupy the North Drome sector with the Mabboux Section in Saint Uzes.

He has now, so to speak, widened his circle of relations. It was not only M. Beroullet in Beaurepaire who was transmitting clandestinely for him, but also, thanks to the mediation of Jean Chancel, Commandant Azur in Saint-Donat.

Moreover, Captain Noir never ceases to demand arms and ammunition directly from Algiers. Every night, big planes are flying overhead and containers are raining down. The Germans say to themselves: "Yes, it's raining," but they always open their umbrellas too late.

Thanks to this, the kids of the Maquis can start training and learn the handling of the new explosives. Their teacher is an extraordinary man: Major Menieres (*Manierre*), who also fell from the sky. Unfortunately, this did not prevent him from falling into the hands of the militia and dying *(fortunately not true)*.

In July, the sedentary Company of Lieutenant Monnot took up arms again, as well as the F.T.P. Company under the command of Major Phi-Phi. With the active assistance of Major Menieres, who is never so happy as when he makes a noise and demolishes something, the Bozambo Company blows up the electric factory at Beaumont-Monteux. As a result, the industrial production of the whole region, as well as that of Saint-Etienne and Saint-Chamond, is completely stopped.

But don't ask Bozambo to stay in place. He has made a master-stroke and here he is now in Grenoble where he contacts the organization COMAC$_g$ (Committee of Military Organization of Combatant Action) and helps to develop it. It is that the fateful moment is approaching.

Danton asked for "audacity, audacity and more audacity." Bozambo agreed with him on this point, but he also asked for men and more men. In turn, the sedentary companies of Saint-Donat (Captain Cote), Hauterive (Captain Gateau), Tain (Captain Martin), the Maquis of Saint-Uzes (Lieutenant Mabboux) and the F.T.P. (Lieutenant Baumier) were born.

At the end of July, tragedy struck in the Vercors. Supported by Darnand's militia, the Germans decided to finish it once and for all. For several nights, the Maquis had been waiting not only for weapons, but also for men. They had been promised men. Many men. And to receive them, runways have been prepared. The planes only have to come.

The Germans do bomb these fields every day, but curiously enough, they do not damage the runways themselves. This should be an eye opener, but the conflict is so great that we are content to joke about their clumsiness.

At last, one night, planes arrive, pulling with them the gliders, but as we rush to welcome them, we realize the mistake. They are the Germans; The attack on Vercors has begun.

The men who have just taken the field have sophisticated weapons, but they also have a hunting knife in their calves. They will use it to finish off the wounded, suddenly with a blow in the belly, when by chance, they will not put out their eyes.

Also, if later you are told that a German prisoner, like in Saint-Donat, was shot, do not feel sorry for yourself and do not blame yourself. The Vercors, which saw its own people tortured and massacred, has the sole right to judge.

The attack did not succeed completely, and many of the men whom the Germans hoped to surprise, were able - God knows at what price - to make their retreat. But alas, so many dead, not to mention villages completely destroyed, inhabitants slaughtered, shot, burned, houses doused with gasoline and delivered to the flames, without mercy of the victims prevented from leaving.

The attack on the Vercors led Bozambo to take position in the woods of Lens Lestang. It is not the place we wanted and the danger is everywhere. He stayed there for a while and then, as the Germans gradually relaxed their surveillance - people were getting tired of everything, even looting, raping and stealing - he quietly returned to his previous positions.

As soon as it was reinstalled, it resumed its activity. On July 14, following an aerial battle, he took Captain Walter (of the German fighter squadron) prisoner with the help of Second Lieutenant Phillipe and transferred him to the Vercors. In retaliation, the enemy seized some hostages, shot them and left, forbidding the population to attend the funeral.

On the morning of August 5, a German column surprised a van on the road bringing supplies to Maquis Bozambo and shot the two little guys occupying it. The same day, probably thanks to the documents found on the two poor dead men, a German column, returning from the Vercors, under the orders of Major Oberland, attacked the Maquis Mabboux in Saint- Uzes. The latter's men blew up two enemy cars and alerted Bozambo. The latter did not hide the risks they were going to run from his men and left on the spot with them. He reached the plateau of Lens Lestang and fell on the German column which was still on the outskirts of Hauterives. The engagement lasted from one hour to seven hours, and when it ended, the toll was as follows:

German losses: 35 killed, 58 trucks demolished,
4 light cars out of order.

Maquis losses: 3 killed, 4 wounded, 4 shot.

Only Hauterives, who could expect to be burned could breathe, Bozambo's energetic action had soothed them.
August 10th saw a new phase in the great battle of the French people against the invader for liberation.

The radio brings an order from London and all the companies are set up. Each one takes the positions assigned to it and Bozambo, always in the vanguard, operates in the Rhone Valley. Night and day, he machine-gunned the Germans on the road who were fleeing back along the national road no 7.

He arrived in Tain and, despite the weakness of his group, attacked the 3,000-strong German garrison. The Germans refused to surrender and, although surrounded, did not dare to try anything. Unfortunately, after eight days, a new arrival of tanks allowed them to break through the lines and to cross towards Lyon. They did not go far, others finished the work so well begun.

The liberation of the Drome was in full swing and two of Bozambo's groups participated in the capture of Romans by

Captain Thivollet. In turn during this heroic month which will remain in the annals of France as one of the most admirable months. - It was a month of legends and chivalry, with Tain, Saint-Vallier, taking prisoners, accumulating material, and cleansing the national soil of Nazi leprosy. The end of August arrives and the Drome, then almost all France, can breathe. The enemy is in fruit, crushed, frightened, fleeing both the living and the memory of his crimes.

I do not say that Bozambo did all this, but I say and I repeat that all this was because there was a Bozambo and his legend, and that next to him, there were all the Bozambos of France, with legends as beautiful, as heroic, as vibrant.

Heroes who are proud to be honored for doing what they believe was their duty. Not to mention those who fell before the end and who also have the right to our thoughts.

Below is a letter from a friend of my father's who found it amusing to read about his being shot, and so wrote the Director of the magazine.


```
Direction-Redaction.
"AUX ARMES!"
32, Place Bellecour
LYON - Rhone.
                 Paris, le 28 juillet 1945


Monsieur le Directeur,

    Je me permets de vous ecrire au sujet
d'un article intitule "La legende de
```

Bozambo" paru dans le numero 9 du 15 juin
1945 de votre excellente revue.

Il y est dit, a la page 27, 2eme
paragraphe, que le major americain
Menieres aveit ete tue par la milice.

Il se trouve, fort heureusement pour
le Major (dont le nom exact MANIERRE) qui
est un de mon amis, que la nouvelle est
inexacte. Il eteit bien tombe en effet
entre les mains de la milice au moment de
l'operation indique dans l'article.

Mais apres avoir passe de longs mois
dans un camp de prisonniers en Allemagne,
il est revenu sain et sauf en France au
mois de Juin dernier et il est reparti
presque aussitot pour les Etats-Unis.

A titre d'indication, je voua
communique son adresse:

Major C. Manierre,
O.S.S. Detachment,
A.P.O. 413, U.S. Army

Je me permettrai de faire la
suggestion suivante: etant donne d'une
part que le Major serait pour le moins...
amuse de voir en photographie reproduite a
titre posthume dans une revue francaise,
etant donne d'autre part qu'il eprouverait
un vif plaisir a lire l'excellent article

sur le VERCORS, puis-je vous demander de
me faire parvenir un exemplaire du numero
en question que je lui remettrei moi-meme
a mon prochain voyage aux Etets-Unis.

Veuilley croire, Monsieur le Directeur, a
mes sentiments les plus cordiaux.

Lt. Marcel VIGNERAS
OSS Detachment,
A.P.O. 887,U.S. Army

(Translated below)

Director-Redaction   Paris, July 28, 1945.
"AUX ARMES!"
32, Place Bellecour
LYON – Rhone.

Dear Mr. Director,

I am writing to you regarding an article entitled "La legende de Bozambo" which appeared as the 9th article of the June 15, 1945 issue of your excellent magazine. It says, on page 27, 2nd paragraph, that the American Major Menieres was killed by the militia.

Fortunately for the Major (whose exact name is MANIERRE), who is a friend of mine, that news is inaccurate. He had indeed fallen into the hands of the militia at the time of the operation mentioned in the article. But after spending many months in a prison camp in Germany, he returned safely

160

to France last June and left almost immediately for the United
States.

> For your information, here is his address:
> Major C. Manierre,
> O.S.S. Detachment,
> A.P.0. 413, U.S. Army

Allow me to make the following suggestion given that,
on the one hand, the Major would be, to say the least ...
amused to see his photograph reproduced posthumously in a
French magazine, and given that he would take great pleasure
in reading the excellent article on the VERCORS, may I ask
you to send me a copy of the issue in question, which I can
give him myself on my next trip to the United States.

Yours sincerely, Monsieur le Directeur, my most cordial
sentiments.

> Lt. Marcel VIGNERAS
> 0SS Detachment,
> A.P.O. 887, U.S. Army

Chapter 15

Report by Col. Roger

The next two pages are copies of the re-typed multi-generation copies of the report which had been typed and copied on onion-skin paper that did not reproduce well on a scanner. Below is an example of that report:

Ref: F/OPS/1/22/ *veganin*   15. 11. '44   **17 AUG 1945** (2)

To: Lt.Col. Musgrave   From: F/OPS/1
            Carelton-Smith
____

     I enclose herewith copy of a report made by our agent Lt.Col. CAMMAERTS (ROGER) on the JEDBURGH Mission of Major MARTIN, Commandant NOIR and Capt. MANYERS

Report on JEDBURGH Mission
Major MARTIN, Commandant NOIR, Captain MANYERS

    This Mission was sent to me early in June, at a time when I was unable to move from the Hautes Alpes, but I had left directives with my Reception Committee who knew with whom they should most profitably be put to work. Unfortunately their briefing was an impossible one, as guerilla work in the Rhone Valley north of Valence was impossible, owing to the concentration of German troops, and the flat nature of the country. As I needed at that moment very urgently an officer to carry plans of Col. Zeller and myself for the S.E. to Algiers, I detached Major Martin and sent him back to Algiers with reports. Commandant Noir was appointed F.F.I. Commander of that portion of the Drome which is north of the River Isere, and in co-operation with Capt. Manyers *[Manierre]* and with the aid of Sgt. de la Rocque who worked magnificently as Radio Operator, they did *[Durocher]* all that was possible in this extremely difficult and dangerous sector. Capt. Manyers was unfortunately arrested, and as far as we know was treated as a normal prisoner-of-war.

    Major Martin and Commandant Noir will have made fuller reports on their work, including a report on the death of S.Lt. Gardiner who was killed because his parachute did not open. The troops with which they worked spoke very highly of them, and after the landing on August 15th played a magnificent part in harassing the German retreat.

    After the Liberation the body of 2nd.Lt. *[Sgt]* Gardiner was exhumed, and buried in the Cemetery at Beaurepaire with F.F.I. military honours.

(signed)   ROGER

Lieutenant-Colonel ROGER
British Liaison Officer F.F.I. -
R.1 - R

Here is a more legible copy:

Report on JEDBURGH Mission
<u>Major MARTIN, Commandant NOIR, Captain MANYERS</u>

This Mission was sent to me early in June, at a time when I was unable to move from the Hautes Alpes, but I had left directives with my Reception Committee who knew with whom they should most profitably be put to work. Unfortunately their briefing was an impossible one, as guerilla work in the Rhone Valley north of Valence was impossible, owing to the concentration of German troops, and the flat nature of the country. As I needed at that moment very urgently an officer to carry plans of Col. Zeller and myself for the S.E. to Algiers, I detached Major Martin and sent him back to Algiers with reports. Commandant Noir was appointed F.F.I. Commander of that portion of the Drome which is north of the River Isere, and in co-operation with Capt. Manierre and with the aid of Sgt. Durocher who worked magnificently as Radio Operator, they did all that was possible in this extremely difficult and dangerous sector. Capt. Manierre was unfortunately arrested, and as far as we know was treated as a normal prisoner-of-war.

Major Martin and Commandant Noir will have made fuller reports on their work, including a report on the death of Sgt. Gardner who was killed because his parachute did not open. The troops with which they worked spoke very highly of them, and after the landing on August 15th played a magnificent part in harassing the German retreat.

After the Liberation the body of Sgt. Gardiner was exhumed, and buried in the Cemetery at Beaurepaire with F.F.I. military honours.

(signed) *Roger*

Lieutenant-Colonel ROGER
British Liaison Officer F.F.I.
R.1 – R

164

CODE NAME: VEGANIN

OPERATION CODE PLAN: BECK

CENTRAL PLAN CODE NAME:VEGANIN   Signal Times:-

                                             Odd Days:

                                             Even Days:

                                             Night Transmissions:

MEMBERS OF TEAM: Major H. Marten   (B) (CUTHBERT) Pers.Code CARBOLIC
                    Capt. C.L. Noir   (F) (DEREK)
                    Sgt. D. Gardner   (B) (ERNEST)   Killed on landing

SERIAL NO. OF TEAM:

OPERATION ORDER NO:

COUNTRY SECTION OVERHEAD: Massingham

AREA: JOCKEY circuit Nr. Valence, Drome and Isere

MISSION: To assist resistance movement and to stimulate
                            sustained guerilla action in the area of main
                            lines of communication east bank of Rhone
S.A.S. BASE: Mil   between Avignon and Vienne.

DROPPING GROUND: Tarsis

DATE OF DEPARTURE: 8/9.6.44.

INITIAL CONTACT:

OPERATIVES:
    DATE OF RETURN: -   *MAJ. MARTEN - 21/10/44*
                                   CAPT. NOIR |
                                SGT. GARDNER
                            See Team DODGE sent to re-inforce TeamVEGANIN:
                            Major Marten exfiltrated 10th July

MAJ. H.N.MARTEN   CAPT. C.L. NOIR   SGT: D. GARDNER

The following is the report of Major Marten whom my father replaced in the Vercors.

(ATTACHMENT "B" is missing...)

I left Algiers at the end of the first week in June in company with a French officer and an English radio operator to be dropped by parachute in the area BEAUREPAIRE with orders to report to _____ who would place us with a Maquis Group in that region. Our mission was to stimulate and where necessary direct the harassing of the enemy and his lines of communication in the RHONE VALLEY from approximately ST. RAMBERT to LIVRON, and also to train and arm groups of 20 men as shock troops capable of carrying out coups-de-main on our target area on the day when the Allies landed in the South of France.

Our arrival was marred by these events: firstly, the radio operator was killed because his parachute failed; secondly, both wireless sets were rendered useless, one because the parachute failed, and the other because the crystals belonging to it were carried by the operator and consequently smashed, and thirdly, our contact was not there and his whereabouts were unknown. Our reception committee therefore placed the French officer and myself in a safe house in BEAUREPAIRE in civilian clothes, and buried the operator in a wood. Five days went by and there was still no sign of him, but during that time we managed to get a message through to London on a local wireless; we decided it was useless waiting any longer so we asked the owner of the safe house to find us the nearest Maquis group to which we could go.

On our sixth day in France we arrived at a small Maquis south of HAUTRIVES; it was commanded by a youth of 21 years who was quite irresponsible and appeared to have little appreciation of elementary precautions against the enemy; however, it was a Maquis. In the afternoon we went to a meeting of all the company commanders in the region and there, of course, met the local leader himself. It appeared that he had under command some 300 men divided into eight companies, and moderately armed. At that juncture, I gave them the orders of the Allied High Command which I had brought with me, but as they received them I noticed a certain hollowness in their attitude. It transpired that before serious operations could be carried out, there was much to be done, such as straightening out the political differences which existed between the A.S. and the F.T.P., intensive training and instruction, arming and equipping of those who needed it, and tactfully changing the gangster methods of some groups to that of a properly organized Maquis. So, that night we saw the local head of the F.T.P., and agreed in principal that they would work in harmony with the A.S. under the Allied Mission, and that a joint committee would be formed consisting of one representative from each party and the Allied Mission. The details were discussed the following day, and it looked as though everything was fixed for a period of co-operation and hard training, but the following day the Germans attacked ST. DONAT, the main town in our area.

They bombed it with incendiaries first, and after that some five hundred troops entered with support of six tanks, and searched the town, pillaged the shops and the Maquis hospital, raped 15 women and then withdrew. The Maquis offered little resistance as it was not prepared, and the numbers were too great for them. As a result, civilian opinion tended to go against the Maquis for it was due to their presence in the region that the town was attacked. The following day we received news at our camp that we were going to be attacked, so we ordered removal of all stores to a hidden cave in the woods and a state of alert amongst the

Maquis; the removal was effected, but the attack did not develop, so we remained at that camp.

The next night we got three reports that we were to be attacked within two to four hours, so we ordered an evacuation of that area and a move to the North of some 15 kms. and a concentration there of about four of the companies. This move was carried out by night. In order not to desert the civilians in the nearest village, we left two sections of twenty men to defend it, hoping that this would not make them turn against the Maquis; the attack however, did not develop.

Our new Headquarters was in a deserted farm in a wood; certain difficulties were encountered, namely rations and accommodation for all. For three days we lived in comparative discomfort, eating two small meals a day, consisting of newly killed cow and bread; it rained hard all the time and there was complete disorganization, as a result of which the question of A.S. against F.T.P. reared its head again. After long discussions it was decided to let all those who were in the A.S., but who inclined towards F.T.P., join the F.T.P., and vice-versa at their own risk. The result that 64 men went from the A.S. to the F.T.P., and none from F.T.P. to A.S. The following points may be brought out of all this:-

(a) If the Maquis had been a military organization with military discipline, they would have stood the slight hardships encountered.

It must be remembered that in a Maquis, civilians are in the majority and cannot understand the necessity for some military actions; therefore the greatest tact must be used in handling them, from both the low level of an allied Mission and the high level of the Allied High Command.

(b) There is a need for good officers who can lead their companies and train them – these should be Frenchmen.

(c) The Maquis to which I have referred was far too transport minded – a mere 15 kms. move by night gave rise to a lot of grumbling. Their transport, although up to a degree necessary, was used far too much, at the expense of security of the headquarters.

(d) This Maquis was not capable of doing a quick move efficiently.

(e) The rationing was an eternal problem. At times they would requisition food from local farmers, at times they would raid the establishment of a collaborator and take his livestock. (I was not always convinced that these raids were confined exclusively to collaborators) and at times they would raid the enemy for food. It is imperative that they have money to purchase food, I am certain that there would be, as a result, much better relations between civilians and Maquis.

(f) A certain amount of disharmony existed within the A.S. itself in this case because they were receiving orders from their superior chief whom they accused of deserting them and going to the safety of the VOSAGES MOUNTAINS[g]; they were not, therefore, very inclined to obey his orders.

(g) It was apparent that the F.T.P. were the better organized and had carried out better work than the A.S.

(h) The policy of the Maquis operating in towns is wrong, unless the town is one in a liberated region, such as the VOSAGES. The case of ST. DONAT is good evidence of this and as a result of the German raid, the excellent Maquis hospital was completely denuded of all its stores, where-as if it had been in a secluded part of the country it would not have been touched.

(i) The area North of the River – ISERE to HAUTRIVES is a very difficult area for a large Maquis to operate in. It is undulating country and very open to enemy attack and observation. It is impossible to carry out firing practice as at once one's position is given away. Attacks on the German communications are very difficult as the approaches to the target area are generally very open, and where they are not open, the target is too heavily guarded. However, operations are not entirely impossible if the Maquis are in small groups of not more than 20 and targets are carefully chosen, both in the ISERE valley and on the River ISERE.

(j) They must have more arms and ammunition.
All the above concern one particular type of Maquis in, of course, one particular area. I then left my French officer to carry on with that Maquis while I went South to find the next higher formation and to further our field of work. My journey was made mainly on foot and started off by a large meal at the Maquis Group, which was providing my guides. After dinner I asked to see their "state of alert" plans go into operation – so the alarm was given, and the actual alertness was very good, but during my tour of inspection of the gun positions, I was astonished to find that when I talked to the gunners that not one of them had ever fired their weapons – it was not their fault, it was entirely due to their locality and the lack of ammunition. This has since been rectified. My astonishment was then somewhat mellowed, as when I left the guard turned out and sang "God Save the King" and asked if they might use my name for the password for that night, and also presented

me with an excellent rum omelet. I think the sight of an Allied officer in uniform, of whatever species, who had been sent from the Allied High Command by parachute gave them the hope that something would happen soon. In this connection it must be remembered that a B.W.C$_g$. directive was given the men of France to take to the Maquis the day before the invasion in the North of France. This they did, and they naturally expected an invasion force in their area. While myself aware of the difficulties of high level planning and security thereof, it is difficult for them to realize why nothing has yet happened in the South, particularly as the majority are young and have not done military service, and therefore, don't understand discipline in the military arena. And for those who are older it is more difficult as although they probably understand military discipline up to a point, they have, in the majority of cases, left their families, wives and children whom they were supporting, in the hope of speedy action and liberation of their region, and now that nothing has happened in the South they are very discouraged, and must in many cases be wanting to return home. Something must be done to rectify this forthwith.

I eventually arrived at the next higher formation and found there a better organized Maquis holding the plateau of GAMBOVIN. During the short time I was there they appeared better trained, better equipped and more disciplined than my former experience. The sorriest sight at this Camp was the quantity of arms and ammunition absolutely ruined by faulty parachuting. I spoke with their Commandant on this subject and he showed me fifteen broken rifles, several 30 mm. Browning M.Gs. with bent binds, belts of ammunition either ruined before despatch from Algiers or damaged on hitting the ground. I saw places where a container of ammunition had exploded on arrival and likewise with grenades. He told me that 30 per cent of his material had been ruined either at Algiers or in the air when the containers opened and jettisoned their load, or on hitting the ground, either due to insufficient packing or the parachute not opening. He also told me that members of reception committees had been killed by containers opening in the air. I spoke to other reception committee personnel on this subject and it was confirmed, and myself attended receptions from London and Algiers and saw it with my own eyes. Perhaps it is best summed up by the remark of one person, which I overheard when they were told that there was a reception that night; he said: "Is it worth going for if it's from Algiers," but that was the strangest comment I ever heard. The details are set out in Appendix "D".

At GAMBOVIN I learnt that the order of General KOENIG was being applied and that therefore my mission as given in my brief was no longer entirely applicable; that was only a presumption, of course, as without a radio, I had received no orders on the subject. I therefore set out on a further tour as I still heard no news from (_____) and to me it seemed likely that he had been arrested and that there was no Allied military representative in the area of the VERCORS, where fighting was taking place. So explaining that my visit was unofficial at that time, I set out to see as much as I could, my guide being (_____).

I met nearly all the local Commanders and the C. in C. of S.E. France and discussed with them their situation and heard their problems. I went to the North of the VERCORS, where I spoke to two machine gunners who ten minutes before had driven back 300 Germans. I went to the South where 150 to 250 Maquis were delaying the advance of 2,000 Germans, I spoke to the men who had been fighting at ST NAZAIR and other places, and it became evident that the plan – "OLIVE", set out in Appendix "A" hereto, was a feasible and workable plan acceptable by all Commanders, and in fact one which from the Resistance point of view was the most satisfactory to the Allied cause. I will deal no further with that here. The following points were also evident:

(a) Requirements in Equipment   (See Appendix "B".)
(b) General requirements   (-do-   "C")
(c) Complaints   (-do-   "D")
(d) General points   (-do-   "E")

In the above report I have been critical of the people who are working for the Resistance Movement inside France, it is purely by way of constructive criticism, with the view to rectifying their sufferings, and not adverse criticism. I have nothing but deep admiration for the way they are working against great odds, fighting against greater numbers and winning nothing but admiration for the Maquis who are living in the hills, and those who are trying to live in the plains or the foothills, for the semi-sedentaires who are doing great sabotage, the civilians who help those in need of a living hiding place, the couriers who walk or ride many kilometers each day in great danger, and the highly-placed officers and liaison officers who move between their departments in an effort to co-ordinate the resistance. Is this great array of 15,000 armed men and 17,000 unarmed men, to which will be added many thousands of helpers on "D" day, to be wasted? Why should it wait there in daily suspense, ignorant of its final role, and wondering whether it will be let down again as it was on 6th. June, 1944? There, in France, one wonders whether its true importance in the role of an Allied advance guard to invading forces is really realized. It needs a definite plan of action NOW.

<u>APPENDIX "B"</u>

1. Heavy weapons, i.e., artillery and A/tank guns.
2. Browning 30 and 50 mm.
3. Brens$_g$
4. Plats and Bazookas
5. 2" and 3" Mortars
6. U.S.A. Carbines.
7. Common, Mills and Phosphorus grenades.
8. Explosives for sabotage, normal demolitions and road mining.
9. Ammunition for new weapons and those already held.
10. Cup discharges
11. Batteries for Bazookas
12. Battledresses, Socks and Shoes.
13. Hard rations
14. Some medical supplies.
15. STENS$_g$, AND FOREIGN WEAPONS NOT REQUIRED.

Priority dropping in each department at once for morale, followed by large-scale droppings according to requirements or effectives.

<u>APPENDIX "C"</u>

GENERAL REQUIREMENTS.

1. Money. Ten million francs to each department per month until "D"-day. This should be in Francs, pounds, dollars or even invasion money. Without money it is impossible to continue in "liberated" regions, such as the VERCORS, as there are public services, food, soldiers and their families, gendarmes and their families to pay for and maintain. This existing shortage of money is appallingly bad for morale.

2. Immediate units to be dropped in each "liberated" region, NOW. This has a tremendous effect on morale as well as providing a mobile reserve and a pool of instructors; it is also, of course, real evidence of Allied support.

Apparion OCs *(?)*, French Batallion de Ovs and British S.A.S. should be employed.

3. Many French officers could easily be absorbed to great advantage for leadership.

4. French instructors are urgently needed.

5. Regions, such as the VERCORS could easily absorb 1,500 men and feed them. Above that figure food would have to be sent. It would be invaluable to have these "liberated" regions really strongly held, from which strong forces could emerge to attack German strong points.

APPENDIX "D"

COMPLAINTS.

1. Bad parachuting from Algiers. 50 and 60 per cent losses reported. I have examined the containers and the faults are:

(a) Opening in the air.
(b) Parachutes not opening.
(c) Pins not put in buckles
(d) Metal strips holding buckle to containers breaking away.
    This appears to be the fault of the bolts.
(e) Cardboard containers not strong enough for Brownings.
(f) Packing for wireless sets not good enough. I have seen
    several smashed sets, but this may be due to faults in (b)

(g) Faulty ammunition packed at Base
(h) Damp and ruined cigarettes received covered in mildew.
(i) Petrol asked for – creosote received by Allen.

It is pathetic to see so much material unnecessarily wasted when the men are wanting everything they can get. I walked over a ground after an Algiers parachutage and was constantly picking up smashed rifles, bands of ammunition, D-rations, explosives, etc. In addition it is pathetic to see a cow which has eaten a stick of plastic explosive!

It is apparent from the French point of view that daylight droppings can be made quite easily.

It is incredible to believe that pilots were not warned that on 22 June there is a festivity in France called Feu de St.Jean, when the French people light fires all over the countryside. Containers were dropped on these fires, and not to the right reception committees in some cases.

2. B.B.C. must give more precise and general directives.

3. W.O.C. Codes indistinctively printed.

<u>APPENDIX "E"</u>

GENERAL POINTS

1. Early advice must be given as to which of the four Cols. on the line of German withdrawal from ITALY are to be blown.

2. Further, Jed Teams required in VAUCHERE and BASSES ALPES at once. In principle one Jed Team per department in S.F.

3. Jed Teams to be instructed in weapons sent to Resistance Groups, i.e., Bazookas, Brownings, etc.

4. Precise directives must be given to Jeds about which factories to blow and what to blow in those which are chosen.

5. The question of collection of arms after regions are "liberated" by Allied invasion deserves early thought, and if nothing is done there will arise a menace to public security in post-war France.

6. It cannot be too strongly stressed that if more arms are sent an immediate increase in the Maquis in all regions will result.

<u>ATTACHMENT 'D'</u>

TOP SECRET
                    Serial No...*24*..

- 1 -

<u>REPORT ON JED TEAMS "VEGANINE" & "DODGE"</u>
                    By Commandant Noir

I. <u>Mission.</u>   To harass to the maximum German communications on the left bank of the Rhone (R.N.7. and railway Lyon - Marseille) and eventually roads and railways Lyon - Grenoble and Grenoble - Valence.
                    To pursue guerilla warfare.

Zone of action: Between Valence and Vienne.

II. <u>Teams</u>   VEGANINE.
                 Major Marten,   B. *CUTHBERT*
                 Cmdt Noir.   F *DEREK*
                 Sgt Gardener.   B. *ERNEST*

                 DODGE
                 Major Manniere A. *RUPERT*
                 Sgt Durocher   B. *OSWALD*

III. <u>Arrival in France and first contact.</u>

Ground: Tanit, between Beaurepaire and Sonnay

Date: 9 Jun.44.   0215 hrs   Veganine
       24 Jun.44   0030 hrs   Dodge.
              (Dodge DZ was Tarsis, not Tanit)
"We jumped in the order of Major Marten, myself, Gardener. The jump by myself and Major Marten was successful, but Sgt Gardener was killed in the jump. The static line came with the parachute, the hook was intact, the parachute was still folded in the bag and only one metre of the line had come out. It looked as though the hook had not been well pinned to the aircraft.

"On the ground the reception party were waiting for us. They were led by M. Berruyer from Beaurepaire. The reception was very cordial and gay, but we were soon worried about Gardener because nobody had seen him jump.

"The search for the containers was long and laborious, the drop having been made at an altitude of about 600 - 700 metres and the parachutes had spread over a large area. The reception party did not seem very anxious at that. The fall of the containers had not been followed and the search was being made here and there. It was during that search that with a young man from Beaurepaire, I discovered the body of Gardener.

"Two panniers, three packages, and three containers were not found. The two radio packages were smashed on landing, the parachutes not opening.

"The return was made by vehicles, at the break of dawn. The body of Gardener and the material were hidden in a shed near Beaurepaire on the road to Nanthes. Major Marten and myself stayed in a little house nearly in the middle of a small wood. A few hours later M. Berruyer brought us some civilian clothes and took us to his home.

"That night Sgt. Gardener was temporarily buried in the proximity of the little house where we were hidden. His body was simply rolled in his parachute and placed in a container, because the people told us it was impossible at the time to make a coffin. Sgt. Gardener was solemnly buried on September 30th. 1944. His body now lies in the vault of the Berruyer family in the cemetery of Beaurepaire.

"The information given us by Algiers was that we were at first to contact Major Roger. He was at the time doing a tour in the south and M. Berruyer did not know when he would return. We waited four days at Beaurepaire for him to come back. This gave us time to notice that the German and Milice activity seemed to be more or less restricted. We contacted Major Roger's radio operator Albert, which permitted us to communicate with Algiers via London.

"On 12th June M. Berruyer brought us to Montchenu to a maquis chief named Bozambo, who was able to guide us to the local chief. He was an athletic young man with a sympathetic face, a strange glitter in his eye, and a bit crazy. He seemed to be flattered to receive Allied officers, and gave us an attractive picture of his maquis.

"It was a matter of extreme urgency to:
     Inculcate into the maquis a sense of discipline
     To instruct them
     Officer them
     Urge them to military action.

"For all that, one had to have cadres, and I had no one available suitable to put in cadres. They had to come from outside. So, strange though it may seem, I began with the instruction. I used for this purpose Major Manniere. I ordered the groups of Bozambo's maquis to come week by week for instruction at my H.Q. Manniere taught them how to handle explosives and the rudiments of battle drill. I also sent my colleague for the same purpose to pass a few days with the Malboux maquis and to the F.T.P. As exercises I sent teams with Manniere to attack the Grenoble - Romans railway. The attack on the factory of Basses Isere also served as training.

"I sent the Malboux maquis, which was relatively the most experienced, to make attacks on the railway Lyon - Marseille. At the same time I looked for officers and N.C.O.s or men who could be made into these. I contacted, or had contacted, the regular and reserve officers in the region. I found amongst them not the slightest enthusiasm. They either refused to come to the maquis whom they regarded as bands of pillagers, terrorists, communists (those whom were spoken about by Radio Vichy) or they pretended that the moment was not yet ripe, but that they would come on D-Day. I brought to their attention the fact that as they did not reckon the disembarkation in Normandy to be D-day, there was absolutely no reason why they should not wait until the Allies were in Lyon or even Berlin before deciding D-day had arrived. They refused to appreciate the irony and changed the conversation.

"Most often they declared that they did not want to come to the maquis because they were unorganised bands of young people too inclined to pillage.

"First period.
   Attacks on electric plants.

"The attacks on the Basse-Isere plant was minutely prepared through the help of an engineer who worked there. He supplied all the plans and sketch maps necessary and gave me the keys of some of the doors. We made a point of not destroying apparatus which would require a great deal of mending, or too long a wait for spare parts. We decided on the control panels as a target, and these were successfully destroyed.

"The operation was not at all difficult from the point of view of the attack as the guard consisted merely of 11 rather ineffective Gendarmes. But the attack had to be carried out rapidly and discreetly as a German detachment was stationed less than 200 metres from the plant.

"This operation was illuminating as it was the first to be carried out with fairly strong forces (two sections under the command of a Lieutenant, with Rupert as sabotage expert), and because of the varied jobs to be carried out (covering look-outs, capture by surprise of certain men, different demolitions etc.), all requiring strict coordination. Certain things could be deduced; although the group employed was composed of selected personnel, the officer had to intervene strongly before the leading elements crossed the road separating the last cover from the plant well – during the withdrawal there was some confusion among the sections, although the Germans had not moved.

"There was still a great deal to do from the point of view of instruction.

ATTACHMENT 'E'

To: Commanding Officer
S.P.O.C.g   11 Oct 44.

"DODGE DEBRIEFING
The completeness of this report leaves little to be added. I was with this team myself in June and any comments which would normally be put into debriefing notes will be found in my own report. Commandant Noir had a very difficult time with political differences and in changes in command and I cannot speak too highly of the work he did, knowing as I do, the personalities he had to deal with.

(Signed) H. N. MARTEN
Major
Northamptonshire Yeoman

"RADIO REPORT - TEAM "DODGE"

Sgt. Durocher. "OSWALD"
Dropped 24th June 1944
Ground Tarsis 9 kms N.E. of Beaurepaire
               11 kms S.W. of Rouillon

"Reception was very good. Crew of aircraft and despatcher especially did a very good job. Material and teams came down on centre of ground, very close together. Did not have to show any papers on arrival. From there despatched to region of Vercors, where I met Major Marten who was chief of the Veganin team. Stayed there for twelve days. Did not get own W/T equipment. Had to use an American set which had to be repaired. It took four days before I made my first contact. Because of urgent messages I had to use emergency link quite often for three days. Base sent a message saying to use another plan giving me four liaisons a day. Work was very tiresome because I had to do all ciphering and deciphering by myself. Equipment that came with me was the only one that was not damaged. Three other B. Mk. II were completely smashed.

"Used B. Mk II set for most of the time. Contacts with base were very good in general. Used an American set for the last 7 days, which worked very well. I found that the quarter wave aerial at right angles to base station worked best. Experimented with aerial quite often. Also noticed that aerial making an angle, instead of being parallel to the ground gave a better outgoing signal.

"Uniform made it impossible to circulate at times. When I came out of the Vercors I had to procure myself some civilian clothes which were very hard to find. Had to buy them at a very high cost. Had to leave all my equipment and uniform because enemy action made it impossible to take it. Due to that I lost quite a few things, including money belt containing 20,000 frs and 50$ American. That region was attacked by a strong enemy force 4 days later. That is why only part of my kit and equipment was brought back to me.

"I do not intend to go on any operations before I have leave to go home to Canada, as I have been two years without leave because of operational reasons, and also I have been overseas for nearly five years. After I get leave, I am willing to go on any mission you wish to send me on.

L.J. Durocher. Sgt."

The Memorial to Sergeant Gardner of Team Veganin,
placed at DZ "Tanit" - the site of his unfortunate demise.
(Photo be Gerald Rix)

Chapter 16
More About Teams
Veganin and Dodge

(by Commandant Noir)

"Historical context:

Two similar Jedburgh teams, starting from the Blida aerodrome near Algiers, are parachuted into the north of the Drôme: the Veganin and Dodge missions. Commanded by British Major Neil Marten, the Veganin mission included Captain Gaston Claude Vuchot ("Black", *later Major Noir*) and British radio sergeant Denis Gardener who was killed during the parachute drop on June 9, 1944 at 2:15 AM on the "Tanit" field, between Sonnay and Beaurepaire. The parachuting was carried out badly: the drop altitude of between 600 and 700 meters led to a wide dispersion on the ground, several containers were not found and, to make matters worse, the two radio packages were found badly damaged, the quartz preset frequencies broken.

"The mission assigned to the Veganin team consists mainly of harassing German communications as much as possible on the left bank of the Rhône (RN 7 and railway lines from Lyon to Marseille) and, possibly, along the railway lines of rail from Lyon to Grenoble and from Grenoble to Valence, then to trigger guerrilla actions between Valence and Vienne. First in date of the "Jedburgh" missions for the Drôme, Véganine will soon be talked about because of the effectiveness of Vuchot who articulates his command plan by retaining four objectives to be achieved: instilling a sense of discipline in the maquis, giving them basic instruction and collective training, command on a daily basis by offloading service details to only two chiefs, one AS, the other FTP so that he can better devote himself to intelligence and the operations and, finally, lead his companies into battle.

"The second *(first)* team to be deployed from Algiers, Veganin, was made up of Major Neil Marten of the Northamptonshire Yeomanry ('Cuthbert'), Capt Claude Vuchot, who took the name Noir ('Derek') and Sgt Dennis 'Jesse' Gardner of the Royal Armoured Corps ('Ernest'). It was to operate in the Drôme and Isère departments east of the Rhône in support of SOE F Section's Jockey circuit, run by 'Roger' (Maj Francis Cammaerts), and by the time it was inserted, on the night of 8 June, the maquisards of an adjacent area, the Vercors Plateau, had risen up against the Germans. The Germans were somewhat slow to react, and it was 13 June before they struck, moving into the village of St-Nizier-du-Moucherotte on the north-east shoulder of the Vercors massif$_g$. This toe-hold on the plateau allowed them to control much of its northern end, but surprisingly no further offensive ensued until mid-July, and by that time two massive parachutages, part of Operations Zebra and Cadillac, had ensured that all the partisans on the Plateau, who by now numbered perhaps 4,000, were armed.

"Jedburgh team Veganin was inserted at Roger's request 'to assist resistance movement and to stimulate guerilla [sic] action in the area of main lines of communication east bank of the Rhône between Avignon and Vienne'. Marten's report adds that the plan was for the team to recruit, arm and train teams of partisans to carry out coup-de-main operations in the Rhône Valley on the day the Allies landed in the south of France.

"The aircraft located the DZ, 'Tanit', west of the village of Beaurepaire, and Marten, then Vuchot, then Gardner jumped from a height of about 600 metres. Marten and the Frenchman landed safely and soon met up, but there was no sign of Sgt Gardner. The containers and packages dropped with the men were spread over a wide area and it took some time to locate them; some, including those containing both radio sets, were smashed. In the course of the search Vuchot came upon Sgt Gardner's body. His parachute had failed to open due to the static line not being hooked up correctly (there was no provision for manual release with this type of chute), and he was killed on impact.

"The team's briefing had said they would be met by Roger, and they waited for him at Beaurepaire for four days, eventually leaving only after they had been put in contact with his radio operator. On 12 June they began to move southward in the direction of St-Donat-sur-Herbasse and meet other maquisard leaders in the region, notably 'Capt René', who commanded the Northern Battalion of the Régiment du Drôme. This, he claimed, ran to nine companies, and more manpower was available, but since he lacked weapons, it was only barely effective. Marten coded a message, to be sent by Roger's radio operator, asking for arms for these men, but it was seemingly never sent. In fact, it soon became obvious that there was very considerable unrest within the so-called battalion – which actually numbered less than 200 men at this time – due to friction between leftist and rightist factions, men of both persuasions having been mustered together under 'officers' from the Armée Secrète chosen for their political motivation rather than for their leadership abilities or military experience.

"The situation had been steadily deteriorating long before D-Day, but came to a head when, after the Resistance leaders in the area gave the signal for a general rising, two companies attacked the German garrison at St-Rambert. The Germans responded by attacking St-Donat in strength, taking many hostages and burning their houses, and then repeated the exercise in villages and farms across the region. Far from offering resistance, the partisan groups began to fall apart, the

FTP faction blaming the AS for showing poor leadership, while the population at large blamed the maquisards as a group for first stirring up the Germans, and then being able to do nothing to contain them.

"By this time Vuchot seems to have assumed the leadership of Veganin. Arthur Brown, in his Brief History of the Jedburghs, says that Marten was badly affected by Gardner's death, and was prematurely withdrawn from the field in consequence; but it is unclear whether this was due to his grief or to the official explanation – that he was required to convince the planners of Operation Anvil/Dragoon of the viability of the Route Napoléon – Vuchot decided that the only solution was to separate the two factions, and give FTP supporters the chance to constitute themselves into separate groups. He achieved this by about 20 June, by which time total active membership of the AS groups stood at around 180 and that of the FTP at around a hundred. There was a temporary improvement in morale as a result, but it soon became apparent that the situation was out of hand; no permanent resolution was achieved, and the groups in question were never entirely reliable during the eight weeks before the area was liberated. Vuchot later came to believe that the picture which had been painted for Veganin on their arrival, which portrayed the maquisards in the area as well led, keen and eager, was completely illusory. He said of the AS bands: "Most of them came to the maquis to escape compulsory work in Germany, above all to lead a better and larger life than in their family; what attracted them was the requisitioning expeditions for rations, scrounging in certain places with submachine guns ready."

"I have rarely experienced anything so painful, as when I saw the astonishing joy on their faces, when the maquis chief announced an expedition for supplies, and, on their return, when we unpacked the jars of jam and barrels of pork. They had the souls of looters and constantly they would go and see the chief to tell him of another victim, saying that he was a war profiteer or collaborator or sympathising milicien, but actually, most of the time, it was some enemy of their family or themselves … In the FTP the same characteristics were found, but exaggerated even more by the lack of leaders.

"On 19 June Marten left Vuchot, and made his way on foot to Combovin on the edge of the Vercors, where 'Hermine' (Cmdt Druout, commander of the Régiment du Drôme) had his headquarters. Two days later Hermine ordered René to join him, with all his men, but Vuchot countermanded the order. On 24 June, he says, he was joined by Capt Cyrus Manierre ('Rupert') and Sgt L.T. Durocher, of the Royal Canadian Corps of Signals, ('Oswald') who made up team Dodge, which had been inserted on to the same ground Veganin had used, but without mishap. This was one of only two cases of a Jedburgh team being sent into France without a French liaison officer; under the circumstances, it seems possible that SPOC$_g$ had already decided to withdraw Neil Marten and consolidate Manierre, Vuchot and Durocher into a single team.

Dodge

"The Dodge mission was Jedburgh's second action-charged mission against the Rhone Valley thoroughfares. In reality, this action would essentially consist of strengthening the Veganin team, which was very quickly reduced to only the "Black" commander. Composed of American Major Cyrus E. Manniere Jr. and Canadian radio sergeant Lucien Durocher, with two radios, the Dodge mission was dropped on June 24, 1944 on Tarsis airfield near Beaurepaire.

"The decision was made on June 26 when Manniere and Durocher went with Vuchot to a command meeting at La Chapelle-en-Vercors attended by Huet "Hervieux", Drouot "L'Hermine", Cammaerts "Roger" and Major Marten. Colonel Zeller "Joseph" presided. After having heard Vuchot protest against the fact that a planned removal of his device from the Rhone Valley would be contrary to his mission, then Hervieux and Roger argued firmly and persuasively by affirming the priority of strengthening the Vercors fortress in the eyes of the

Allies, "Joseph" decided the attachment of Manniere to the Veganin team, Manniere becoming Vuchot's deputy, and the temporary assignment to the Vercors of radio sergeant Durocher with his two radio sets, the radio links of Veganin having to be ensured by Berruyer agent of Major Roger in Beaurepaire. At the end of the meeting, Marten announced his departure for Algiers. Vuchot and Major Manniere then formed a close-knit pair, well supported by Marcel Desgranges, Noir's intelligence officer. They shared the command tasks. Vuchot traveled dressed in civilian clothes, night and day, throughout the territory of the Drôme to contact the leaders of the maquis and solicit their cooperation by tempting them, if necessary, with offers of equipment and money.

"The following day Marten sent word for Vuchot to join him at La Chapelle-en-Vercors, and he and Dodge set off on foot on 26 June, arriving two days later. Manierre stated that they were fired on by maquis sentries and had some problems identifying themselves, but were eventually taken to meet Marten, Roger, 'Col Joseph' (Henri Zeller), Hermine and 'Hervieux' (Cmdt François Huet, leader of the Vercors maquisards). Disappointed by the lack of enthusiasm observed in the Drôme, he decided to recruit in Isère and in the Rhône. To this end, he was recommended by Commander Faure, Berruyer in Beaurepaire and the leader of the Free French in Lyon. Thanks to this support, he made contact with active or reserve officers as well as with non-commissioned officers to encourage them to join him but, alas, few were those who agreed to follow him: only two officers from the regular army and some non-commissioned officers.

"While Vuchot strived to recruit active and reserve cadres, Manniere periodically visited the maquis AS and the maquis FTP, sharing lodging and meals. Each visit was structured over three days: a day and a half of instruction on the weapons and explosives available in the maquis visited, a day and a half for shooting and combat methods in the field. The last hour was used to inventory the equipment made available.

"These visits followed the initial training given to the PC and which the sections received in turn, week after week. They were also very useful for ensuring the cohesion of the companies to which Vuchot was keen to give as much independence as possible. Each company must be able to quickly dodge in the event of a surprise attack.

According to Richter: "There is not in all the maquis a figure more beloved and more obeyed. It's because it has everything you need to please those maquisards who, yesterday were going to school. He's a kid like them. He has come to teach them how to use the new explosives and his greatest joy is making noise. If the Dark Commander let him, he would detonate every five minutes. The Black Commander, he says, doesn't like noise, too bad. A rider trained in the USA, considered too clumsy to become an airplane pilot, Manniere became an expert parachutist in the use of explosives.

"During the period between Overlord and Dragoon, the actions in North Drôme are carried out by favoring the instruction of the men and that of their leaders. The attacks targeted the electrical installations: that of the Beaumont-Monteux power station, meticulously prepared with the help of the foreman Paul Dubois and the expert Manniere, was a success, that of Pizançon failed in part. Attacks against enemy vehicles on the roads were carried out by small teams of 5 to 6 men who approached by car as close as possible to the locations chosen to lay the most successful ambushes. The biggest losses were recorded on July 13 when the Militia surprised a vehicle: the guerrillas deplored two killed, three wounded including one seriously and a prisoner.

"The Germans tightened the guard of the railways more and more by placing men every 200 meters, by cutting the trees at the edge of the tracks, by multiplying the patrols along and at a distance from them, by increasing the lighting and by increasing the firepower of their weapons. The biggest guerrilla action took place on August 5 when four German convoys moved towards Beaurepaire to encircle the locality: the first on the road from Romans-sur-Isère to Hauterives, the second between Saint-Sorlin-en-Valloire and Lens-Lestang, the third on the D1 at Anneyron and the fourth coming from the north via the Jarcieu road.

"Captured by militiamen, Manniere was transferred to Lyon as a prisoner of war. Thus ended the Dodge mission. Despite the obstacles and many difficulties he encountered in the exercise of his command, Vuchot succeeded in the mission assigned to the Veganin team. The total strength of his maquis increased, in twelve weeks, from 200 to more than 650 men who caused the enemy the losses of several hundred killed and 300 prisoners. Admittedly, it would have been possible for him to do much better in the last week of August 1944, but on condition that the local command grant him reinforcements to fight the enemy in the narrow corridor between Tain-L'Hermitage and Saint-Vallier. Unfortunately, the priority was elsewhere: we had to take Romans and Valence.

(Authors: Pierre Balliot
Source: "Report on Jeds Teams Veganin and Dodge".
Jedburgh Alumni Association.
For the love of France,
Federation of Resistance and FFI combat units of the Drôme. Valence - Peuple Libre 1989.
North Drôme, land of asylum and revolt.
Valence-Peuple Libre 1993. Troupes de Montagne n°12, page 20. De Richter, pages 196-197.

Study by Bertrand Souquet published in the bulletin n°191 of Symbols & Traditions) *Translated from French.*

"It soon became clear that Joseph and Roger had an agenda to which the Jedburghs were not privy: to turn the Vercors Plateau, where the maquisards had risen in open revolt as soon as news of the Normandy landings reached them, into an impregnable redoubt. From here forces could sortie to support the Allied advance up the Rhône Valley and – crucially – up the Route Napoléon$_g$ to the east of the Massif$_g$, an alternative way north from the Côte-d'Azur, through Gap, to Grenoble, which the Emperor himself had followed in his northward passage to reclaim his throne after his escape from Elba in 1815. To assure the invulnerability of the Vercors, Roger avowed, it would be necessary to bring in all the partisan units from the surrounding area, which, of course, immediately rendered the Jedburgh team redundant. Nor was that the only surprise in store for Vuchot: Our interviewers were firm; Roger was persuasive. I noticed that Marten was silent; it seemed as if he were assisting (this in the French sense, of being a spectator at an event) at a discussion that did not concern him. As he was the team leader I hesitated at times to say something. It was only after the conference that I found out he had other functions; Marten thought I knew what it was all about; he had evidently sent me a letter informing me about it; that letter had never reached me unfortunately.

"One of the 'other functions' was apparently to act as a courier/emissary; Marten boarded a Westland Lysander aircraft at an LZ$_g$ known as Spitfire, south of Sault in the Vaucluse, on the night of 10 July and returned to Algiers via Corsica; according to some reports the purpose of his return was to press Joseph's plan to utilise the Route Napoléon, though this may have been justification for withdrawing him. (In fact, Joseph himself was brought out of France, also by

Lysander from Spitfire, on the night of 2 August, and it was he who, during a lengthy meeting at his headquarters in Naples, persuaded Lt-Gen Alexander Patch, the Supreme Commander of Operation Anvil/Dragoon$_g$, to make use of the Route Napoléon$_g$; as a result, the Allies were in Grenoble on D+6, instead of D+90, as the original plan had predicted. If one relatively low-ranking officer personally shortened World War Two in Europe, it was probably Henri Zeller.)

"Perhaps Vuchot was an able negotiator, or perhaps Roger (and/or his colleagues; Hervieux, for one, was no friend of the Communists) had foreseen problems integrating the FTP into the overall structure of resistance on the Vercors Plateau. In any event, a compromise was finally struck on the matter of the disposition of forces: Vuchot and Manierre would be allowed to remain in the valley and operate there in the conventional Jedburgh role, and would keep the 'troublesome' FTP, along with two AS companies of his choosing. He opted for the maquisards from St-Uze, under 'Malboux' and another which had taken the nom de guerre of its rather idiosyncratic leader 'Bozambo' (Lt Marcellin) as its own. Roger, however, insisted on retaining the radio operator, Sgt Durocher, arguing that Manierre and Vuchot would have little need of a direct conduit to Algiers, and that any messages they did need to send could be transmitted, with the highest priority, by Roger's headquarters. Vuchot gave in, but with rage in my heart I descended to the valley. It seemed to me essential to organise something in the northern sector of the Drôme. If not, who would utilise this region, useful as it was for work on the lines of communication running along the Rhône valley?

"It is clear from Vuchot's account that he had an uphill struggle to turn the maquisards at his disposal, barely 200 men in all, into anything like an effective fighting force, and he had to resort to most extreme measures to get his message across:

The maquis chiefs each wanted to raise, organise and dispose his little band at his own will and pleasure. The principal interest was feeding. Good fare being the condition of recruitment, it was the maquis where one ate the best that was the most prosperous and the chief the most famous. Malboux did not hesitate at forgery, and used my name to make more or less unreasonable requisitions. He took arms destined for others at parachutages, to equip his men better. His maquis he felt should be the only one in the region; he attempted to organise his own personal police etc.

"One might ask why, with so many drawbacks, I kept people like Bozambo and Malboux. Malboux was remarkably brave and audacious, with no military experience; he had a genius for coups de main and ambushes. If he was without scruple, he was on the other hand, almost the only chief of a Corps Franc on whom I could depend at all. He died heroically at the very moment when I was planning to have him arrested.

"Bozambo was unbalanced, versatile, susceptible, always listening to the last who spoke, getting enthusiastic, and losing enthusiasm with equal rapidity. He seemed to me to be the perfect example of the maquis leader to get rid of. But he had a very real popularity in the region …

"Over the course of the next week, Major Desmond Longe, the leader of Eucalyptus, sent urgent radio messages to London and Algiers, asking for reinforcements, heavier weapons and air support, while Roger attempted to persuade London to launch air raids on local airfields, where he had seen troop- carrying gliders being readied for action. The pleas fell on deaf ears, but it was probably too late anyway.

"When the German assault came, on 18 July, it was rebuffed initially by defenders on the heights who were able to control the roads up on to the plateau, but on 21 July troop- carrying gliders landed in the zone at Vassieux which the partisans had just finished clearing for Allied airborne operations. The German airborne forces were soon reinforced, and the perimeter they established and held was never in serious danger. Assaults from St-Nizier-du-Moucherotte, as well as from the south and east, followed and proved to be overwhelming. On 23 July, Hervieux gave the order for the maquisards to disperse, but by that time a reinforced division of German mountain troops, with artillery and heavy armour, had spread out over the plateau and were blocking every road that led down from it. Those who escaped did so chiefly in ones and twos, and even the men of the Operational Group were sorely tested.

"Hervieux's decision to delay the order to disperse until long after it had become the only obvious course of action has been criticised widely ever since. The death toll was high – at least 630 men died in the fighting on the plateau – and more were taken, the majority of them being killed out of hand while trying to get away. Moreover, some 200 non-résistants were killed in reprisals, which saw whole villages leveled and many hundreds of houses burned.

"The arrival of the rest of Mission Eucalyptus, which had no less than three radio operators, freed Sgt Durocher, and he returned to the Jedburgh team about 10 July, by which time Veganin/Dodge was starting to get its activities on a more level footing. While Vuchot was trying to increase the numbers of men at his disposal, to introduce a more stable element and instill some discipline into them, Manierre – a career soldier who had graduated from West Point in 1942 – was trying to improve their military effectiveness, instructing the more reliable elements in the handling of weapons and explosives and leading them on raids. He achieved little at first, but as July wore on, the men's confidence began to grow, and he was able to turn his attention to more important targets, among them the power station at Beaumont-Monteux.

Chapter 17
Missions to destroy Power Plants

Major Manierre continues:

The formation of our resistance network was as follows: Major Noir and I set up a Command Post at St. Bonnet de Valclerieux. We established a guard of about 70 men, under the command of a French Foreign Legion Captain. We lived in a barn in the woods, with our guards. We retained contact with all other resistance units through the means of messengers and by means of our own transportation, which consisted of approximately five automobiles, several trucks and a large number of bicycles. We required each Maquis to keep a liaison man at our Command Post. Each liaison man attended all conferences and was present when all operations were planned.

During this time we had received some instructions from Algiers and, deeming it necessary that we should have a radio operator so as to be in continual contact, we sent for Sgt. Durocher and he duly returned to us. We were now ready to being fulfilling our mission.

One mission of high priority, which I had been instructed in before leaving Algiers, was the destruction of electrical power. It was therefore resolved that our first big operation would consist of wiping out all electrical power in the Drome. A secondary effort would be the cutting off of electricity to the coal refineries at St. Etienne, which depended on the power plant at Beaumont-Monteux and l'Isere

"The purpose of this raid was to knock out the power supply of the plants in the area, especially coal-processing plants at St. Etienne. The plants were to be temporarily damaged; that is, damaged to the extent they could be repaired in six months after the area was conquered by the Allies.

"For this project, Manierre headed the men who were to blow up the Beaumont plant. Another group was sent to a small generating plant farther up the river, and a detachment of Communist troops was to overturn the steel towers which carried power lines. The attempt to blow up the other plant was unsuccessful. Instead of meeting French Vichy militia. the men met Germans, and unprepared for this opposition, were routed, "pretty badly shot up," Manierre said.

"His men, though, were successful——quite successful——he later had the gratification of knowing. At 2:30 AM one summer morning, a force of 80 men crept through the outer lines of the guards about the plant, and at a given signal, overpowered the guards. Overpowering, the major explained, meant to disarm, knock out, or kill."

In our Maquis was M. Dubois, who had been a foreman at Beaumont-Monteux. M. Dubois furnished us with complete details of the interior of the plant and on the stations of the guards. However, we had no accurate information as to the interior of the Isere power plant. Nevertheless we decided to go ahead, and on the night of about 25 June we prepared our operation. The FTP, whose Maquis were very ardent but somewhat disorderly, was assigned the mission of attacking the Isere power plant; purpose to do temporary damage, lasting about two months. To another Maquis was assigned the mission of lopping off high-tension pylons within a certain area.

To our own Maquis I assigned the mission of doing temporary damage, lasting about two months, on the plant at Beaumont-Monteux. I resolved to lead this coup-de-main myself, despite the energetic protests of Major Noir.

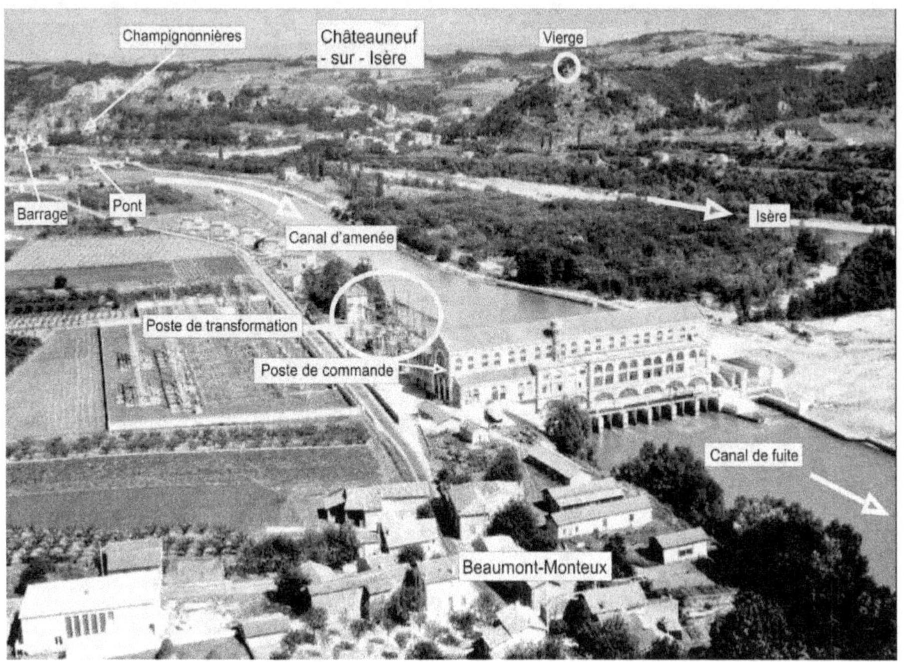

I will give a brief description of the mission. Careful study of the plans of the power plant, and consultation with M. Dubois, convinced me that the best method of attacking the plant would be to take about 25 men and creep up at night in the manner of the training which we had received in Scotland and at Peterborough. Four silent scouts were to be sent ahead, preceding us by 200 yards, and they were to eliminate any guards and anyone who showed signs of resistance. The rest of us were to follow them into the compound of the plant, where any sleeping guards were to be secured. Then Lt. Desgranges and I were to go alone into the plant, and I was to place the explosive charges on the central board, while Lt. Desgranges cleaned out any guards who were inside.

Substantially the mission was carried out in this way. The plant, it turned out, was guarded by gendarmes. They seemed to be a very useless lot, who would not have resisted even if they had not been attacked in as determined a manner as we did attack. I placed the charges in the power plant on the control board through which practically every wire in the entire plant had to pass. I then turned on all 12 generators and got them going at maximum speed.

"At this point, Manierre took charge, for he was the only man in the group who was trained in demolition work. First he went to the large switchboard and turned on the turbine generators which were to be damaged. The generators were turned on so that the current would be in the wires when the explosions went off. Damage from short-circuited wires and connections was expected to be as great as from the actual bomb damage.

"As the turbines hummed into action, Manierre directed that hand grenades be thrown into the giant machines. Surprisingly enough, the grenades made little damage, and he turned next to blowing out the switchboard, the heart of the plant. "

I lit a 45 seconds fuse and ran out of the building. When I was seen to come running out, all the people ran as well, the rest of the Maquis running with them. In a few seconds the explosion took place. Not only did the 30 kilos of plastic destroy the control board, it seemed to blow off the roof of the power plant, smashing all the windows of the houses in the vicinity. The explosion was followed by numerous secondary explosions inside the plant, accompanied by violent cracklings of electricity and further explosions from the transformers outside the plant. We felt that we had succeeded.

This was at 5 AM. On returning to our position we discovered that the FTP mission to the Isere power plant had failed completely and that the Maquis had suffered heavy losses, due to the plant being guarded by the Germans. Our intelligence had told us that it was guarded by gendarmes or the Milice, and we were still sure that this had been the case. Nevertheless, about 24 hours before the attack was made, a company of German soldiers was put on duty at this plant. The result was that the Maquis were caught in a cross fire, and half of them were wiped out before the rest could withdraw. However, the third mission was successful in that the three only arteries of high-tension wires had been cut over such a long distance that it required approximately six days to repair it.

"Days later, Manierre learned that the manager of the plan wrote to Vichy, reporting that the damage would take three months to be repaired, if the materials could be obtained. But the materials were vital copper and rubber and steel, and in less than three months, the Nazis were driven from south France."

Two days later a young girl, Mlle Cabouillet, who lived at St. Donat and who was an intelligence operator of ours, came to us with an almost complete record of the destruction of the Beaumont-Monteux plant, which had been prepared by the manager of the plant, apparently a Milician, and purported to explain why and how his plant had been demolished. He claimed that it had been an inside job, but that a certain number of terrorists, led by an American, had apparently engineered the sabotage. He went on to assess the damage, and we gathered that even the most optimistic of electricians could not have hoped to repair the plant in less than a month. We also discovered that a German roadblock of about 50 men had been established on the road about a 1000 yards from the power plant. The Germans had heard the alarm bell at the plant ringing, and had milled around trying to decide whether or not to see what the trouble was, when they heard the explosion and saw the roof flying in the air, at which time they deserted the road block and ran away.

An interesting operation conducted by another Maquis involved the destruction of telephone and telegraph communications in the region. Instructions from Algiers had reached us that such a mission would serve a very useful purpose. Therefore it was decided that a certain Maquis from the region just north of Valence, under the command of a man who had been in the service ITT$_g$ in Valence, should carry it out. The mission was executed by ambushing a truck of ITT workers. The workmen were placed under guard in a comfortable barn, treated very well, and their uniforms were confiscated. The uniforms were donned by members of the Maquis, who entered the Post Office at Valence and went down into the manhole below the switchboard through which all wires connecting telephone communications had to pass. They pretended to be on a repair job, and nobody interfered with them. They placed demolition charges in the manhole and ran out, herding all the people in the Post Office out with them, slamming the door behind them. They got into their truck and drove merrily away, leaving a bewildered group behind to hear a violent explosion from the basement of the Post Office. This act effectively cut communications for a period of time the length of which I do not know.

Chapter 18
Handling of the "Gangsters"

At this time, about 10 July, a diplomatic situation arose between ourselves and the civilian population of the region. Gangs of young boys had joined the resistance, found the living easy, and had become hoodlums. Instead of fighting the Germans, these young bandits set out on lives of crime; robbing and murdering their fellow country-men in the guise of serving the underground.

Although they were not aware of the presence of bonafide American and French officers in the area, they nevertheless knew the location of most of the Maquis. We were certain that it was but a question of time before someone would betray us. Moreover, a section of six men of the Maquis Bozambo had turned gangster. These six men were known as the "equipe speciale", and their mission had been to retrieve all the supplies for the Maquis which were not sent by air from Algiers or London. This work was supposed to entail the orderly requisitioning of food, gasoline, and other supplies. In fact it involved the looting, pillaging and robbing of the farms and homes of the region.

The "equipe speciale" had set themselves up in a deserted chateau, where they were living with their women and from which they would make wild excursions in automobiles decorated with tricolors and the Cross of Lorraine, the object of these trips being robbery and banditry. They were known to have entered houses, taken everything out from money and silverware to bed linens and household effects, and they were keeping all this property in the stables and barn of the chateau in which they lived. Naturally their activity was creating a terrible impression throughout the region, and was causing ill feeling towards the French resistance. The "equipe speciale" had not turned over the money or supplies they got, but kept them for themselves. Therefore it was determined that we would arrest them, try them by court martial, and either execute them or put them in jail.

We surrounded their chateau early one morning and called on them to give themselves up. This they refused to do. A brisk fire ensued, reminiscent of prohibition days in Chicago, the result was that two of the six were killed and two of the women also, the others wounded. Then we threw four hand grenades in through the window and fired rockets into the house. The "equipe speciale" was very effectively liquidated, and an observation of their loot indicated that all six were criminals and that they deserved capital punishment. Their booty consisted of many very valuable items stolen from houses in the vicinity, and also included the most inconsequential items, such as children's dolls, and the saber of a fine old French cavalry Colonel who lived in retirement nearby and whose home had been looted.

"They were criminals in the eyes of the law, and more seriously, they were a hindrance to the resistance. "We were forced to control them," Manierre said. Asked to explain what "control" meant, he said simply, "We eliminated them."

Meanwhile our intelligence operators, most of whom were very brave and determined women, had notified us of great activity being conducted at a certain chateau on the left bank of the Rhone, across the river from Tournon. We reconnoitered this chateau, and found that the Germans were massing large numbers of tanks, trucks, 88 mm guns, similar supplies and personnel. We suspected that this preparation foretold an attack upon the Vercors. Therefore we notified the Vercors. Likewise we sent urgent messages to Algiers, pinpointing the chateau and requesting aerial bombardment. We repeated this request for about three days, and were rewarded by a lovely bombardment, conducted by the 15th Air Force from Italy. Unfortunately the Germans had evacuated about half of their supplies. Nevertheless a good deal of damage was done. Shortly afterwards the 15th Air Force bombed the German airfield at Portes, near Valence. Algiers requested us to assess the bomb damage and notify them.

This we did, and sent back a message giving details of the damage insofar as we had been able to observe it, through our operators who worked on the field, and who would certainly have been able to see what specifically had been done. In addition to this message I protested to Algiers that I did not wish my position to deteriorate into that of a spy. Other espionage missions included descriptions and pinpointing of PLM_g bridge, Pont de l'Isere at Valence.

Since this bridge was surrounded by mine fields and was protected at each end by two batteries of 88 mm Flak guns plus a company of Infantry it was decided to attack it with a company of Maquis. Even if we had succeeded our losses would have been too high, and we would have required about 150 men with automatic weapons, mortars (which we did not have), and other equipment difficult to obtain. Therefore we pinpointed it in a message to Algiers describing the conditions of its defense, and requested aerial bombardment.

Later, while in Germany, I met an aviator who had taken part in a raid about 10 August. He said that the 15th Air Force had destroyed the bridge.

Chapter 19
In Civilian Clothes

By this time – mid-July – events were starting to come to a head up on the Vercors Plateau. The Vercors maquisards had received their first big parachutage of weapons and equipment as part of Operation Zebra on 25 June, when thirty-five aircraft dropped a total of 420 containers; and the arrival of the advanced elements of an Inter-Allied mission, Eucalyptus, and a fifteen-strong Operational Group, Justine, on the night of 29 June, seemed to indicate that SHAEF$_g$ was, at least belatedly, taking the rising seriously. The partisans, however, mistakenly assumed the parachutists to be the advance party for a much larger airborne force, and that impression was reinforced when a French military engineering team, Mission Paquebot, was parachuted in on 6 July to begin work on fashioning a landing strip big enough to take a twin-engined aircraft at Vassieux, in a large, shallow bowl near the geographical centre of the plateau.

By 14 July, Hervieux having issued a proclamation calling for every able-bodied man in the region around the plateau to join the rising, there were around 4,000 partisans assembled at Vassieux, many of them armed.

That morning, even as they began to assemble for a Bastille Day parade, seventy-two B-17 Flying Fortresses dropped 862 canisters of arms, suspended beneath red, white and blue parachutes, as part of Operation Cadillac, whereupon the Luftwaffe promptly reacted, dropping incendiary bombs and strafing the DZ with machine- gun fire. The pick-up operation had to wait until nightfall, but by the end of the next day there were weapons – though only, and this was to be crucial, light weapons – for all.

Around the middle of July we were thrilled to see whole masses of Fortresses flying towards the Vercors, where they dropped thousands of containers and returned directly over our heads. They were accompanied by Mustangs and while overhead they were attacked by six or seven German fighters. At about 11 o'clock we observed one of the German fighters shot down. We saw someone bail out and saw his parachute open. We rushed to where he was, but he was no longer there.

On our return to my Command Post we discovered that Bozambo had gone out in a car and had arrested the German aviator. The aviator was interrogated by Major Noir. He was well treated, and although at first he seemed terrified he soon regained his poise and Hun swank. We dispatched him to the Vercors, where he was placed in a so-called prison, actually a hotel in which a few Germans were kept under guard.

On the following day six German armored cars appeared in the town close to where the aviator had disappeared. Without any warning whatever they opened fire with machine guns on the people in the street and in the public square, which was crowded with women washing clothes and children playing games. When the Germans had finished shooting, the officer in charge of the party read a proclamation stating that if the aviator was not returned to German control by a given time and date, about three days later, that the Germans would return and completely demolish the village and kill a large number of hostages. It was decided at our consultation that same day that the aviator would not be returned. He was kept in custody, and the German threat was found to be a bluff, because they never came back to the village again. Similar German atrocities could be seen in any village in the Vercors. The Luftwaffe made it a policy to bomb and strafe everything there, including isolated houses, barns, herds of dairy cattle, and particularly small villages. Absolutely no harm was done to the armed forces in the Vercors by this and the result was simply slaughter of the innocents.

The fighting in the Vercors (21 July – mid August 1944).

"The Germans, worried about the high concentration of men in the Vercors at a time when the defeat of the Third Reich was looming, feared that these Resistance fighters might, during an Allied landing in Provence, carry out raids in the Rhone valley to hinder their withdrawal from the south of France. In order to remove these threats, after a few targeted attacks (battle of Saint-Nizier-du- Moucherotte (bataille de Saint-Nizier-du-Moucherotte), in the north of the massif, in mid-June), the German general staff prepared a general offensive against the liberated area of the Vercors, entrusted to General Karl Pflaum and called "Bettina". With more than 10,000 men, it was one of the largest Wehrmacht operations against a maquis in Europe.

"From mid-July, German troops deployed on the foothills of the Vercors, encircling the massif. Aware of the imminence of the attack, those in charge increased their requests to the Allies for reinforcements and heavy weapons. The Resistance fighters on the outskirts of the Vercors tried to slow down the enemy pressure here and there.

"On 21 July, the Wehrmacht launched an offensive with the simultaneous opening of four axes of attack: to the north of the massif, from Grenoble, the German soldiers seized the canton of Villard-de-Lans; at the end of the day, they were stopped at the hamlet of Valchevrière. Resistance fighters held this strategic sector for two days, but on 23 July the position fell, opening up the south of the massif to German troops. On the eastern flanks, from the Trièves, mountain troops seized the numerous passes between 21 and 23 July. They thus crossed the imposing barrier of cliffs and progressed rapidly on the high plateaus.

"In Vassieux$_g$, the order was to strike quickly and hard, without sparing civilians, as the German general staff believed that the village was home to the Resistance's supreme command. On the morning of 21 July, twenty-two German gliders landed on the outskirts of the village and the hamlets. On board were some two hundred men. A fierce battle ensued, complicated by the rain. It was only on 23 July, with the arrival of a second wave of gliders, that the Germans took control of the situation and forced the resistance fighters to end the battle of Vassieux. Finally, the Zabel group of the 9th Panzer from Die reached Vassieux via the Rousset and Vassieux passes.

"By the evening of 23 July, the fate of the Vercors was sealed. The German troops had gained decisive advantages on all fronts and were advancing throughout the massif. At the end of the afternoon, François Huet, military leader of the maquis, gave the order to disperse. The men had to stop fighting and "nomadize" by going into the forests.

"The German soldiers were ordered to sweep the Vercors to track down the Resistance fighters and destroy their hideouts. Executions multiplied: massacre of sixteen men in a farmyard at La Chapelle-en-Vercors on 25 July; destruction of the maquis hospital entrenched in the La Luire cave on 28 July; execution of twenty young men from the Vercors in Grenoble on 14 August, etc. Many farms were burnt down. Many resistance fighters managed to hide and survive in the forest. Among those who tried to leave the massif, some two hundred were intercepted at the foot of the Vercors by the cordon of soldiers surrounding the massif and then executed (Saint-Nazaire-en-Royans, Beauvoir-en-Royans, Noyarey…).

"The German troops left the Vercors in mid-August 1944, leaving the massif in a state of total desolation. The human toll in the whole of the Vercors was heavy; several estimates have been made and the number of deaths is generally between 500 and 800, depending on the files, dates, geographical areas and conditions of death used. The material damage was considerable. In Vassieux, more than two hundred people lost their lives (including 73 civilians) and 97% of the buildings were destroyed. However, more than three thousand combatants survived and many of them took up the fight again, particularly within the 6th BCA and the 11th cuirassier regiment." (From this website: <https://www.vercors-resistance.fr/en/the-resistant-vercors/>)

I will not discuss the attack the Germans made on the Vercors. Since I was not there myself at that time I am not qualified to give an account of what happened. Let me say that it took two German divisions to force the Maquis to withdraw temporarily from the Vercors, that those divisions suffered very heavy casualties and that the losses of the Maquis were extremely low.

While this attack was taking place, I believe beginning on about 20 July, we continued our sabotage and espionage activities in that region. I had been approached by Roselle, a small Frenchman with a withered right arm, who identified himself to me as an American agent. He wished me to keep this a secret, since he did not wish to identify himself to Major Noir. With some misgivings I did keep this secret from Major Noir, who thought he was simply another Maquisard. Roselle supplied me with messages to send to Algiers. Actually those messages had nothing to do with my mission and were relayed by me simply because Roselle's radio had been captured by the Germans.

At the end of July we contacted an American agent from Marseille, whose name I do not remember. He informed us that he had lost his radio and all his codes, and was unable to send messages, and asked us to send some for him. We did this, and succeeded in getting another radio set parachuted to him.

Throughout this entire period we had requested more Jedburgh teams, and had specifically asked for ten French speaking non-coms, preferably Frenchmen who would be willing to operate either in civilian clothes or in uniform. Our purpose was to man each Maquis in our region with a responsible individual, loyal to us.

Algiers promised us five such men, together with a large quantity of explosives, weapons, and ammunition which we had requested. Our situation was that up to six or seven thousand men in the region had flocked as recruits to our group of Maquis. This constituted a problem rather than an asset. They had to be fed, they had to be armed, they had to be checked for security, and they had to be trained. Major Noir and myself did not have the time to perform all those things.
It was absolutely imperative that we be sent as many French speaking officers or NCOs$_G$ as possible, willing to work as civilians, in order to control the enormous flock that we were attracting. Therefore every night was spent waiting for a parachute drop.

We finally received a drop which brought us about half of the supplies we had asked for, but none of the men. The supplies were placed temporarily in a storehouse operated by a man known as Bebe. Bebe was most untrustworthy. We suspected him, with good reason, of selling weapons, clothing and food on the black market. There the weapons found their way into the hands of the Milice. Therefore I was not surprised when I attempted to take an inventory to discover that all of the containers had been opened and that much of the equipment was missing. I assumed a diplomatic attitude towards Bebe, accusing him of nothing and resolving to myself that I would be more careful next time.

Major Noir however, became very angry with Bebe, accused him of being a racketeer and became involved in a bitter quarrel with him, the result of which was that Bebe and his valuable if not entirely honest resistance unit separated from us. Since most of the supplies coming from Algiers were dropped to Bebe through previous arrangement by radio, and not to us or to anyone else in the vicinity, this made our work more difficult.

Numerous other operations were carried out by the Maquis under our direct control. However, neither Major Noir nor myself took a physical part in these. Major Noir protested whenever I told him of my desire to lead the Maquis in coup-de-main operations. However, I decided that I would go to work for a time with the Maquis of Captain Martin, who lived at Chantemerle les Bles.

This town is located about three miles from the Rhone River. The area, being close to this important line of supply and communication, was regularly patrolled by German foot, bicycle and motor cycle patrols. Therefore I decided to don civilian clothes and to avail myself of forged identity documents. I had been warned in Algiers that it was very dangerous to take off my uniform, and that by doing so I would relinquish any claim that I had to being a bonafide soldier. Algiers, however did not understand the situation in which I now found myself, since it would have been totally impossible to do any operations whatsoever in uniform at this point.

It was decided by Captain Martin and myself that we would operate for about three weeks together, and would do everything in our power to cut off completely and permanently all railroad traffic on the left bank of the Rhone. Captain Martin's Maquis was composed of young men of an exceptionally superior quality. He himself was a man of 50 years of age, a former French regular army cavalry officer, before World War I, who had then been an aviator in that war and had been connected with aviation in France until the beginning of this one. The men in his Maquis were mostly between the ages of 18 and 25. All of them were extremely intelligent, responsible and interesting men. Many of them were St. Cyr cadets, who had been forced to leave the Military Academy when the Germans closed it, also Naval and Air Force cadets; one young man who had been a vice administrator in the colonies and one who had been preparing for the diplomatic service.

Of all the Maquis that I had ever visited, this one impressed me the most favorably. The following day I got a truck with a driver, and since the Maquis with whom I was working had very few explosives and demolition equipment I was going to use this truck to go to a nearby Maquis, load up with the necessary demolitions, and return to my present location. The driver and I went out and drove about 20 miles to a small town near Beaurepaire. Here we were stopped by Roselle, whom I have previously mentioned. Roselle told me that it would be dangerous to proceed any further. He said that the Germans were in the process of surrounding a Maquis camp in the vicinity and that in order for us to go further down the road it would be necessary for me to run the risk of passing German patrols. Since I was in French laborer's clothes, with an identity card, and since the truck was loaded with peaches, I told him that I expected to continue en route and would tell any Germans who stopped me that I was going to deliver some peaches to the fruit cooperative market that I knew existed somewhere to the north. He agreed that this would be a good plan, and volunteered to come with me to show me the camp where Major Noir, whom I had not seen for about two and a half weeks, and my radio operator were located. He thereupon got into the truck and the three of us drove to the camp. We met no resistance of any kind, and we saw no Germans, but we noticed that in two of the towns we had to pass through there was a good deal of excitement, and that the Maquis was systematically requisitioning all useful property in the town.

At the camp I was greeted by Major Noir, and I asked him if he would give me the necessary explosives and also my knapsack, which I had left with him at another location some time previously. I had never been to this present camp before. Major Noir told me that the camp was in the process of being evacuated. He stated that the Germans were surrounding the area and said that the safest thing for me to do was stay with him and forget about my plan to blow up the troop train. I told him that I was determined to attack the train, and he thereupon told me where he had hidden the explosives and my knapsack. I went to the cave in which the equipment was, and got it out, loaded it on the truck, said goodbye to Major Noir and my radio operator and set out again on the return trip. As I left, Major Noir and his Maquis were shouldering their packs preparatory to leaving. It was the last time I ever saw him.

Chapter 20
The Railway Missions

For the following week I devoted myself to visiting other Maquis, four of who were of the AS$_g$, one of who was of the FTP$_g$. On these visits I would spend a half a day instructing in weapons and explosives that were available at

Major Manierre Demonstrating a Colt 45 to maquisards

the Maquis, and half a day on practical application of arms, and an hour was put in taking inventory of what equipment they had. Therefore I lived with the Maquisards, slept in the same lofts, and ate the same food. I will not dwell on a criticism of the FFI$_g$. Certain units of the AS were very clean and military, while others left a great deal to be desired.

The FTP on the other hand, impressed me as being an extremely dirty, disorderly, ruffianly crew who in great part consisted of Italian communists and Spanish republicans. The FTP thoroughly deserved the name "terrorists", since they were more preoccupied with throwing bombs through the windows of the collaborators homes or the homes of suspected royalists than they were with fighting the Germans. On my visit to the FTP I was given the dubious honor of inspecting the corpses of three Milicians who had been executed about half an hour before I got there. I gathered that those men had been tied to posts for about three days, subjected to beating and starvation until they were finally shot through the head. I pretended to be very enthusiastic about this fine patriotic display, and I think that I made a favorable impression on the FTP.

In any case I led the FTP on a mission on the railroad track of the Rhone River at a place near St. Vallier, but directly on the Rhone, I do not remember the name. We had intelligence that a freight train carrying German troops was coming up the river at night. We therefore determined to knock out a culvert while the train was crossing it, and after the train had stopped we would fire with bazookas into the train, throwing down hand grenades and gammon$_g$ grenades and incendiary bombs and firing on any Germans who got off the train.

We selected as our attacking position the ridge overlooking the railroad. This ridge was very high and very steep, so that at the point selected we were almost directly above the line.

The charges were placed on the railroad track by one of the Maquis, and the rest of us, about 70 in all, took position on the ridge above track about 100 yards from the culvert, in the direction from which the train was to come. We did this in

about half an hour's time, during which we saw and heard not a sign of the Germans. At about 11:30 hours we heard a train approaching. It was not preceded by the usual single locomotive to set off demolition charges. The locomotive hit our charges and was blown up.

Naturally the train stopped, and our lads immediately began firing on the train with anti-tank rockets, three Bren guns, three Browning LMGs$_g$, Sten guns, hand grenades and gammon grenades. I am sure that we inflicted high losses on the Germans in the train. Since I have never seen, except in pictures, such a scene of destruction. Germans were rushing off the train, which was a mixed freight and passenger one, only to be mown down by heavy fire from almost directly above their heads. In the meanwhile, grenades and rockets were destroying personnel and material alike.

There was a loud explosion, followed by another from one of the freight cars and so we assumed that some of their ammunition had gone up. This skirmish lasted about 12 minutes. We were completely preoccupied with firing at the train, and were surprised to hear shots behind us. Our security guards, a detail of about 8 men, informed us that a German patrol was on the ridge and was attacking us. We immediately withdrew from the ridge, feeling that we had accomplished the mission, and made our way across country to the previously arranged rendezvous. It was pitch dark of course, and when we first withdrew from the ridge we encountered small arms fire from all directions except the direction of the railroad line.

Apparently we had been discovered by a small German patrol. However, since we had about 70 men, the patrol doubtless was frightened to do more than shoot at us from a distance of about 50 yards, and remained hiding in the dark. We made no attempt to clean out the patrol, but simply returned to the rendezvous, where we counted our losses. I don't remember the figure, but it was not more than four or

five. We then separated, the FTP returning to their camp and I to our Command Post to report to Major Noir.

During all this time all the other Maquis were opening up on the Germans with sabotage operations on a big scale. Not a night went by that the Rhone railroad line, which is the main line of the PLM_g railway, was not cut in numerous places. No great effect was caused however, by simply cutting the line, since a single cut could be repaired in 20 minutes. Nevertheless, combining this with the destruction of pylons on the high tension lines, the cutting of telephone and telegraph lines, the ambushing of German patrols and the laying of trees and similar obstacles across the roads in places where the German trucks would hit them, made life disagreeable for the Germans in the region.

The Maquis of Mabou, the unit I had first gone to in the Maquis and with whom I was on very cordial and friendly terms, conducted an attack on the railroad line at least twice a week. On one occasion a party of 25 men had been ambushed by a German patrol, and all but 3 men were wiped out. On another occasion they had succeeded in wrecking a German train carrying tanks, and it had taken the Huns two days to clear the railroad line, an exceptionally long time considering that most repairs were done in a matter of an hour. Although neither Major Noir nor myself took part in the operations of Mabou, we nevertheless were responsible for directing his efforts, and felt some share in his success. An unfortunate incident occurred when Mabou blew up and destroyed a passenger train carrying French civilians, causing the death of numerous innocents.

In order to avail ourselves of all possible information of the coming and going of trains, on the appearance of German patrols on the railroad tracks, and on the alertness of the Germans in the region, it was necessary for the Captain and myself to visit towns and localities along about 20 miles of the railroad line. We did this on bicycles. In my civilian clothes, which were those of a French laborer, I went unnoticed by numerous Germans with whom I rubbed elbows in bistros, whom I have passed in the street and whom have in turn passed me in their trucks while I was riding a bicycle. At no time did I ever have to produce my identification papers.

When he received intelligence that a train carrying German troops was to move north up the Rhône Valley, Manierre resolved to ambush it at St-Vallier, where the valley narrows almost into a low gorge, with roads and railway lines on both banks. He chose a spot where the line crossed a culvert beneath a bluff; when the line was blown and the train derailed, his ambush party on the crest created carnage among the Germans at no cost to itself.

A day or two spent in reconnoitering the railroad line was all that we needed. We had foolishly amused ourselves by sniping at German patrols from a ridge overlooking the railroad line. Although we had liquidated a few Germans, we accomplished nothing but to make the patrols more alert and to make them send reinforced patrols on the ridge by the line. We had just hindered ourselves.

By the end of July Manierre was no longer participating personally in operations, but was persuaded, over Vuchot's objections, to work for a time with a group based near Chantmerle-les-Blés, a little way north-east of Tain, in an attempt to cut definitively the railway on the left bank of the Rhône. The group in question, composed of young men of an exceptionally superior quality, many of whom had been cadets at the St Cyr military academy, was under the leadership of 'Capt Martin', a man in his fifties, for whom Manierre clearly had the highest respect. Manierre decided that the best way to take the line out of commission was to demolish a bridge at Serves-sur-Rhône, and planned the operation to coincide with the passage of a train carrying elements of a Panzer Division (and its vehicles), which intelligence said was due on the night of 5 August. We finally decided that the best place to blow up a train would be at the bridge at Serves-sur-Rhone, and we estimated that 70 kilos of explosives would not only destroy the bridge but would probably blow any train on the bridge into smithereens, and everybody in it.

"Reconnoitering the bridge on 4 August, he elected to place a total of seventy kilograms of plastic explosive in peach baskets (an important local crop, the peaches were just then being picked), and wired them to the rails from beneath, the charges to be fired both by pull switches and fog signals placed on the tracks. Manierre had to work harder, and takegreater risks, to cut the railway lines in the Rhône and Isère valleys, as the Germans improved protective measures along them – reducing the distance between sentry posts from 500 to 200 metres; increasing patrols; installing lighting at key points and cutting down undergrowth near the permanent way. Some opportunities, however, were simply too good to ignore."

Bridge at Serves-sur-Rhone

Our intelligence, which was still functioning very well, informed us that a German troop train would be coming up the river at about midnight on the night of 5 August. This troop train was presumed to contain one regiment from the 6th or 9th Panzer division, together with tanks and material. We therefore determined to attack this train in the same way we had attacked the other troop train in July. We reconnoitered the bridge very carefully. In doing this we came close to being captured by a German patrol. I was under the bridge, deciding where to place the charges. I decided to put explosives in peach baskets, which would be wired to the rails underneath the bridge, connected with cordtex$_g$ and fired by means of a pull switch, as well as by the usual railroad charges we would place on the bridge, when the train got on top of it.

Captain Martin was standing in a vineyard about 50 yards away from the railroad line. He was supposed to be a security guard, to warn me if any German approached. I suddenly heard footsteps on the bridge above my head, I looked out and saw Captain Martin furiously working in the vineyard. He was taking long strands of vines and wrapping them round the poles and tying them in terrific knots. The footsteps passed over my head, and I walked out from under the bridge into the vineyard with my eyes straight to the front. Once in the vineyard I fell flat on my face and looked back at the railroad track. Six German soldiers had walked over the bridge, and had not observed me until they had seen me fall flat on my stomach. This was certainly a suspicious action. I got up and began to do the same thing I had seen Captain Martin doing, working furiously at trimming the vines and tying them into large knots around the poles. This did not appear to deceive the Germans, since they shouted at me, and when they did so, I bolted from the vineyard, across the field and into some woods. In the woods I found Captain Martin, who had done the same thing a few seconds before. The Germans shot at me as I ran from them, but did not chase me.

We returned to Captain Martin's house and laid our plans for demolishing the bridge the following night. We did not believe that the Germans would take any particular precautions about the bridge, and since we had a large well armed and well trained Maquis, we were not afraid of running into German resistance.

"The next day he set off in a borrowed truck to collect the explosives, which were cached near Beaurepaire, and met up with Vuchot, who tried to dissuade him from blowing the bridge."

Chapter 21
Captured

According to Commander Noir: "A small school for cadres for the company of sedentaires of Captain Martin had been organized near Chantemerle les Bles. Major Manniere was there as an instructor. He taught the future chiefs of groups the handling of explosives, and made them go through combat exercise. He also carried out reconnaissance on $RN7_g$ and on the railway line Lyon - Marseille, for future operations. He had the habit on reconnaissance of dressing himself in civilian clothes as a peasant and carrying a false identity card - quite useless because of his accent. The 5th August he came to the H.Q. situated near Moras in a lorry to fetch explosives and to see what was happening to Martin's command. He wore civilian clothes and had his false identity card. The lorry belonged to M. Fort of Chantemerle, who drove it himself."

On the return route we passed through the little town which was occupied by the Maquis. They were continuing to requisition all possible supplies and were even taking personal property from houses. We drove through the town without stopping and started to go up a little hill about half a mile beyond the village. At the top of the hill our truck overheated and we stopped. The driver had failed to put water in the radiator. We allowed the engine to cool off and were filling the radiator with water when we noticed two armed civilians coming up the road towards the truck. They were coming from the direction in which we were heading. They were both wearing tricolor armbands with the Cross of Lorraine. One of them carried a Thompson submachine gun; the other had a Sten gun. They spoke to the driver, who was standing on the other side of the truck. Roselle remained in the truck, and I stayed on the right side. They said something to the driver, conversed for a short minute, and the two men got into the back of the truck on top of the peaches which we had placed to cover our explosives and my knapsack. The driver got in the truck and so did I. I asked the driver who the men were, and he said that they were from a Maquis which had placed a security guard outside the town, and had put up a roadblock at the bottom of the hill. They had heard our truck stop at the top of the hill, so they had come up to investigate. We were to give them a ride down to the roadblock, where we would presumably be allowed to continue on our way.

We drove down to the roadblock, which consisted of two trees across the road. They had not been there two hours before, on our initial trip. The roadblock was covered with two Bren guns and about 30 armed civilians, some of them, wearing tricolor armbands with Cross of Lorraine, were lying in ready positions, watching our approach. The atmosphere was that of any Maquis, and I felt no suspicions or misgivings.

We stopped the truck, and the driver got out. A young man armed with a Sten gun, addressed the driver. The young man seemed to be in command. He and the driver walked towards the rear of the truck, conversing. I did not understand what they were discussing because I could not hear them, but in a minute or two I heard the sounds of a loud argument behind the truck. I gathered that the truck was going to be confiscated. Since such "high-jacking" was not unknown in the Maquis, I felt no particular misgivings, but felt that I could persuade them not to confiscate our truck. I therefore descended from the truck, walked around to the back, and saw that the driver had his hands in the air and that three or four men were sticking guns into him. I began to protest, when the man in charge pushed his Sten gun into my stomach and told me to hold out my hands. I did so. Somebody handcuffed them, and I was ordered to sit in a deep hole by the side of the road. Still believing that there had been a mistake, I sat in the hole and decided to keep quiet until some responsible person appeared to whom I could explain my identity, and who I expected would give me back my truck and send me on my way.

In the words of Prof. Arthur Funk of the University of Florida, author of **HIDDEN ALLY**: "In early August the team was operating in the northern part of the Drome Department, south of Beaurepaire, along the Rhone river between Vienne and Valence. On August 5 Manierre and a maquisard Jean Grouselle were ambushed by members of the Milice near Albon, about 15 miles north of Valence."

"The place can be identified exactly, as Desgranges, one of the authors of '**DROME NORD**,' who was in the area and later was one of the negotiators to try to get the two men released. He says it was at the bridge where route D122 crosses the river Bancel.

"The men were taken to Milice headquarters in Valence, and efforts by the Resistance were made until August 10 to bribe the Milice officer-in-charge." (*Professor Arthur Funk email – 11 Nov 2001)*

Returning, the lorry carried Manniere's rucksack, plastique, detonators and various accessories. The passengers were as follows: the driver Fort, Manniere and young Grousellan, and an intelligence agent belonging to the H.Q. Along the way they picked up a civilian who asked them to take him a little of the way. Near the Mantille$_g$ bridge the lorry was stopped to fill up the radiator. Nearby there were some men in shorts and khaki shirts, of whom the passengers took no notice, imagining them to be maquisards. When the lorry started to move off these men who were really miliciens jumped on the running board, sticking their pistols into the chests of the passengers and overpowering them before they had the slightest chance of defending themselves. The name of the chief milicien was Jose, late professeur at the technical school in Romans."

Shortly afterwards, I was searched, and my American Army dog tags were found in my pocket. The man in charge, on seeing them, said in French, "You Yankees must understand that there is only one chief in France, and he is Marshal Petain$_g$." I then realized that I was in the hands of the Milice.

A first interrogation took place in a nearby farm. Manniere stated that he was an American Major who came to France to sabotage, and that he had parachuted into the Vercors. He energetically denied that the other three passengers were comrades of his. He had only met the driver by chance, he said, and had insisted on him transporting himself and his kit. Then the prisoners were taken to Valence to the Milice H.Q. (This we only found out later.)

"As soon as I knew of his arrest, thinking it likely that he would be taken to Valence, I sent to that town my intelligence officer and four resolute men; I saw to it that they had 3 million francs, to be used as they thought fit.

"Unhappily when these men had the necessary information to act effectively in Maniere's favor, we found that he had been moved to Lyon (7th Aug), probably to Saint Paul, later to the Montluc$_g$. After that he was transferred to Belfort on the 21st of August. Since then we have lost track of him.

"Two of the men arrested at the same time, Fort and the other civilian, were released several days after their arrest. Grouselle was taken to Lyon. From there, towards the end of the month, he was able to escape. It is certainly due to Maniere's able replies and his sangfroid during his interrogation, that the two men were released and the third not killed. Cmt Noir"

The driver and his truck were taken to some other place, and I did not see them again. Roselle and I were loaded into another truck and taken to Milice Headquarters in Valence. During this trip we were subjected to verbal abuse, and one Milician found it amusing to place the muzzle of his pistol behind my ear, and threaten to shoot me unless I repeated such things as "Down with Roosevelt, Down with the Jews. Long Live Petain." I refused to repeat these slogans, whereupon he raised the muzzle of his pistol above the level of my head and pulled the trigger. He continued this little game three times. My pockets were rifled, and I was robbed of my watch, and my pipe and tobacco, and some personal photographs. My ring was not taken until later. Fortunately I had no American identity papers connecting me with the OSS, except one official order published in London, placing me on parachute duty. This order was later retained by the Milice and not recorded or sent on to the Gestapo.

At Valence my hands were handcuffed behind my back, I was taken into a small earthen cell with a wooden door, and the handcuffs were nailed to the door. I was left in a sitting position with my hands behind my back for 48 hours with no word or visit from the Milice whatsoever. Meanwhile Roselle prevailed upon me to give him my money belt, which contained 100,000 French francs, given to me by the OSS for personal expenses. I took it off with difficulty and passed it under the door to Roselle. He was in a bullpen with about ten other Frenchmen, through which my cell could be reached via the wooden door. The other Frenchmen had planned an escape for the following Thursday night. This date, my date of capture, was Saturday, 5 August 1944.

A French Captain in the jail warned me that the Milice might possibly give me some supposed opportunities to escape. He told me not to attempt to escape for at least two weeks. He said that the Milice made a practice of allowing people to try to escape so that they could shoot them. "Meanwhile," he said, "if you are here on Thursday you will escape with us." The plan for escape of the Frenchmen seemed to have a reasonable hope of success, and my spirits rose considerably.

The following Monday I was taken from my cell and an attempt was made to interrogate me. The Milice of course knew that I was an American agent, and they wanted me to identify myself, who had sent me in, and who the people were who had assisted me in France. I adopted the correct military line of refusing to tell them anything. Unfortunately I was unable to adhere to this line of action because I was subjected to a mild third degree treatment. I therefore told them that I had parachuted into the Vercors four days before, that I had been a Major in an American parachute regiment in England, that one day a British officer had asked me if I would care to go into France to act as a military policeman to prevent the

Maquis from robbing the civilian population and thus creating a bad reputation for the Free French and for the Allies. I said that I had accepted this deal and subsequently been sent to France with no briefing except that I was to go to the Vercors and be interviewed there by the Provost Marshal. I said that my mission was simply to protect the French civilians from being victimized by the FFI so that Allied prestige would not be compromised.

The Milice appeared to swallow this story. They asked me a few questions, attempting to fix the people with whom I had been working. Naturally I did not give away any of my friends. I did not reveal my true mission in any way, and I gave away no information connected with either OSS or SOE.

Then I was asked by the Chief of Milice to give my parole of honor that I would not attempt to commit suicide. I told him that I would give my word of honor only if he in turn gave his word of honor that I would not be turned over to the Germans. I was then given some tomatoes to eat and was returned to my cell without handcuffs.

The following day I was called out again and told that I was being sent to Lyon to the Quartier General of the Milice, where I was to be further interrogated and was then to be placed in a French prisoner of war camp. Together with my knapsack, which had been captured and ransacked, I was placed in an automobile with four guards. I was again handcuffed, this time with my hands in front. I watched the guard to my left pull a pistol out of his pocket, place it on his lap and suddenly seem to go to sleep. He fell forward and woke up, he looked at me to see whether I had noticed it or not, then he looked down at his gun and immediately went to sleep again, falling onto me and then waking up with a very violent start. I had noticed his action, and my first thought was to take his pistol, to shoot the driver and attempt to shoot my way out of my predicament. While I was studying the pistol, a

Belgian make which I had not seen before, and wondering how I could cock it and take off the safety, it suddenly occurred to me that the pistol might not be loaded. I then remembered what the French Captain in the jail had told me. I felt that this would not have been a good opportunity to escape, particularly since I was wearing handcuffs, and since the car was going at about 60 miles an hour along a main highway with much German traffic.

During the ride I attempted to persuade my guards to set me free. I promised them fabulous rewards, wonderful treatment, and positions of importance in the Maquis if they would come with me, but since two of them had families in Valence they very definitely refused. The other two gave me the impression of being somewhat in favor of it. I had succeeded in talking them into allowing me to open my knapsack and put on those parts of my uniform that were in it. This consisted of a pair of paratrooper trousers and a cotton khaki shirt with no insignia of any kind, plus a green Commando beret. The Milicians expressed delighted surprise at seeing an American wear a beret, so I made no effort to disillusion them.

On arriving at Lyon our first stop was Gestapo Headquarters where I was delivered into the control of the Gestapo. I was taken into a dungeon in Gestapo Headquarters and then a large cell with 20 or 30 men and women. I saw and heard some very shocking things in my first half an hour in this cell. It was my first contact with the Gestapo and they seemed to be exactly as they were depicted in the most lurid Hollywood films.

Later that night I was loaded into a truck with many men and women and was taken to the Prison Militaire of Lyon, where I was kept for the night.

Former Health School in Lyon, used as Gestapo Headquarters

The following day I was taken back to Gestapo Headquarters at 5:30 in the morning for my first interrogation. I decided to spin a yarn rather than refuse to give anything besides my name, rank and serial number. My story was the same as it had been with the Milice. I was specifically asked if I were an agent of the Special Operations Executive. I said that I had never heard of it. Strangely enough, the OSS was never mentioned.

My interrogation became extremely difficult for me at the stage where I denied any knowledge of the whereabouts or names of any of the FFI who had assisted me in France. This difficulty continued when I succeeded in concealing my radio and code procedure. Some details of my personal treatment were that on one occasion I was subjected to what in America is known as a "third degree," which consisted of three Gestapo agents punching me, pulling my hair, and knocking me down and kicking me until I got up off the floor. These blows did not seem particularly hard to me, and I daresay that no effort was made to seriously hurt or punish me, nevertheless it was most unpleasant.

"What makes your Dad's experiences so noteworthy is that he was captured; not a lot of Jeds were POWs, and convinced his captors that he was an airman. This gave him the right to be in a 'Stalag Luft' camp and better treatment. Unfortunately, all of the Germans didn't buy it including Klaus Barbie who tortured him for a time. He may relate this in his report. He spent from 5 Aug, 1944 to 25 May, 1945 in a POW Camp. He was captured near Valence, France" *(Letter from Ben Jones)*

(Klaus Barbie was born in the village of Bad Godesberg in 1913. He was the son of a schoolteacher. While studying at the Friedrich-Wilhelm Institute, Barbie became a member of Hitler's youth brigades. After getting his degree in 1934, he enrolled in the security services of Himmler, head of the Gestapo. In 1937 Barbie became a member of the Nazi party.

"In 1940, Barbie traveled to La Haya as a member of a research group with the only purpose of gathering information about the Jews "situation" in that city. Then he went to Amsterdam and finally to Lyon, where he committed his most terrible crimes, as head of the Fourth Section of the Gestapo.

A dedicated sadist, responsible for many individual atrocities, including the capture and deportation to Auschwitz of forty-four Jewish children hidden in the village of Izieu, Barbie owed his postwar notoriety primarily to one of his "cases," the arrest and torture unto death of Jean Moulin, the highest ranking member of the French Resistance ever captured by the Nazis. On behalf of his cruel crimes and especially for the Moulin death, Barbie was awarded, by Hitler himself, the 'Iron Cross First Class with Swords'.

"When the war was over, Barbie was convicted in absence and given the death penalty. During the immediate postwar period (1945-1955) he was protected and employed by American intelligence agents because of his 'police skills' and anti-Communist zeal. With their protection, Barbie, together with his wife and children, escaped to Latin America, where he spent a long and prosperous career. Barbie established residence in Bolivia, where he obtained citizenship in 1957. He lived there several years under an alias (Klaus Altman), working primarily as an interrogator and torturer for dictatorships both in Peru and in Bolivia. He helped the Luis Garcia Meza narco-coup in Bolivia in 1980.

"The 'Butcher of Lyon', responsible for the torture and death of more than 26,000 people, was a wanted man in France, particularly for the torture and death of Jean Moulin. Though he was identified in Bolivia at least as early as 1971 by the Klarsfelds (Nazi hunters), it was only in 1983 that Barbie, left unprotected through the coming to power of a moderate leftist government in Bolivia, was deported to France. In 1987 he was tried in Lyon and sentenced to life imprisonment for his crimes against humanity. Barbie died in prison in 1991."

(from: Bibliography (Yosef Yaakov, **"Escape Routes".**, Jerusalem Post, 08-22-1996, pp 01.* John Felstiner, **"One by One; French Children of** the Holocaust: A Memorial By Serge Klarsfeld", Edited by Susan Cohen, Howard M. Epstein, Serge Klarsfeld; New York Uni., Los Angeles Times, 01-05-1997, pp 4. * "Hotel Terminus - The Life and Times of Klaus Barbie; Uncertain Regard", Magill's Survey of Cinema, 06-15-1995.)

During all this interrogation, including the violent phase, two German girl stenographers sat at a desk, calmly typing and minding their own business except to cast me an occasional curious look.

I was required to witness a disgusting exhibition when two French Maquisards were brought into the next room, were stripped naked and were beaten with belt buckles until they collapsed. I was told that that was what would happen to me.

The Gestapo of course were convinced that I was lying to them, but strange to say, their conviction was first that I was not a Major in the American Army, but was possibly a Lieutenant, and second that I could speak German. Since both of these accusations were incorrect, I felt that I could get away with almost any lies.

A report accompanying me had been sent up by the Milice, and the Gestapo was well aware that I had been taken in civilian clothes, with a truckload of explosives and weapons, with forged identity papers and in the company of notorious terrorists. I was therefore accused of espionage, sabotage and terrorism, and I was told by one of the "higher ups" in the Gestapo that I was to be tried by the German People's Court, a civilian tribunal, and that I would almost certainly be found guilty and sentenced to death. I asked him why I was not being sent to a prisoner of war camp and he told me what I already knew, that my status was that of a spy and an agent, and that I was not entitled to recognition as a military prisoner. I made no discussion over this, since I realized he was correct.

(In a letter to a Mr. Forgan dated August 4, 1947)

"...The French Milice who arrested me had definitely been tipped off as to my whereabouts. Moreover, they were well aware of who I was and what I had been doing, since several of them were men whom I positively identified as people I had seen and even spoken to in the Maquis. In short, they were Vichy informers who were working in the French Forces of the Interior and who had undoubtedly supplied the Milice with plenty of information concerning me, my location, radio set, codes, etc. The Milice being a part of the Gestapo had passed on this information to their German colleagues, with the result that the Germans knew a great about me. The apparent purpose of my interrogation was to determine the location of my radio and operator, the location and identity of my French colleagues, my codes and schedule of broadcasts, and also full details of who had sent me to France. I never revealed any of this information in spite of the fact that I was severely beaten with straps and truncheons on several occasions. I was threatened with real torture unless I gave in and told the truth, and of course I was told that I would be shot. I was actually shown a copy of the charges which were being preferred against me for trial before the Volksgericht (People's Court). I was accused of espionage, sabotage, and terrorism.

"Naturally I don't know whether I would have alleviated my situation by spilling the beans, but the chances are that I would have saved myself a good deal of grief by giving the Germans some of the information they desired. in any case I was spared the alternative by the fortuitous Maquis action which is described in my report."

On the sixth day of my interrogation. I had been returned to my cell for the night when I heard violent explosions, shooting and disorder in the town. This was about 15 August. The next morning an Italian soldier who worked as a janitor in the jail whispered through my door that the

Gestapo had been liquidated by the FFI the previous night. He said that the FFI had blown up part of the Gestapo Headquarters, that many of the Gestapo had been shot and killed, others had been captured and that the rest had burned their documents and had cleared out of town, leaving their prisoners behind them and leaving no instructions as to what was to be done with them.

In a letter dated March 10, 1987, Francis Coleman writes: "I parachuted into France near the village of Dieulefit in the Department of the Drome as a member of a 15 man OSS commando group to work with the resistance. During the month of August we operated against the Germans in the Montelimar – Livron – Chabeuil area. We had nightly radio contact with our HQs in Algiers, and one night we received instructions to try and rescue Captain Manierre from the Gestapo prison in Lyon. Through members of the resistance we verified that Manierre was indeed being held prisoner by the Gestapo in Lyon, that he was considered a very important prisoner, and that he was being severely interrogated. Some of the Resistance in Lyon had contacts among the prison guards, and we developed a plan to try to bribe some of the guards to permit Manierre to escape.

"The Gestapo knew exactly when and where he had parachuted into France, knew much about his activities in France, knew his name in the Resistance, and knew the details of his earlier life which he had told members of the Resistance.

"The Allied invasion of Southern France and subsequent northward advance of the Allied armies persuaded the Germans to send Manierre back to Germany before we could effect our plan...."

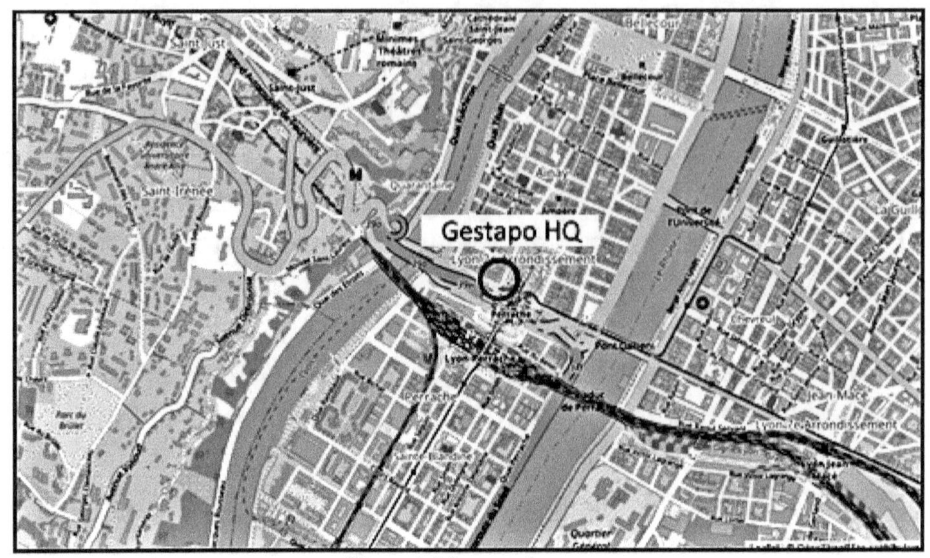

Street Map – Lyon

The following day a German soldier whom I had not seen before entered my cell and spoke to me in German. I told him that I was an American and he looked very surprised and ran out to get a German Army Captain who came into my cell. The Captain spoke English; his name was Boesch, an Infantry Officer. Boesch asked me if I were an American and if so what was I doing in a Gestapo prison wearing what seemed to be an unidentifiable semi-military outfit.

I told him that I was an American aviator, shot down near Valence, that I had been given civilian clothes by the Maquis and was attempting to make my way into Spain when I had been caught by the Milice and given to the Gestapo. The Captain seemed sympathetic, and told me that the German Army always deplored the fact that the Gestapo got hold of military prisoners. He seemed to know nothing of my real record, and he appeared to swallow my story hook, line and sinker. He said that he would send me to a prisoner of war camp right away.

However, I remained in my solitary cell for about 18 days longer. He returned then and told me that the Germans were evacuating Lyon and that the American forces were only 15 miles away. I was again handcuffed, loaded onto a freight train together with Lt. Chester Myers, OSS, of an OG_g which had parachuted into the Vercors, and Mr. Whitmore Hicks, a British agent who had like myself been beaten and sentenced to death and who had told approximately the same story to the German Army as I had done. Also on the train were numerous Russian forced labor prisoners and Russian traitors who had served in the German Army and were undergoing punishment for disciplinary offenses.

Again from F. Coleman's letter: "Throughout his interrogations Manierre stuck to his story that he was only a downed aviator. When sent to Germany by train for further interrogation, the train on which Manierre was a prisoner was heavily bombed and strafed and was largely destroyed. Manierre completed the trip on another train and when he arrived in Germany, he learned that the records of the Lyon Gestapo had been destroyed on the first train and that the Gestapo personnel on the train who knew his background had been killed."

"In the crowded, stinking train he was evacuated from France to Germany with a crowd of prisoners. He was crammed into a box car with 35 Russians who had been forced into the Wehrmacht, five German soldiers who were under arrest, and one Austrian woman who was under sentence of death for spying.

"Handcuffed together in one small box car, they never were allowed to leave the box car for nine days until they arrived in Germany. Frequently the train was strafed by Allied fliers who did not know it contained prisoners. Once the engine was blown up by Maquis troops. Always the train crept slowly along while the prisoners suffered in the cramped stifling space."

Our treatment for the following 15 days on the train was not particularly bad, but it was never good. We were fed a quarter of a loaf of bread a day, while the guards ate tinned meat, fresh vegetables, milk and the contents of French and American prisoner of war Red Cross parcels which had been looted from the Red Cross warehouse. Further details concerning our ride to Germany and subsequent treatment should not be of interest here.

"The train would halt while planes riddled it with bullets. Miraculously the prisoners escaped injury. Nine days later, they were taken from the train at Oberusel, near Frankfurt."

Chapter 22
Capture and Scene at HQ

JEDBURGH TEAM
~~DODGE~~
~~MOUNTAIN~~ DODGE

Maj. Cyrus E. Manierre (US) CAPTURED
Sgt DUROCHER (BR)

FFI/501/FER   16 August 1944

TO: Col. Haskell
FROM: Major Rosell
COPY TO: Lt.Col. Carleton-Smith

ARREST OF MAJOR MANIERRE

1. The first information of the arrest of Major Manierre was received here in SPOC$_g$ telegram No.623 of 8 August; extract follows:

"JEDBURGH DODGE INFORMS US ARREST OF RUPERT"

Further information was received in SPOC telegram No. 647 of 9 August, as follows:

"ONE. INFORMATION RECEIVED 8 AUGUST OF ARREST RUPERT OF JEDBURGH DODGE WORKING IN ISERE.

"TWO. PLEASE ASK GARETT (CARRE) WHETHER HE HAS ANY KNOWLEDGE OF HIS SUBSEQUENT WHEREABOUTS AND IF HE COULD TAKE ANY STEPS TO GET HIM OUT."

2. In a telephone conversation with Major James Champion, who recently came to the U.K. from ALGIERS, I learned the following details of the arrest:

(a) Major Manierre was working on both sides of the RHONE Valley and was carrying out tasks over and above those actually required of him in his mission. It is reported that he was doing a magnificent job in the area where he was working. He has set up a sabotage school for sedentaires. In order to carry out the operation of this school it was necessary for him to operate in civilian clothes.

(b) At the time of his arrest Major Manierre, accompanied by two sedentaires, was proceeding by car to the school for sedentaires. They stopped beside a brook and Major Manierre got out of the car to put some water in the radiator. Several Milice (number unspecified) jumped out, apparently from hiding, and overpowered him before he could get his pistol into operation.

(c) The Milice took Major Manierre to VALENCE where he was turned over to the Gestapo and subsequently placed in the prison at that town. It has been reported that the Gestapo are beating him daily.

(d) The sum of 3,000,000 francs has been offered for his release but without results.

3. CARRE, who was exfiltrated about 8 or 9 August and who is still in the U.K. has been given all of the known details of this case. Upon his return to the field in the near future he will take all steps possible to attempt to secure Major Manierre's release.

NOTE: 17 August

CARRE left for the field last night.

FER

F. E. Rosell

FFI/541/FER   18 August 1944
TO: Col. Haskell
FROM: Major Rosell
COPY TO: Lt.Col. Carleton-Smith

ARREST OF MAJOR MANNIERE

1. With reference to my FFI/501/FER further information has been received. An extract from SPOC telegram number 856, dated 17 Aug. is as follows:

"RUPERT HAS BEEN TAKEN TO VICHY".

2. A telegram was sent to CARRE in the field on 18 Aug informing him of this fact.

FER

F. E. Rosell, Jr.

FFI/562/FER   22 August 1944

TO: Joseph F. Raeskell
FROM: Major Rosell
COPY TO: Lt.Col Carleton-Smith
        U.S. War Diary

ARREST OF MAJOR MANNIERE

1. Further information on the above subject was received in SPOC telegram number 910, dated 18 August, as follows:

"OUR 647. CAN YOU REMIND CARRE OF RUPERT. JOCKEY HAS BEEN RELEASED THROUGH QUICK WITS OF PAULINE. NO (?) LOCAL COOPERATION CASE OF RUPERT. DEREK (?) RPT DEREK HAS WRITTEN PROOF LEGRANDE RPT LEGRANDE STATING QUOTE LES AMERICANS NE L'INTERESSENT PAS UNQUOTE."

2. DEREK is the French officer in the Jed team RUPERT.

3. LEGRANDE is the Commandant FFI of the department of DROME.

4. Extract from SPOC telegram 930 dated 20 August is as follows:

"JED MONOCLE REPORTS RUPERT IN PRISON BUT ALRIGHT. DOES NOT STATE WHERE.

FER

F.E. Rosell, Jr.

<u>Captain Manniere, U.S., Field Name RUPERT, Leader of
Team DODGE which was sent in to reinforce Team
VEGANIN working in the Isere in the Area of
Beaurepaire, on the 26th June.</u>

This Officer was doing brilliant work in the Rhone Valley in the Area of St. RAMBERT in organising sabotage with FTP/Sedentaires, and was responsible for numerous rail and road cuts on both sides of the Rhone Valley.

In order for him to effect this, it was necessary to work in civilian clothes as the East bank of the Rhone is not true Maquis country. On the 6th August Captain Manniere was proceeding in a car with a chauffeur and one other to his School of Saboteurs. He stopped at a brook to re-fill the radiator of the car, and on resuming his seat the car was surrounded by Milice and the occupants arrested.

Captain Manniere was taken to VALENCE where he suffered a day's severe interrogation. He was seen that night to be in a very bad state. The next morning he was handed over to the Gestapo and endured three more days interrogation.

The latest information received is that Captain Manniere is now in prison in Lyons, and up to three days ago was known to be alive.

Note: Captain Manniere has been promoted to Major since his despatch to the field.

COPY

HQ & HQ DETACHMENT
Office of Strategic Services
ETOUSA_g

8 January 1945

TO :   Archbold van Beuron
FROM :   Frederick W. McKinnon, Jr.
SUBJECT: Casualty Reports

Major Millet of the SO Branch has asked our assistance in finding a solution to the problem outlined herein.

I am enclosing a copy of a memorandum dated 18 December 1944 from Major Eubank to Col. Bartlett which sets forth the difficult position resulting from being unable to furnish any information to the families of the men involved. I have reviewed with Major Millett all of the information available on each of the Subjects which I shall summarize as follows:

<u>Major CYRUS MANIERRE.</u>   Based on reliable information contained in the files of the Branch in London it is established that Subject was captured by the Germans in civilian clothes and that at the time he was carrying a false identity card. In order to save his French associates who were with him at the time, Manierre immediately disclaimed any knowledge of them and declared that he was a Major in the American Army and that he had been dropped into France to perform sabotage. As a result of this action his French associates were released and through them, this report ultimately reached London.

254

Nothing further is known as to his treatment. In view of the declaration made by Manierre at the time of his capture, I advised Major Millett that I could see no objection to the release of information to the effect that he was captured.

<u>Capt. PIERRE MARTINOT.</u>   From two reliable and independent sources the Branch has been advised that Subject, although captured in civilian clothes, was known by the Germans to be a Captain in the American Army and was being treated as such. In view of the fact that the Germans have knowledge that the Subject is an American Officer I advised Major Millett that we saw no objection to the release of official notification. In all other cases I advised against the release of official notice.

<u>Major PETER J. ORTIZ.</u> It is definitely known that Subject was in uniform at the time of his capture but it is likely that he was equipped with false papers and may have been able to conceal his identity. You will note from your investigation that Subject had previously escaped from the Germans and that his father is alleged to have been in a German concentration camp.

Major Millett tells me that the Germans had a high price on Major Ortiz' head and he would, therefore, have every reason to try and conceal his identity. On the chance that he may have been successful, it would seem most unwise to furnish the enemy any clue which might lead to his discovery.

1st Lt. REILE MINERAULD. Subject is known to have been caught by the Gestapo in civilian clothes. He possessed both true and false identity cards and may have been able to conceal his identity. Since his connections with the American forces may not be known I recommended against any official notification.

      1st Lt RENE GUINAUD
      2nd Lt MAURICE LEPAGE
      2nd Lt EDMUND LESOUT
      2nd Lt VICTOR SOSKICS

All of these Subjects are known to be, or must be presumed to be, if alive, in the hands of the enemy. All operated in civilian clothes and may have been able to conceal their true names and their connection with the American forces.

For the sake of the individuals concerned, as well as the organization, it would seem unwise to permit notification of capture in any case where the Subject may have been able to conceal his true name or the fact that he is a member of the American Forces. I think we can safely assume that our casualty lists are scrutinized by the enemy and that they may provide them with useful information in cases where the individual may already be under suspicion.

However, as pointed out in Major Eubank's letter, this results in a most difficult situation with respect to the men's families which will grow steadily worse as time goes on. We have discussed the matter with our British friends who tell us that they have an arrangement with the British War Office which permits them to talk, privately, with the Subjects' families. Their practice is merely to advise the families that the individual is missing – they do not indicate him to be captured. The families are told that the individual was engaged in special work and that it is essential that no mention be made of the matter nor any attempt made to obtain information through the Red Cross or otherwise.

There would, of course, be no reason to withhold official notification in any of those cases if word is received, through the Red Cross, or otherwise, indicating that the Germans know the identity of the Subjects.

The problem will surely grow more acute with the passage of time and it would appear highly desirable if some similar arrangement could be made by you in Washington with the AGO$_g$. I have confirmed with Major Andrews, our Adjutant in London, that the AGO in Washington will not release information privately. OSS is prevented from doing so by OSS General Order #54 and I assume by orders of the AGO, as well.

Unless some solution is found, I anticipate that these men's families will ultimately resort to inquiry through the Red Cross which might, especially in a case like Major Ortiz, have most serious results. We shall be interested in knowing whether an arrangement can be made with the AGO.

CC. Major Millett
    Gerald Miller
    Lt Cmdr. Breckinridge

Major Cyrus E. Manniere

1. Chief X-2 SO_g   8 April, 1945
(Fwd)

1. Mr. Brooks Richards of the British Embassy has turned over to us a visiting card given to Mme Vanier (wife of the Canadian Ambassador) when she was on a trip through Lyon.
2. The face of the card reads as follows:

"Madame J. Parent
        Member du Conseil Municipal
        17 Mae Vautelles, Lyon"

On the back side is the following note:

"Commandant Parachutiste Manniere, dit 'Jean Pierre', parachute au Vercors, atait a Montluc le 7 Aout 44 presume fusille le 11/8/44" *("Paratrooper Commander Manniere, known as 'Jean Pierre', parachuted in Vercors, was in Montluc on August 7, 44 presumed shot on 11/8/44")*

3. Major Cyrus E. Manniere was one of our Jedburghs known to have been captured. His personal records in London show nothing beyond the fact that he was captured and taken to Montluc.

4. Would it be possible for someone from your Lyon office to interview Mme Parent with a view toward obtaining all possible details on his "presumed" execution.
For Chief, SO Branch:

                              WENDELL M. HASTINGS
                              2nd Lt. AUS_g

CC to Major S C Millett, Jr
Chief WESO$_g$ (Main)

MEMORANDUM FOR FILE   26 April 1945

1. The undersigned interviewed Sgt Seymour, British Army, member of Jedburgh Team Jacob, at SFHQ$_g$ today with reference to the whereabouts of Major Mannierre

2. Sgt Seymour supplied the following information:
a. Sgt Seymour saw Major Mannierre on or about 13 September 1944 at Wezlar, which he calls a Luft Transit Camp. This camp is located near Frankfurt-am-Main and appeared to accommodate British and American officers and NCOs. Sgt Seymour was unable to speak to Major Mannierre but stated that "he looked all right". He also stated that the Germans pointed out Major Mannierre as a man whom he should know, and that is how he happened to notice him. The Germans knew Major Mannierre by rank and name. Sgt Seymour was unable to get in contact with Major Mannierre as the latter was being moved out of Wezlar that day. He did not know the name of the new camp to which the Major was being moved. Sgt Seymour recognized a photograph of Major Mannierre.

Jane M. Tanner
JANE M. TANNER,
Captain, WAC$_g$.

CC: Major Willard

SECRET

Chapter 23
Prisoner of War

Several days later, having arrived in Germany, I was sent to the Luftwaffe Interrogation Center at Oberroessel, outside Frankfurt, where they seemed to think that I was an American aviator.

"Practically all Air Force personnel captured in German-occupied Europe passed through this camp, which was composed of three installations: the interrogation center at Oberusal, the hospital at Hohemark, and the transit camp ultimately in Wetzlar.

"The number of POW's rose from 1000 per month in late 1943 to an average monthly intake of 2000 in 1944. The peak month was July 1944, when over 3000 Allied airmen and paratroopers passed through Auswertestelle West. Since solitary confinement was the rule, the capacity of the camp was supposedly limited to 200 men; although in rush periods up to five POWs were placed in one cell. Strength on any given day averaged 250.

"Oberusal, near Frankfurt, was established in 1941, a central German Air Force Interrogation Centre, officially termed "Auswertestelle West", meaning Evaluation center West, which was the principle Air Force Intelligence center for the whole of the Western Theater of Operations. Its chief function was to obtain information of an operational character relating to Allied Air Forces through the interrogation of captured crews of Allied planes. Information thus acquired was of course supplemented by the evaluation of documents sometimes recovered from crashed aircraft."

"The only information which a prisoner is required to give consists of his true name and rank or regimental number.

"Upon arrival at Dulag₉ Luft, prisoners were undressed and their clothes searched. They were then put into cells described in solitary confinement. They were there visited by a reception officer, such as the accused Eberhardt, and sometimes by an interpreter as well if the reception officer was not fluent in the language of the prisoner. The reception officer would endeavor to persuade the prisoner to answer all the questions on the Red Cross form. The interrogation officers would compile from the form and the prisoner's statements the information which they had gleaned as a result of their oral examination of the prisoners, and these statements would then be forwarded to the German Air force Operations staff. "

THE COOLER!
This is the building called the "Cooler" at Oberursel. It was a jail that had a large number of solitary cells and nearly every flyer shot down by the Germans spent a few days in this facility while being interrogated.

I was given the usual treatment here, starved for 8 days, and finally was interviewed by a German officer who was eating a juicy sandwich. Upon finishing the sandwich he then lit a cigar and, addressing me very fraternally, wanted to know what kind of airplane I was flying, and about the bomb load, and other details. Realizing that I was in the hands of the correct authorities, I told him that I would give him no information of any kind except my name, rank and serial number. He told me I was a very silly boy, and said that the Luftwaffe knew all about me anyway, and all he wanted to do was check my story and see if it coincided with their records. I felt great misgivings at this statement, but then he produced a dossier which he read to me, and which identified me as Cyrus E. Manierre, born in Chicago, graduated from West Point in 1942, commissioned in the Cavalry, and known to have taken pilot training with the Air Corps. Omitted from this dossier was the fact that I had failed in my pilot training, had subsequently taken parachute training, and had joined the OSS.

He then told me that I would be sent to an Air Force prison camp. In order to avoid this, since I wished to be sent to a ground forces camp in the hope of meeting other Jedburghs and paratroopers from my old regiment, I told him that I was a paratrooper. He insisted on knowing what regiment I was in, and when I would not tell him he sent me back to my cell, where I was kept for three more days on a starvation diet.

Since I had been sick for about a week, and was still sick, I decided to tell him that I was in the 508th Parachute Infantry Regiment, and had jumped into southern France. He checked his records and produced the history of the 508th Regiment, which had jumped into Normandy and had never been connected with southern France. He then asked me if I were in the Office of Strategic Services. I said I had never heard of it.

He then made a little speech about the OSS, in which he mentioned the names of Colonel Eddy, Colonel Obolensky, and several other names which I had never heard before and which I do not remember. I denied ever having heard of them and clung to my story of being in the 508th Regiment. I told him that his information was all false. He appeared to lose interest in my case, and the following day I was sent to Wetzler, a transit camp. The camp was built on level ground. There were large white rocks that covered the length of the front lawn forming the words "Prisoner of War Camp".

There I was standing in a chow line when I saw a soldier ahead of me who resembled my brother. I tapped the guy in front of me on the shoulder and said, "Gee, that guy looks like my brother," pointing to the man I meant. He called ahead saying, "Hey Bill, this guy says you look like his brother." When he turned around, sure enough it was my younger brother Bill, who had been in the Air Force. As we flung our arms around each other the Germans took notice and hearing that two brothers had met they pulled us out of line to get our story. They made much of this and there was evidently publicity to the effect that "due to the kindness of the Germans, two brothers have been united and will be together in prison camp."

This news *(eventually)* went to the United States via ham radio operators on Christmas Eve, 1944 and our mother in Lake Forest, Illinois was called by two of them and given the good news. *(Both of her sons had been listed as "Missing" since August, and for 5 months she had no news, despite frequent calls and visits to offices in Washington.)*

Bill had been shot down a week after I had been captured. I decided to resume my role as an aviator so that I might live with my brother. Thereupon my brother and I were sent to Stalag Luft I at Barth, on the Baltic, where we remained for nine months *(unfortunately in different compounds.)*

POWs being marched through the streets of Barth

Colonel Stark, senior American Officer in the camp, gave me some Air Force insignia. I told Colonel Stark that I was a paratrooper, and had landed in France before the invasion. Since he was a West Pointer whom I had known before, I saw no harm in telling him that, naturally I did not mention OSS.

Air Corps POWs arriving at Stalag-Luft 1

Christmas Eve, 1944

And back in Chicago, their mother, who had received no news of either of her sons since August 1944, received a telephone call from a stranger, a Ham Radio Operator, who had heard a radio broadcast from Berlin, and so wrote the following POW Post letter to her older son:

NO. 18
CHRISTMAS EVE, 1944
MY OWN DARLING CY,
    I WILL BEGIN THIS TO-NIGHT AND
FINISH IT TOMORROW. YOU ARE IN MY
HEART AND I AM LOVING YOU AN

AWFUL LOT, I HAD A VERY WONDERFUL
XMAS PRESENT AS I GOT THE OFFICIAL
NEWS THAT YOU ARE IN LUFT I AND I
NOW HAVE YOUR P. OF W. NUMBER. I AM
SO GRATEFUL AND HAPPY TO THINK THAT
YOU AND MY DARLING BILL ARE TO-
GETHER, IT IS THE MOST UTTERLY
FANTASTIC THING IN ALL THE WORLD AND
COULD ONLY HAPPEN TO THE MANIERRE
FAMILY...... ISNT THAT TRUE? EVEN NOW I
CAN'T QUITE BELIEVE IT, IT IS TOO
WONDERFUL TO BE TRUE. TO THINK THAT
YOU SHOULD MEET IN THAT WAY AND BE
PUT IN THE SAME CAMP... GOD BLESS YOU
MY SON, AND GOOD NIGHT FOR NOW.

CHRISTMAS NIGHT

MY DARLING,

I AM INDEED A HAPPY WOMAN AND SO
GRATEFUL, I WILL TELL YOU ABOUT IT.
THE PHONE RANG AT I0.00 TO-NIGHT
WITH A COLLECT CALL FROM DAYTON,
OHIO, FROM A MAN I HAD NEVER HEARD
OF THE OPERATOR SAID" IT IS ABOUT
YOUR SONS"... WELL, THIS MAN HAD HEARD
A BRAODCAST FROM BERLIN IN WHICH THE
NEWS WAS INTERRUPTED TO TELL THE
STORY OF ONE OF THE MOST FANTASTIC
TALES OF THE WAR AND THE STORY WAS

ABOUT YOU AND BILL, AND HOW YOU HAD
BEEN ASSIGNED TO DIFFERENT PRISON
CAMPS AND JUST RAN INTO EACH OTHER
AND THEN WERE PUT TO-GETHER, AND
THAT YOU WERE BOTH WELL AND SENT ME
YOUR LOVE….. OH, CY. YOU CAN WELL
IMAGINE WHAT THAT MESSAGE MEANT TO
ME, AND ESPECIALLY TO-NIGHT. I AM
JUST ON AIR WITH HAPPINESS AND
GRATITUDE. MY DARLING SONS, AT LEAST
YOU ARE TO-GETHER AND WELL AND SAFE.
WHAT A WONDERFUL THING THAT
BRAODCAST WAS, THE MOST UTTERLY
LOVELY THING THAT HAS COME OUT OF
THIS WAR. I AM OH SO HAPPY. I HAD
TRIED TO MAKE IT CHRISTMAS AFTER AL
AND I WAS REPAID FOR MY REALLY HARD
EFFORT. AT THE LAST MINUTE I DASHED
UP (XMAS EVE) AND GOT A WREATH FOR
THE DOOR AND A TURKEY AND PUT ON THE
TABLE A TINY TREE THAT I HAD NOT
SENT TO BILL AS I HAD AN AWFUL NEWS
THAT HE WAS "MISSING" AT THAT TIME,
YOURS HAD GONE ALREADY, WELL OGIE,
MAMIE AND I HAD OUR LITTLE DINNER
WITH YOU BOTH IN OUR HEARTS, ALL MY
LOVE DEAREST CY, I WILL FINISH THIS
IN BILLS LETTER, YOUR OWN GRATEFUL
AND HAPPY   *Ma*

Chapter 24
The Saga of Passion Pit

44th Bomb Group * 2nd Air Division *
8th Air Force *
World War ll
USAAF Station 115

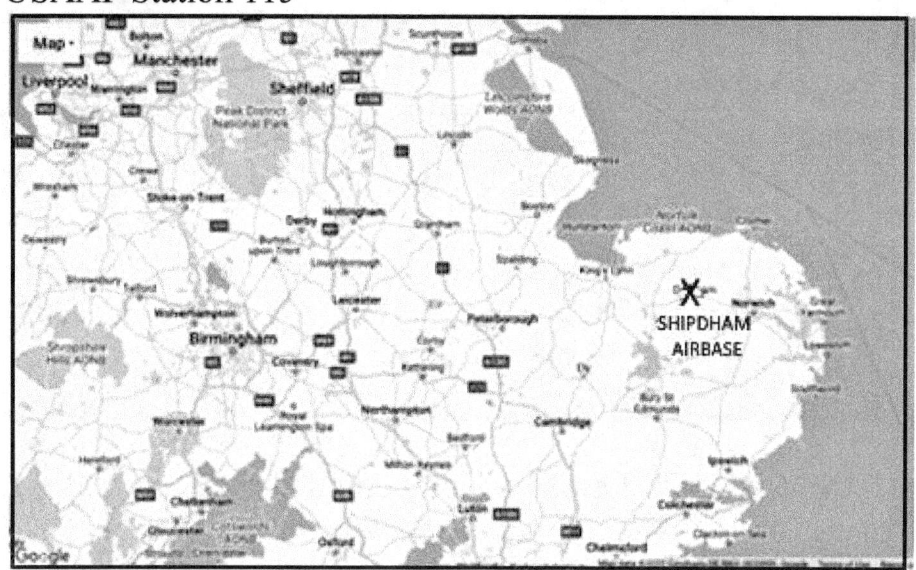

Aircraft #: 42-95150
City: Le Havre/Rouen
Country: France
Mission #: 207
Target: Road Junction (Lisieux)
Date: 8/13/1944
Formation Type: B-24 Aircraft Pos.: Unknown
Squadron Pos.: Unknown Group Pos.: Unknown
Aircraft Name: Passion Pit
Aircraft Remarks: Bombing results were very good
for the 25 aircraft dispatched against this target
No. Crew Member   Rank   Duties
Manierre, William R.   1st Lieutenant,   Co-Pilot

Remarks: "PASSION PIT STORY"

RAF Shipdham:

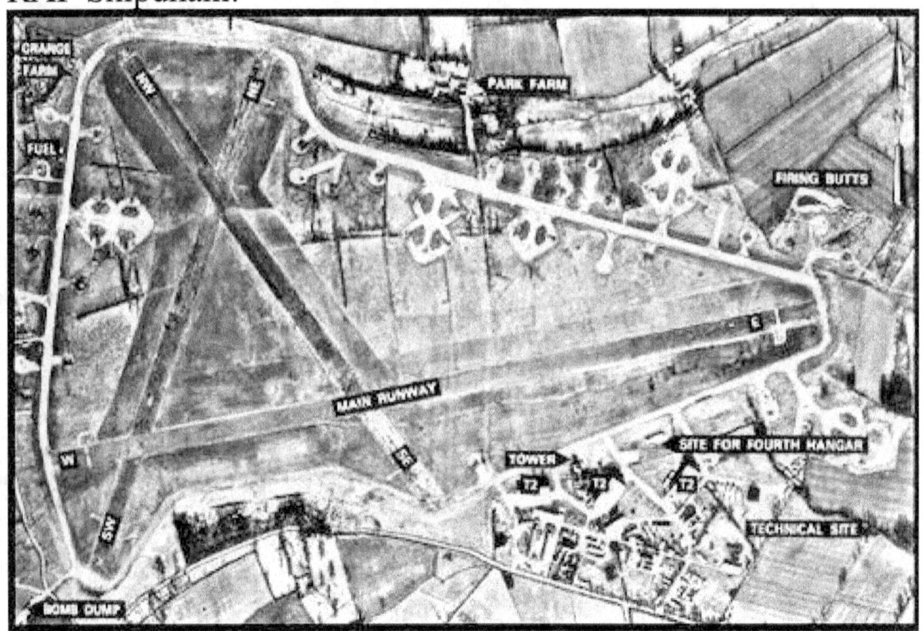

(PASSION PIT'S Last Mission - compiled from narratives of Uncle Will, Irwin Stovroff and other crew for 44th Bomb Group Reunion)

Aircraft Remarks: Bombing results were very good for the 25 aircraft dispatched against this target. No enemy aircraft was observed, but the flak was heavy and accurate, causing the loss of another 506 Squadron aircraft and crew. Statements in the MACR (Missing Air Crew Report) include, "At 1321 hours, this aircraft was hit by flak. #1 and #2 engines burst into flames and it slid out of formation, under control.

Nine chutes observed to open before aircraft exploded and crashed." Six other 506th aircraft received heavy damage."

Lt. John Milliken stated that, "Your information (MACR) is quite accurate. Our plane's name was PASSION PIT, which was named after the basement bar of the Santa Rita hotel in Tuscon, Arizona where we took our phase training. This plane had been our regular one since 14 June 1944. We had arrived on the 6th of June and were assigned this one on the 14th. It belonged to the 506th Squadron and was designated "B: for Baker.

Back row – Kenneth Beckwith, Irwin Sovroff -Bombardier, Uncle Bill - center, Lt Milliken - Skipper, Navigator

They had raised the tour requirement to 33 missions and this one was our 31st. I found out later that they had lowered it to 31 that day. If we had returned, they would have told us it was our last mission! (Beckwith was on 30th)

"This raid required a long bomb run over the Falaise pocket. We had three road intersections in a direct line where we were supposed to drop 1/3 of our bombs on each one to stop the Germans from escaping Patton's pincher. It was too long and straight a run. The first flak burst did knock out both #1 & #2 engines and set us on fire. I was flying deputy group lead (#2) and had a hard time sliding out of the box without hitting others.

"I knew we were gone, so I gave the signal to get out," Millikan said. "I thought everyone was out, so I let go of the wheel and jumped out the bomb bay."

Kenneth Beckwith, 77, of Woodward, Oklahoma, a retired tanner and cafe owner was the "Passion Pit's" radio operator. When the plane got hit, they were trying to kick open the bomb bay doors which would open only partially.

"We took a direct hit between No. 1 and No. 2 engines," he said. "The flak came through the bomb bay doors, cut all the hydraulic lines. We caught on fire." He recalled thinking, "This can't be happening to us."

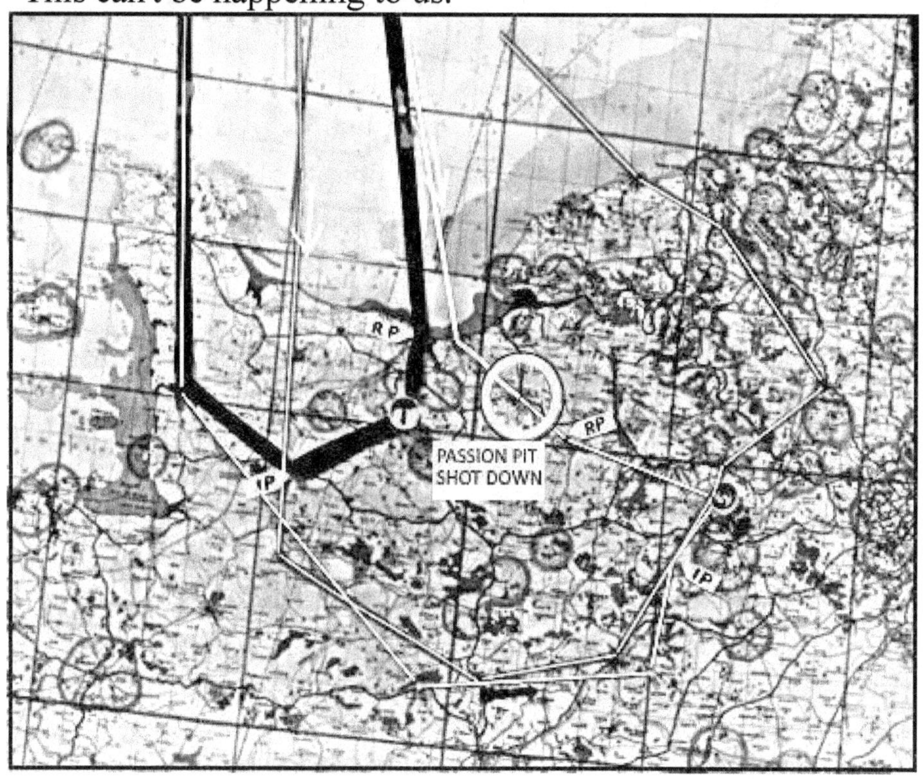

(Photo of Mission Briefing Map 13 Aug 1944)

About that time, Beckwith got a "kick in the butt" that sent him soaring over northern France. Behind him was flight engineer Martin Richard, 75, a retired geophysicist who lives in Metairie.

"He froze. I couldn't get out, I had to do it," Richard said. "It all happened so fast; you really don't think about it.

You know, the whole thing was going to blow up. You don't even have time to get nervous."

"We all bailed out and were captured by the Gernans. I escaped that night by jumping out of a canvas-back German G.l. truck that was taking us back to Germany. I walked through the German front lines and joined the advancing Canadian 1st Army four days later.

"No one was hurt as far as I know except Larson, who suffered a wrenched back that he still has today. He escaped before the end of hostilities when he was being marched across central Europe by the Germans. Stovroff, a Jew, was beaten up and given a bad time by the SS.

"The rest of my crew were prisoners 'till the end of the war They are all alive and I correspond with them occasionally.

John McClane, a navigator on Lt. Perittil's 68th Squadron airplane, tells his observation of this event, "The 506th Squadron was perhaps a half mile ahead of us or less. As they approached the river, very heavy and accurate flak burst in their formation. I was looking directly at it when one of their planes (Milliken's) started to burn. The plane fell out of formation and the crew bailed out just in time.

Uncle Will relates: "In a written narrative on display at the reunion, John McCIane, Jr., a crewmember on another plane that day described the demise of the "Passion Pit" as he witnessed it.

"As I looked at it, the plane exploded in front of us. There was a monstrous explosion, the plane literally disintegrated before my eyes. The engines were torn from the wings and went tumbling through the sky with their props windmilling as they fell in a large non-linear arc. The wings and the fuselage and tail were torn to shreds. As the pieces of aluminum drifted and twisted while they fell, with each tum, the sun would be reflected off their surfaces back into my eyes as if they were mirrors. It was like watching a thousand suns tum on and off in a rapid, random fashion. But the most spectacular sight was the fuel cells which had been torn from the wings. They did not explode their gasoline, but rather they burned in huge orange tongues of flames streaming out behind the tanks as they fell in a wavy fashion toward the earth below.

"But now we must fly straight through that same shooting gallery, and would we suffer the same fate? It was very frightening, terribly frightening, but they missed us."

"Unbeknownst to McCIane, the "Passion Pit" crew escaped. For about 20 minutes, ten shaken, but generally uninjured young airmen floated from 18,000 feet. Like the others, Richard landed in a field amid the Nazi front lines. He saw a German scout vehicle heading in his direction and he ran to hide in a thick hedgerow. The Nazis called for him to come out.

"Finally, they started shooting up the hedgerow, and that's when I came out," Richard said.

"Stovroff was one of two Jews in the crew. While still in the air, he threw away his dogtags to avoid being identified as a Jew in Hitler's Germany," he said.

"I was captured immediately," he said. "I was taken to an area where they were actually burying the German soldiers who were killed at the front. A German officer told me, "Nein! Nein! We don't kill our prisoners."

The other Jew was Morris Larkin, 80, a retired businessman from Massachusetts. The oldest in the crew, he was a staff sergeant and the "Passion Pit's" tail gunner.

"Three Germans came running up, two with machine guns and one with a rifle," he said. "They were calling, "Halt!"

"Hey, I ain't going anywhere. That was it for me."

Unlike Stovroff, Larkin was not able to conceal what he was. "Aren't you afraid to come here as a Jew?" he said he was asked by the German officer - a Harvard graduate - who interrogated him. "I came over here as an American soldier," Larkin said he replied.

Milliken was a prisoner of war for about 15 hours. He escaped while being transported in a canvas-top troop truck. "I found a flap in the damned thing, so I just bailed out," he said. "I don't know why they didn't see me. He found a farmhouse where German troops were sleeping. A French woman gave him a shirt and hat.

Stovroff relates it thus: "It was to be our 35th, our last scheduled mission, we were to complete our tour. Together we had flown very dangerous missions, many of which were deep into Germany. This trip was just over the Channel, the Falais Pocket in France, a 'milk run.'

"We were on a straight run, and were to drop our bombs on three sites, one third each time. Then BOOM! We got a direct hit at the first target. Numbers one and two engines were on fire. We all bailed out, right into the German front lines. On the way down I threw away my dog tags, not wanting them to know I was Jewish.

"Our pilot John Milliken, somehow on a truck taking us away from the front lines fell thru the canvas cover and escaped, getting to the allied front lines days later.

"Within a week's time we were taken to a major Interrogation center outside of Frankfort, Germany. I think it was called Wetzler. We were separated and placed in solitary, and individually taken out for continued interrogations. The German officer, my Interrogator, asked me questions I could not and would not answer. I gave him the usual name, rank and serial number, and told him that was all I had to give, and knew very little else. On my third trip with him, he said, " I know who you are and what you are (meaning Jewish). He told me he could save my life, then proceeded to name my father, mother, brother, sister, the grammar school I had attended, even the name of a former girlfriend. He then said he lived on Ashland Avenue, next to the girl I was dating pre-war. He had lived on the next street - Claremont Avenue in Buffalo, New York. He said he remembered being in class with my older sister, and then he informed me that I had been his newspaper boy!! He had come to Germany to be with his grandmother, and stayed. He again said he would help me, and he put a question mark on my records next to religion.

"After the Dulag Luft interrogation, I later found myself with my co-pilot Bill Manierre in a large room. Bill pointed out a beat up and dirty POW who was staring at us. Did I know who it was? I looked at the man and said 'No'. Bill said, 'He must know you' and I replied, 'I can't figure out who he is.'

"Suddenly Bill exclaimed, "My God! THAT'S MY BROTHER." His brother immediately recognized Bill, and they met and embraced.

"The Germans were flabbergasted when they found out this was happening. Major Cy Manierre was a West Point graduate who had been dropped into France, and was working with the French Underground when captured and tortured. He told Bill and me to repeat his story, that he was a member of the Air Corps, had been shot down and picked up by the French Underground. If the Germans knew the truth, he could have been shot as a spy. They believed him, and he was sent to the same camp as Bill and I."

Not until Christmas Eve did their mother get the news; she received two telegrams on the same day, 1:00 AM, 1:00 PM on both sons – whose status had until then been "Missing in Action."

"Fact is greater than fiction."

Their mother then wrote the following letter to the Commandant of Cadets at West Point:

"Dear Sir,
I am wondering if you would be interested in hearing some news of Cyrus E. Manierre jr – Class of 1942? He is now a prisoner of war in Germany having been captured Aug 8th. He went over to England in Nov. 1943, and in May went to Algiers. He was made a Major in the Special Forces, he was a paratrooper. Fantastically, he and his brother Bill ,who was a pilot in a B-24 (1st Lt.) and also captured, met in a temporary camp and were then assigned to the same permanent camp - Luft 1. I have received 4 shortwave messages from Berlin since Oct, the last two arriving Xmas night. Cy had been in France since early June. I am always interested in the news of the Class of 1942 and hope this will interest you.
Yours truly, Edith Harrison Manierre"

Stovroff continues, "After solitary at Dulag Luft, I like all others, was packed into a boxcar for a 3 day transport to Stalag Luft I. Our train was strafed by Allied fighters because the Germans did not put POW markings on the train. We were also left in the marshaling yards in Berlin during a bombing raid.

"Later in Stalag Luft #1, on January 19, 1945, I was separated from the main compound of prisoners because I was Jewish. I know the reason we were not killed was because of the courageous speeches of Col. Zemke and Col. Spicer, who warned the German commander that if any American officers were harmed, they would be held responsible. Col. Spicer was put in solitary and sentenced to death for his speech. He survived until the end of the war."

Uncle Will adds to the story in a letter dated 30 March 1995: "This fiftieth anniversary of the last year of the war in Europe has made my blood flow rather less sluggishly on occasion this year than usual. It started on June 6, which was the anniversary of "D-Day" and of my first mission. This was followed (after a series of other fiftieth anniversaries of missions I will never forget--Hamburg, Bremen, Kiel, Stettin, Munich – you name it we did it-) by a date I will never forget - August 13, 1944 - our thirty-first mission as a crew following which we would have headed back to the States presumably to be re-tooled for the Pacific - (but with a great deal of intervening pleasure), on which memorable Sunday a burst of Flak got us along the Normandy Coast and for us - as our captors used to say, 'the war is over.'

"I will now tell you one story of what should go down as one of the great parachute jumps in the history of air combat. To describe it properly would take many pages, so please be content with a shortened version. Anyway, the plane was on fire and the proper thing to do was to get out. But first, two facts. First is that we had been briefed that if parachuting became necessary we should refrain from opening our chutes until the last moment because German fighter pilots had been strafing people dangling from parachutes in the area with disastrous effect on said people.

"Second, I was wearing an electric flying suit complete with electrically heated boots which were made for flying and not for walking. So, as was usual when using the electric boots, I had tied the shoelaces of my G.I. boots tightly together so as to be able to grab them and carry them with me for possible use on the ground. A third relevant fact is that we had been briefed repeatedly that when bailing out over enemy territory we should make every effort to avoid landing near large buildings of any kind because they would undoubtedly be occupied by German military.

"So I gathered my wits together and made a terrified journey to the bomb bay which provided the only exit from the plane. But as I left my seat (with considerable reluctance, as you may well imagine), I reached down, grabbed my walking boots, and slung them round my neck.

"When I got to the bomb bay I noticed for the first time (in spite of having flown hundreds of hours in B-24's) the series of metal bars running horizontally across the fuselage and realized that there was a distinct and ghastly possibility that if things turned out unfortunately one might easily be decapitated as one attempted to drop down between them, the front end of the bay and the rafter of bombs that had not yet been dropped. So I solved that problem by adopting a fetal position and just sort of letting go.

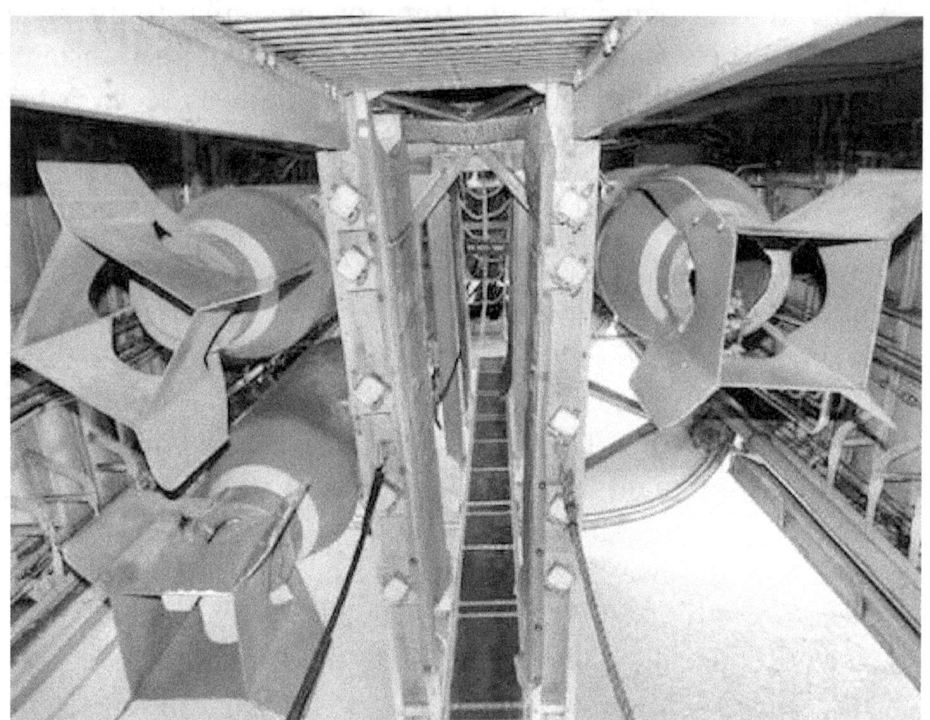

"Well, it worked and I was not decapitated but an unforeseen consequence was that once I got into free fall I found myself tumbling (as it was called) - simply spinning about in a fashion predictable from my hitting the air in the fetal position. Tumbling was a bad idea - blood rushing to the head and all that sort of stuff, leading to unconsciousness and consequent failure ever to pull the rip cord with a result just as total as decapitation would have been. But before jumping, in the full realization of just how scared I really was, the thought came to me that once in free fall I would probably not be able to find the rip cord - So I grabbed it firmly before leaping.

"So there I was, tumbling away ferociously when I suddenly realized that, in addition to all my other troubles, the rip cord which I had grabbed before jumping was about 2/3's pulled so that I thought it should already have opened. So to heck with tumbling and the same with the long free fall of the briefing - and I pulled it out fully. The chute opened at once with a kind of popping sound (ominously similar to the sound of the 88 shell that had hit us). The free fall stopped instantly as did the tumbling, but the pop of the chute was accompanied by another, lighter pop and kind of snap around my shoulders as the shoe laces safeguarding my walking boots snapped apart and the boots went hurtling off on their own personal free fall of some four miles (the formation was flying at 20,000 feet), providing the only equivalent of a bombing provided by our crew on that particular mission. Imagine being conked by a military boot that had a 20,000-foot vertical advantage on you - but then also, that was the end of proper walking equipment for yours truly, something that became highly important to me in the following week or two -.

"Gently swaying back and forth, comfortably dangling but not exactly master of all I surveyed, I proceeded to survey the world beneath and the first thing that caught my eye was a very large building in the middle of gently rolling French farmland. Remembering the briefing about avoiding large buildings, I seized (tentatively you may be sure) and guided my descent (or so I thought) with the sole purpose of avoiding that large farmhouse. Though I had never bailed out before I was reasonably sure I'd be able to miss it, as after all I had almost four miles in which to avoid one small object on all the earth below. Simple task.

"Meanwhile, or should I say, rather suddenly, large pieces of various metal objects began to flutter past me. I had tried before this to spot the formation l had so suddenly left but without success - I could see neither planes (and after all there were hundreds of them up there) - anyway I saw nothing and stopped looking when these more or less flying objects appeared on the scene. I could only think that they were parts of our plane which presumably had blown up. That is precisely what I thought they were then, and what I still think they were. But on the rare occasions when I recount this ancient tale, I have not mentioned this part of it because it seemed unlikely that somebody who had bailed out would then actually encounter parts of the plane he had jumped from. That would demand rather peculiar wind conditions or what have you; So I have always left that out in order to instill doubt in the mind of dubious, non-combat experienced auditors. There will be a brief comment on this aspect of the tale at the end of this letter.

"Actually, the tale is about done. As I approached the ground I heard the sound of a very rapid sort of staccato machine gun-like burst followed by others. Well, I was right about that at any rate - The lovely people below were actually shooting at me with what I later learned were what our troops called "burp guns", machine guns with an excessively rapid firing rate that shot wooden bullets. That didn't last long because obviously I was approaching the end of my 18,000 or so foot guided descent. But the really marvelous thing was that the single, reasonably tiny object I had steered away from for all that distance turned out to be the very object I landed on - right smack dab on the roof! And the briefing was correct. The building was serving as the temporary barrack for a detachment of the Waffen SS$_g$ - not just what we nowadays refer to as "the bad guys" but the very worst of all possible bad guys. At that moment I was in a situation almost the equivalent of that in which your father found himself at pretty much the same time - in a Gestapo prison in Lyon, having been picked up in civilian clothes and the rest of it.

"There is more to the tale but I'm exhausted and you must be fed up but a couple of rather amazing things happened subsequently that really make up part of the story. When I finally got back to Lake Forest what should I find on my wall but an honest-to-God photograph of OUR very B-24 just after it was hit, we had pulled away from the formation and the smoke had begun to pour out of #'s one and two engines.

Someday I'll tell you how it got there. - The picture, not the smoke.

"And then about two years ago in the mail comes a copy of something called COMBAT magazine sent by one of my old crew members. It contained an article written by a person who had been flying off our wing on the 13th of August 1944. The article describes in detail the shooting down of our plane - with a full description of the mission as planned, how our plane burst into flame, blew up with engines going in one direction and other things going in others - date, locations, group and squadron numbers - the whole bit. And he describes with great accuracy the maneuvers we performed before bailing out. The author adds that for fifty - no - forty-some years or so he, not having seen any chutes, assumed that all the crew had been killed. He had finally gone to a 44th Bomb Group Reunion where he had met one of the enlisted men who had been on our crew and found out forty plus years after the fact that rather than being dead we were all still breathing though with some difficulty.

"The article demonstrated, albeit somewhat ex-post fact, that our plane did in fact blow up shortly after we all got out - thus making it possible for me to include the detail about the bits of smashed up portions of B-24 that hurtled past me during my anything but controlled journey from bomb bay to French farmhouse roof…

Uncle Will"

Chapter 25
Stalag-Luft 1, A Short History
(Courtesy of Pegasus Archive,
used with permission)

Stalag Luft I had opened its gates in July 1940, prior to which RAF personnel had been sent to Dulag Luft, but their increasing number had called for more permanent accommodation to be made available. Situated in the largely featureless area of Barth, very close to the Baltic Sea, the region was a popular yachting resort and from a certain vantage point in the camp the tops of masts could be seen in the distance. Neighboring the camp was a training school for Luftwaffe anti-aircraft recruits.

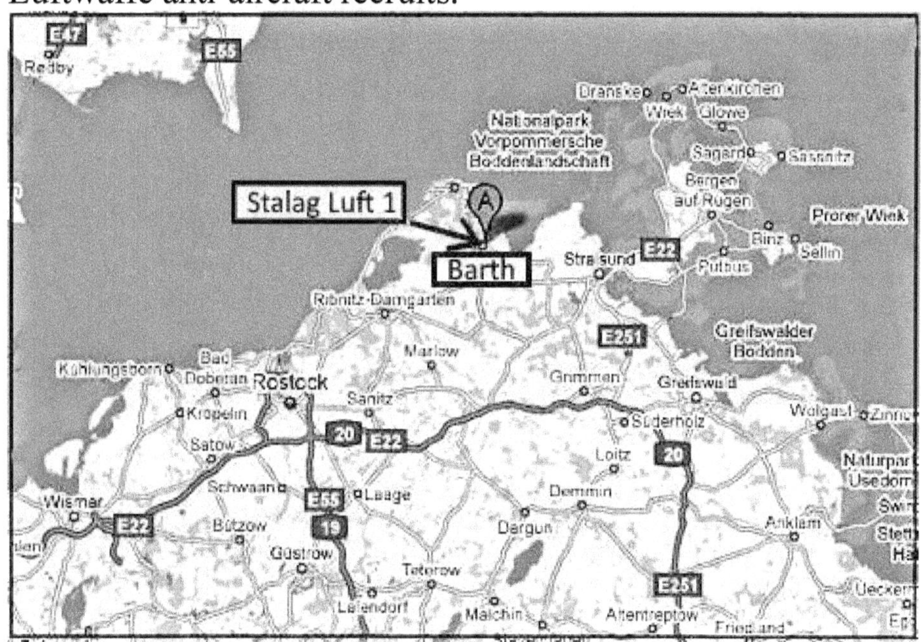

1940 – Starvation
In May 1940 the Air Ministry ordered that all qualified aircrew below the rank of Sergeant, be they captured or not,

should be raised to that rank. For prisoners this meant that under the terms of the Geneva Convention they could not be used as labourers, however Germany decided to partially ignore this fact by putting men to work who were captured before their elevation to a higher rank. These men were known as "Erks", and they laboured on the railway sidings or in a factory canning fish. Truth be told, those who were regarded as senior NCO's and were not forced to work were somewhat envious of the Erks, because while they were in the limited space and entertainment that Stalag Luft I had to offer, the Erks at least saw some of the world beyond the wire, received slightly extra rations for their trouble, and had the opportunity to pilfer rare items such as fish.

In the first party of prisoners who took up residence at Barth was Flight Sergeant Graham Hall, who with his first letter home attempted to establish a coded link between the camp and England. He had informed his wife that if he was captured then in his letters home any word that followed a full stop would be a code word. It was a primitive system that was quickly deciphered when his wife passed the letter on to the Air Ministry. Some time later Sergeant Neil Prendergast was taken prisoner and arrived at Stalag Luft I with orders to report to Hall and pass on a superior and almost unbreakable code which he had memorized. Delighted with this development the two men began to teach it to others. Amongst those introduced to the system was Squadron Leader Roger Bushell, who later organized the Great Escape from Stalag Luft III.

Despite there being no shortage throughout Germany, very little food ended up on the tables inside POW camps, and that which was sent was in a far from wholesome condition.

Roger Bushell, talking with German guard and another POW at Stalaq-Luft III)

Winter 1940 was a most miserable time in the war and their Christmas meal, a very weak soup, did nothing to improve spirits. Red Cross parcels did not arrive regularly enough to take up the slack, and when they did, there was not a great deal inside them. On that rare occasion that meat arrived it usually contained maggots, which were hastily swept off, and most other foods if not in an equal state were too foul tasting for even starving men to stomach. The potatoes and swedes (Chiefly British - rutabaga) that had been poorly delivered to the camp were already rotten before they had arrived and stank badly, but faced with a choice between starvation and dysentery the prisoners opted for the latter. Lice began to emerge, but so did the prisoners natural ability to adapt to their circumstances and make the best of what they had. The lice eggs were sought out with a naked flame, as men had done in the trenches during the First World War, and the technique of shaving and bathing the whole of ones body using only a mug full of water was mastered. However, the men were weak and prone to injury and infection, so Senior British Officer banned any form of outdoor games until better times came.

Spurred on by the poor conditions and the forced restraints of camp life, the prisoners began to go on the attack. After receiving news of how badly the war was going for the Allies, they conducted their own propaganda campaign concerning the depth of Allied military might, and began to hone their subtle skills at goon baiting, gradually chipping away at the morale of their guards and becoming friendly with them to a degree where blackmailing or bribing them became an option. A few of the guards brought in war magazines for the prisoners to read, all of a highly biased nature, but the prisoners took heart from reading of the steadily increasing loss of life on the German side.

1941 - Food at Last

Once winter was behind them, the Kriegies$_g$ began to perk up, especially when the Red Cross managed to arrange proper supply routes through Sweden and Switzerland, and by May the parcels began to arrive at Barth. Until this time the hunger of the prisoners was such that food had become an obsession and they were unable to seriously contemplate thoughts on a different topic, but with this nourishment their minds turned elsewhere, some to the outdoor games which were now permitted, others to escape. So daunting was the prospect of an escape so deep inside Germany that only a few would contemplate it, but all were willing to help in any way that they could. A number of escapes were tried, but as at all camps the art of escape had to be learned the hard way through trial and error, mostly error. But the techniques developed;

tunneling was contemplated, and the boards which supported the bunks began to disappear for the purpose of shoring. However due to the high water table, Barth was far from ideal ground for tunnels.

Though the war was going badly, morale was boosted, in spite of the subsequent loss of privileges from the tightening of security, when Flight Lieutenant Harry Burton escaped from, of all places, the cooler and successfully made it to Sweden on the 31st May. When new prisoners arrived at the camp they were asked if they had any news of Burton and they learned that he had been returned to England where he toured RAF bases, offering instruction on escape methods.

When men who for one misdeed or another ended up in the cooler, their fellow prisoners refused to accept that they were in solitary confinement. Initially they simply shouted messages of encouragement directly towards the building, but the German guards were quick to put a stop to this. After a little more thought it was noticed that most of the guards could not speak English, and none had a full appreciation of RAF slang and obscene phraseology, therefore communication continued using this special code. To the casual observer, the deliverer of the message did not direct his words to the men in the cooler, but instead appeared to be doing nothing more than offering comment on a football game that was conveniently taking place in front of him. As prisoners began to arrive in POW camps from the conflict with Russia, the Germans were greatly fearful of the Russians bringing typhus with them and so the order was given to inoculate all German troops and Allied prisoners. Needless to say the men at Stalag Luft I would have nothing to do with the injection, after hearing rumours of concentration camp killings by injection they had cause to fear something similar, or perhaps a drug that would make them impotent. In the end the men accepted the injection after a compromise was suggested by Sergeant James "Dixie" Deans who proposed that for every prisoner who was given the jab a serviceman in the adjacent flak school should also be inoculated. The 26 year old "Dixie" Deans had been shot down on the 10th November 1940 after a bombing raid on Berlin and, although junior in rank to other men in the NCO's Compound, he was observed to possess a number of key leadership qualities and was elected as their leader, a concept which baffled the Germans.

The Kommandant of Stalag Luft I was Major Burchardt, a most rational man. He had been a POW himself in South Africa during the First World War and as a consequence took no pleasure in his job, once commenting to one of his prisoners, "I do not like to see men in cages. I am a soldier, not a jailer."

He came out to watch football matches and chatted pleasantly with those on the sidelines, and in the Spring he granted permission to 20 prisoners to swim. The senior German NCO at the camp, Oberfeldwebel Hermann Glemnitz, (later re-posted to Stalag-Luft III) had a considerably deceptive manner and was regarded by the prisoners as their most dangerous

opponent. He had a sense of humour which the British were able to appreciate, and to the untrained eye he appeared very casual and friendly, creating the impression that it was possible to pull off any trick in his presence without him noticing. The truth was this was only an act and he was in fact hyper-aware and constantly probing to test the prisoners. It became lore that if this man was around, any subversive attempt would be doomed to fail.

1942

The new year got off to an unfortunate start one morning when the Ferrets$_g$ ordered prisoners out of a hut so they could search it. While they were about their business the prisoners were outside and close to the warning wire, beyond which it was forbidden to cross on pain of death. One man rolled over, quite innocently, and let his foot stray within inches of the wire, upon which he was shot in the ankle by a German guard. Some prisoners rushed to help him while others turned furiously at the guard, who after ignoring a little provocation then gave notice that he was prepared to fire again. Oberfeldwebel Glemnitz arrived and hastily replaced the guard. "Dixie" Deans meanwhile issued a strong protest to the Kommandant and assured him that the guard could not be assured of his safety if he was to re-enter the NCO's Compound.

The guard was posted away. Although "Dixie" Dean's threat was a total bluff as the consequences of taking such action would be heavy indeed, it did send a shiver down the spines of a few guards who from that point onward were open to exploitation by the Kriegies.

On the 22nd April the British NCOs were transferred to Stalag Luft VI. Their departure made way for the conversion of Barth into a camp for British and American officers only.

(The above photograph shows barracks huts in the North 2

compound, looking north-west from a guard tower. The buildings were raised above ground level to enable guard dogs to search beneath for escape tunnels. Excavations beside the huts are trenches dug as air raid precautions at the end of the war in case the camp was mistakenly attacked by Allied aircraft after the Germans departed. - Linn C. Stuckenbruck)

1944

In April 1944 the prisoners were wandering about the camp when in the distance they could hear the distinctive drone of Merlin engines. They spotted two British Mosquitos attacking the airfield at Barth and roared them on as the sound of explosions could be heard. The guards did not like this activity at all as they assumed the cheering was a distraction for an escape that was in progress, but for all they tried to restore order using rifle butts and bayonets, nothing could dampen the atmosphere for the Kriegies.

A typical guard tower in which Luftwaffe personnel were constantly on duty during PoW occupation of the camp. This one was on the inner division bordering South compound and overlooked the shower block, parade area and solitary confinement cooler. Barth church can be seen in the distance under the tower steps. (Linn C Stuckenbruck)

1945 – Revolt?

As the war drew to an end in 1945, the young and healthy guards that had once been stationed here had departed to fight on the front line, leaving their duties to elder servicemen of the Home Guard variety, and the daily news of heavy German defeats on all fronts naturally had an effect upon their morale. The prisoners took cheer as their freedom was at hand, however the thought did occur to them that this might be far from certain. There was a very real possibility that Hitler and a hardcore of his followers would make a final and prolonged stand at his mountain retreat, and if this were done then some POW's would be forced to accompany the Nazis to work as slave labour. In such an eventuality there was also the possibility that those who were not taken may be executed on the spot. Work began to ensure that the men of Stalag Luft I would not succumb to either fate.

A contingency plan was drawn up where the prisoners would rebel and take control of the camp by force, and for this purpose the men were organized into platoons. It was decided that one platoon would break through the gate that led to th German sleeping quarters and deal with the guards, while a section of other would seize the electrical sub-station and the auxiliary lighting plant, both conveniently situated in the same building, and put them out of action. At the same time as these attacks were being carried out, the occupants of the huts nearest the gate would set their buildings on fire to create a smokescreen, which would be aided by the mass of damp straw that they had in place under the floorboards. Under cover of smoke bombs, other men would take out the machine-gunners in the watchtowers that overlooked the assault area.

This last detail was the brainwave of the American troops in the camp, who decided to take out the towers using Molotov cocktails$_g$ to set both the position and the guards alight. However, to lob such a bomb over a distance of approximately 50 yards was by no means a formality, and so those whose task it was began their training before the eyes of the Germans under the guise of a new game loosely centered on baseball. The "game" in question involved two men standing 60 yards apart, each inside a circle four feet in diameter, lobbing lumps of firewood, which were the same size, shape, and weight as the Molotovs, at each other and hopefully scoring a hit within the circle. Eventually the throwers could guarantee accuracy on three out of every five throws. The remaining watchtowers would be taken out by men firing on them with captured German arms. The prisoners were confident that if it became necessary they could brush aside their elderly opposition without too much difficulty.

Liberation

The revolution, however, did not come. With the Russians very near, the prisoners awoke one morning to find their guards had abandoned them. With or without the presence of an enemy the organization did not go to waste and so the platoons came out into the open to perform a range of duties. Some guarded the camp against attack, while others carried out patrol and reconnaissance sorties in the general area, looking for food, weapons, and transport.

Men were even sent to capture the airfield 5 miles to the south, and after VE Day a direct link with MI6$_g$ was established to arrange for the transportation of all prisoners back to England. Before this could happen the Russians arrived, and their political officer was determined to be as uncooperative as possible, insisting that as the prisoners were in Russian territory they must therefore possess Russian passports before they are allowed to leave. However, a deal was struck whereby the prisoners could make their own passports for the Russian officials to stamp, and so a US officer, who could both speak and write Russian, instructed 50 of the camp's forgers how to write the Russian characters, and by working in shifts the prisoners managed to produce 4,600 passports in just three days. Amazed at their rate of work, the Russian officials stamped the passports and gave the men leave to board the American B-17 Flying Fortresses which had landed at the airfield the men of Stalag Luft I had captured. Before going, several Russians, including the bureaucratic political officer, gladly chatted with and shook the hands of those who departed.

(Source: https://www.pegasusarchive.org/pow/cSL_1_History1.htm)

Roll Call - Even after liberation, the Sr. American Officer, Colonel Hubert "Hub" Zemke insisted on daily roll calls as a means of maintaining some degree of military decorum. It helped in keeping track of those who chose to get back to the Allied front lines rather than wait to be repatriated as a group. Illegal but no penalty imposed.

In the latter stages of the air campaign the numbers of downed American aircrew was steadily increasing, so the Luftwaffe was forced to add a new compound to the camp. They built the fourth and final compound called "North 3" and Col. Zemke made the newly arrived Col. "Gabby" Gabreski the officer in charge of that compound. *(My father, as a Major and the next highest ranking officer, went with him as his Adjutant.)* Termed "Gabreski's Rock", the complete area within the wire enclosure surrounding this compound totaled no more than ten acres. Approximately 2,500 prisoners were held here. Nine barracks, two latrines, and a large stagnant pool of water filled the greater part of the compound. Each barracks housed approximately 270 men. Each was completely inadequate in both size and structure. The beds, sarcastically but approximately 270 men. Each was completely inadequate in both size and structure. The beds, sarcastically but appropriately called "the catacombs" by the Kriegies, were nothing more than wooden shelves constructed around two walls of the room in four decks. These decks were so close together that it was impossible for a person to sit up without striking his head on the deck above. A straw tick, one blanket, sometimes a pillow and very rarely a second blanket comprised the bedding issued by the Germans.

The only pieces of furniture in the room were a table, seating eight at a time, the accompanying benches, and a small heating stove which was necessarily converted to a cook stove. To further illustrate the crowded condition, it was impossible for all the occupants of a room to stand at one time.

North 3 Compound

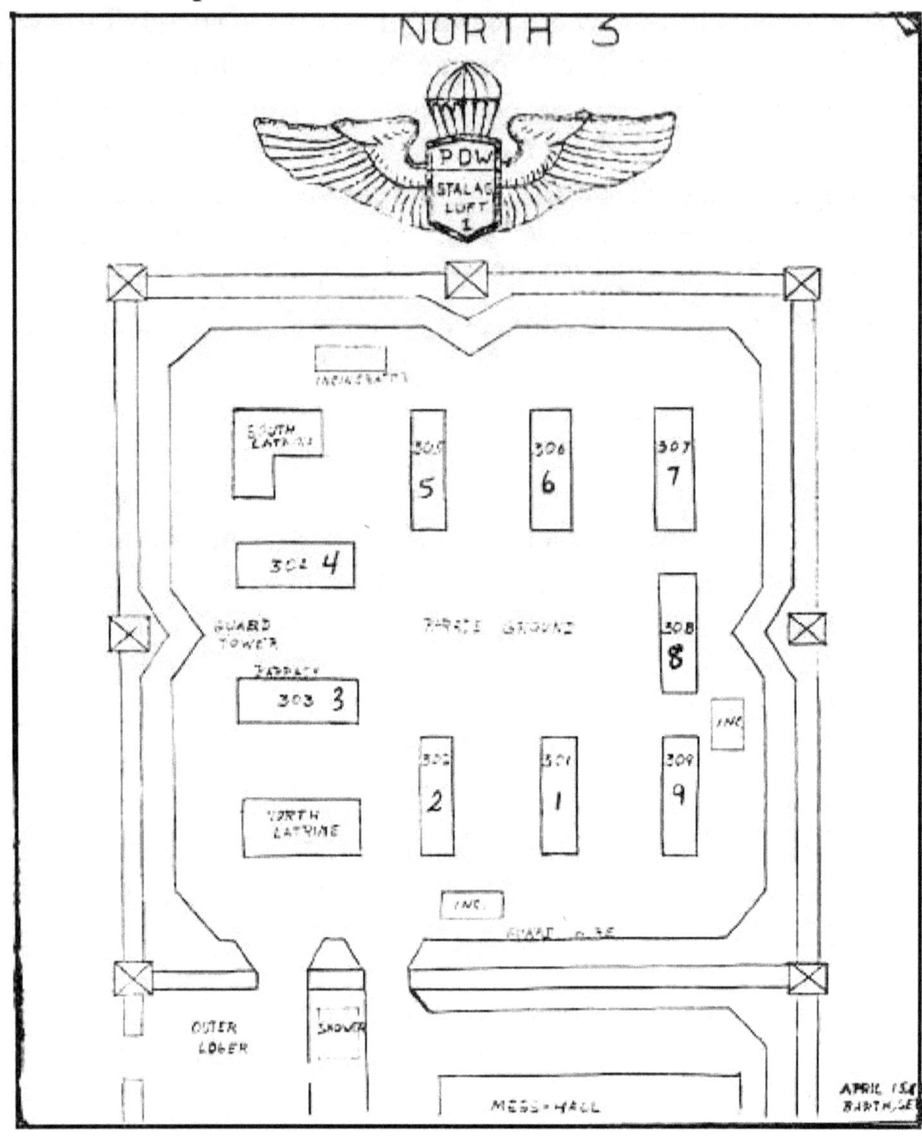

About Col Zemke:

As October 1945 drew to a close and his combat hours passed 450, Zemke knew his days as a group commander were about to end. He was ordered to 65th Fighter Wing headquarters as chief of staff. With his bags packed, he decided to fly one more mission before taking over a desk. On that mission he ran into the worst turbulence he had ever encountered. He ordered his formation to turn back, but before he could do so, his P-51 lost a wing. Parachuting from the wreckage, Zemke was soon taken prisoner and ended up in Stalag Luft I at Barth, Germany, on the Baltic Sea.

Newly arrived, Colonel Zemke found himself senior officer in command of 7,000 Allied prisoners, some of whom had been there for several years. Conditions were deplorable: insufficient food, inadequate clothing and medical attention, a lack of military discipline among some POWs, and indifferent or hostile German officials.

Zemke quickly established his leadership of the POWs, who numbered about 9,000 by V-E Day. Gradually he developed working relations with the prison commandant and staff and achieved some improvements in living conditions. As it became apparent that their war was lost, the Germans became more cooperative, especially as Soviet armies approached from the east. Zemke and his staff negotiated an arrangement with the camp commandant for the Germans to depart quietly at night, bearing only small arms, and turn the camp over to the Allied POW wing.

To avoid conflict between some POWs and the hated guards, Zemke's staff kept the arrangement secret until the morning after the German departure. Zemke then nurtured friendly relations with the arriving Soviets. (In 1941, he had spent several months in the USSR teaching Russian pilots to fly the P-40. He spoke some Russian and fluent German.) Ultimately, Zemke arranged for the POWs to be flown to Allied territory. His strong leadership saved the lives of many POWs.

Col. Hub Zemke retired from the Air Force in 1966, and died Aug. 30, 1994, at Oroville, Calif. He was an extraordinary man, outspoken, courageous, and of unflagging personal integrity and conviction. These qualities, which made him one of our greatest wartime leaders, did not endear him to some of his military superiors and probably denied him the rank and responsibilities he deserved. Nevertheless, he will remain a symbol of military excellence long after others are forgotten.

(Courtesy of AIR & SPACE FORCES Magazine - Published April 1995.)

About Col. Gabreski On May 22, Gabreski shot down three Fw_g 190s over an airfield in northwest Germany. He tied *(Jonnie)* Johnson as the leading ace in the European Theater of Operations on June 27 (passing Eddie Rickenbacker's record from World War I in the process), and on July 5, 1944, became America's leading ace in the ETO, with his score of 28 destroyed, matching the total at the time of confirmed victories of the Pacific Theatre's top American ace, Richard Bong. This total was never surpassed by any U.S. pilot fighting the Luftwaffe.

Col. Francis S. "Gabby" Gabreski

Prisoner of war

On July 20, 1944, Gabreski had reached the 300-hour combat time limit for Eighth Air Force fighter pilots and was awaiting an aircraft to return him to the United States on leave and reassignment. He had already advised Kay Cochran to proceed with wedding plans, and his hometown of Oil City, Pennsylvania, had raised $2,000 for a wedding present in anticipation of his return. Gabreski found, however, that a bomber escort mission to Russelheim, Germany, was scheduled for that morning, and, instead of boarding the transport, he requested to "fly just one more." Returning from the mission, Gabreski observed Heinkels parked on the airfield at Niedermendig, Germany and took his airplane down to attack.

He was dissatisfied with his first strafing run on an He 111, and he reversed for a second pass. When his tracers went over the parked bomber, he dropped the nose of his Thunderbolt to adjust, and its propeller clipped the runway, bending the tips. The damage caused his engine to vibrate violently and he was forced to crash land. Gabreski then ran into the nearby woods and eluded capture for five days. After being captured, he was taken to Dulag Luft at Oberursel, the German Interrogation center for allied airmen where he was interrogated by Obergefreiter Hanns Scharff. *It is reported that Herr Scharff greeted him thusly: "Gabby, we've been waiting for you."* He was eventually sent to Stalag Luft I.

(Wikipedia-https://en.wikipedia.org/wiki/Gabby_Gabreski)

Chapter 26
Life in North 3

A further German attempt was made to interrogate me, but since I was now in good health and had been mentally fortified by living with other Americans, I simply laughed at them, and defied my interrogator. This was the usual attitude on the part of American personnel, and the interrogator did not try to question me for more than 15 minutes. The American security cell inside the camp interrogated and identified all prisoners to make sure that no German agents were put in the camp. Since several West Point classmates were in the camp I had no difficulty in identifying myself without mentioning OSS. Although I freely told responsible American senior officers at the camp that I had been on a sabotage mission behind German lines before the invasion, I never told them who had sent me or connected myself with either OSS or SOE.

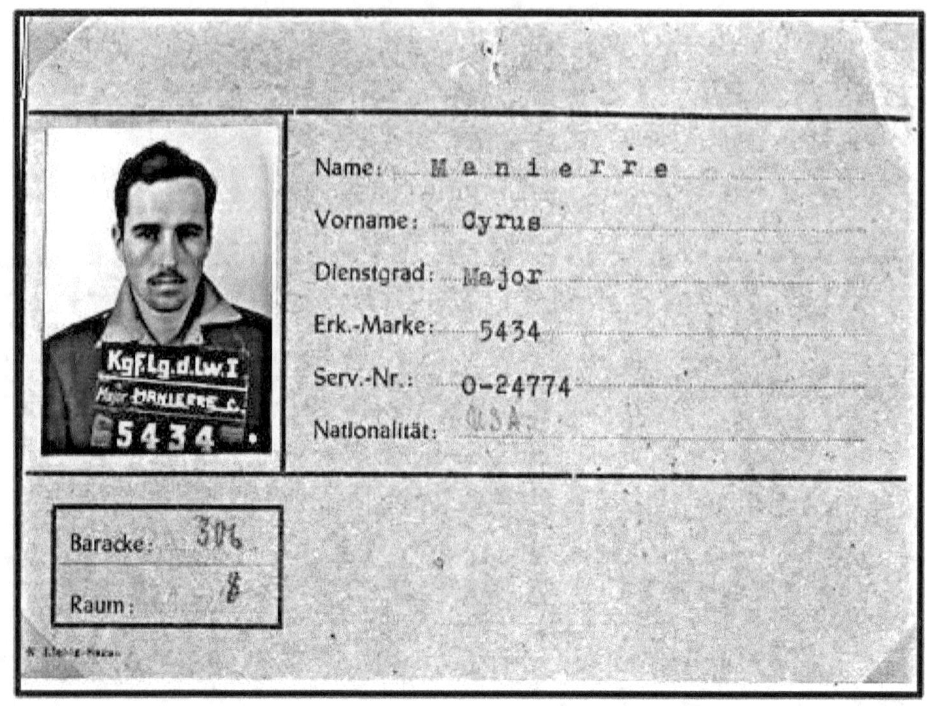

*Roger Armstrong, another "guest of the Luftwaffe," had this to say about him in his book **USA THE HARD WAY** (Quail House Publishing Co. Orange County, CA):* "Major Cy Manierre, who was all 'spit and polish,' with his shined paratrooper boots, was an enigma to the POWs. We heard that paratroopers were shot when captured. But he was alive, hungry and cold like the rest of us. Later I learned from Col. Gabreski that he had been in the infantry. Most of us thought he was a captured OSS Officer. In any event, he also waited for Captain Probst to salute him first before returning the salute."

*From the book **JOURNEY TO A STAR**, by William J. Blum, excerpts:* "The entire camp was considered to be a Wing, which was composed of several Groups… At Stalag-Luft 1, it was Wing X, comprised of four Groups, one for each compound.   Each individual barracks in the compound of

Group 4, or North 3, was designated a Squadron, totaling nine for the Group.

Example of barracks room in Stalag Luft 1

"In regard to personnel of this bastard organization, it paralleled closely that of actual Wings operating in England. The Wing Commander was Colonel Hubert Zemke, former Commanding Officer of the famous 56th Fighter Group of the Eighth Air Force. Working under his supervision… In Group 4, Lt. Colonel Francis S. Gabreski, the world's top living ace, was Commanding Officer; Major Cyrus E. Manierre, a paratrooper captured while working with the Free French Forces, was Adjutant…" (page 73)

"…my evenings were usually spent at the bridge table or in discussions of various subjects with my three roommates, Major McCafferty, Major Manierre, and a French Air Force pilot, Lt. Roger Receveau. I felt very fortunate to be living with these three fine gentlemen. Their varied talents, educational backgrounds, and general knowledge of world affairs, and sense of humor were far above average—so I feel as though, in at least one way, I gained materially from my seven and a half months confinement." (page 88)

(Re: living conditions: It should be remembered that the camp was located in the very northern part of Germany, right on the shore of the Baltic, so the weather there was very cold and damp. Plus the winter of 1944-45 was one of the coldest in many years... Imagine being in that cold and snow while eating only several pieces of bread a day, with very little decent food.)

Watercolor Painting by Col. Ross Greening, from the book **NOT AS BRIEFED,** *From the Doolittle Raid to a German* **Stalag** *Another piece of the story I found in Hub Zemke's*

*book **ZEMKE'S STALAG** (Smithsonian University Press, Washington and London). This concerns the various "extra-curricular" activities that kriegies became involved in, one of which was a boxing match which Col. Zemke offered to fight; many were eager to take a poke at the S.A.O.*

Accordingly: "To ensure the selection was seen to be fair, all names of would-be opponents were written on slips of paper and Group Captain Weir was asked to draw one from the hat. The chosen name was that of Major Cyrus Manierre, Gabreski's Adjutant in North 3, a big lean US paratrooper who professed to have done a bit of boxing at West Point as a cadet. As can be seen from the particulars that were displayed in a Provisional Wing X bulletin, about the only advantage I had was experience.

"Vital statistics of the two opponents:

	Colonel Zemke vs.	**Major Manierre**
Weight:	10 st. 10 lbs	11 st. 6 lbs
Height:	5 ft. 9 ins.	6 ft. 1 in.
Age:	31 years	25 years
Eyes:	Steel gray	Now dark blue
Hair:	Brown (graying)	Curly black
Training Diet:	Distilled water and cigar butts	Kriegbrot, schnapps schrimpers and rice
Ability:	55 bloody matches all in rings	Intercollegiate matches, street and bar room clashes

Round 2. Manierre on the ground while referee T. A. G. Pritchard makes the count and a relieved SAO takes a breather on the ropes. In the audience, directly behind me, sit the Luftwaffe staff and Ross Greening (legs crossed).

(Photo from **ZEMKE'S STALAG**)

"The moment arrived when my opponent and I ducked under the ropes. My only misgiving was that I had not had any time to get in a little training to limber up. In the opening round the stringy Manierre showed a good straight left but began to tire and waste away after a few punches had been landed on his torso.

"In the second round he was decked with a solid right hook cross and from then on I carried him through the last round. Zemke received a unanimous decision for what was to be his last boxing match in any ring."

The following is from a letter received from George McCafferty (one of Pop's roommates in Room 8, Barracks

306, dated 12 Nov 2001: "I was shot down over Magdeburg, Germany on Sept 11, 1944. Was taken prisoner almost immediately and after being shunted around for several days I ended up in the POW interrogation center at Oberursal just outside of Frankfort. My best recollection is that I was there for about three weeks in solitary confinement. I was interrogated three times in a manner that was mostly a propaganda briefing. From Oberursele, as the Germans spell it, I went to Wetzler, a camp set up for staging American Officers of the Air Corps. We were briefed there and provided with a kit with shaving equipment, underwear, sox and the like. We also received shoes and outer clothing.

"After three or four days I left with five others for our permanent camp at Barth in Pomerania on the Baltic Sea. It was here that I met Cy. I am not sure whether he was there already or came shortly after my arrival. At any rate we became roommates and good friends. We were in compound two and in a room with six or seven other guys. I, with most of the others, was very much impressed by Cy. He was obviously a hell of good soldier who had gone through an unbelievable experience. His story was like one from a spy novel. He was certainly most fortunate to be alive and where the Gestapo could not find him. The Germans that ran the camp were also quite impressed with his military bearing and the way that he conducted himself.

"During the first months in camp each of us received a Red Cross package. It contained canned meat, canned milk and other food as well as cigarettes and 'D' bars. We pooled most of the food for our little room mess. This was supplemented by bread, barley, rutabagas and an occasional dead cow or horse (killed in an air raid) that we bought from the Germans. (According to the Geneva Conventions the Germans were required to pay us. We never saw the money but it was used to buy food, books, musical instruments and the like.)

"The food ran out by Jan 1945. Up until then we had plenty to eat and although the menu was limited it was not bad for a POW camp in Germany. During this period your dad did calisthenics every day. We also walked a good bit. Round and round the compound. Sometime near the end of 1944 a group French aviators came into camp and one named Roger Receveau came to our compound. Since Cy was fluent in French they soon became good friends and Cy started to teach him English."

From George McCafferty letter of 18 Nov, 2001 "We had some boxing matches or better expressed as fights, the contestants coming from all compounds. The American camp commander, Hub Zemke, challenged anyone who washed to give it a try and your father took him up on the challenge. It was not known at the time that Zemke was an experienced fighter who had a number of amateur fights. However, Cy was a tough guy and gave a good account of himself lasting the three rounds. Cy at that time was probably in much better condition than those of us that took life easy. He did calisthenics every day and walked endless rounds of the compound. In early December the Germans opened a new compound next to ours. Francis Gabreski, one of the all time great fighter pilots and an ace in two wars, was made commander of the new compound. He recruited several of us to go with him and form a new staff including Bill Blum, Roger Receveau, Cy and me. Cy, Roger and I roomed together. For a time things went well.

"However, as of January 1, 1945 the Wehrmacht took control of the camp and replaced all the Luftwaffe guards with old men wearing WW 1 uniforms. It was very evident from the start that they hated us. There were two incidents of American POWs being shot and killed. One was in the barracks during an air raid sleeping. He woke up and stepped outside the Barracks door and instantly realized that there was an air raid and turned back in. He was shot and fell in the door.

The Red Cross parcels stopped and it became almost impossible to buy food from the Germans. We got a little bread, and some meat that was mostly rotten. We ended up with one cup of soup and a slice of bread a day. My weight went from 170 to about 130 although I never had a sick day or even a cold.

"Cy kept up his calisthenics all through this time although he cut back a bit. We all got one hot shower about every six weeks. However, Cy took frequent baths or showers by going to the wash basins and turning the faucet upside down so that the water shot up and created a sort of shower. The water was ice cold and stripped to the skin in below freezing weather really took some doing. But as I said he was a very tough guy.

"I think that it was in late January that a Catholic priest came into our compound; I think that he was an army chaplain. He conducted some services each day and he and your father became good friends. At some time near the end Cy converted to Catholicism.

Father Michael Charlton

CERTIFICATE OF BAPTISM.

CYRUS EDSON MANIERRE, MAJOR U.S. ARMY O-24774, BORN 30th AUGUST 1919,

SON OF CYRUS EDSON MANIERRE

AND EDITH OGDEN HARRISON MANIERRE,

WAS, AFTER A COMPLETE COURSE OF INSTRUCTION, AND AFTER MAKING HIS

PROFESSION OF FAITH, BAPTISED CONDITIONALLY AND RECEIVED INTO THE CHURCH

BY ME AT LAGER LUFT I GERMANY ON MAY 1ST 1945.

THE WITNESSES WERE: GEORGE O'DAY McCAFFERTY,

JOSEPH THOMAS McKEON.

Quorum in fidem ego capellanus militum captivorum die 3ª maii 1945 manu mea subscripsi.

Thomas J. E. Lynch.

"I understand that sometime after the war he joined the Episcopal Church but you would certainly know more about that. All through this time Roger Receveau was learning English from Cy and although I was supposed to be learning spoken French from Roger, I must admit it did not take. We received rumor some time in March that we were to be moved on foot to a different camp. It was very worrisome as many of us were not in good enough shape to make any long march."

RATTLED BY RUSSIANS *(Clair Rauth interview)*

"While the men were eating well they played softball and had the vigor to while away the tedium of prison life by wagering, by bartering. or playing cards. Just before the Russians overran eastern Germany in May the Germans became panicky lest the Allied servicemen should be found in poor physical condition. Then the Germans opened up the stores of Red Cross packages, which they had been keeping from the prisoners, and for several weeks in April the men knew what food was again.

Uncle Bill and friend on the way to showers

"The men cooked their own food on small stoves in the frame shacks in which they lived; that was, they cooked whenever they had enough fuel. Manierre recalled some of the fantastic recipes the men tried out with the food from their Red Cross packages.

"There was the cake made with crumbled crackers for flour and toothpaste for baking powder. "It tasted all right then, but I'd hate to have to eat it now," he said.

"No beards were allowed in the camp. The men had razor blades from the packages or, occasionally from the Germans. They were required to shave once every two days, but mustaches were permitted, and many men grew enormous ones.

SPECULATE ON PEACE

"The men bet on the day and hour the war would end, and the pools were paid off in checks which some artists drew.

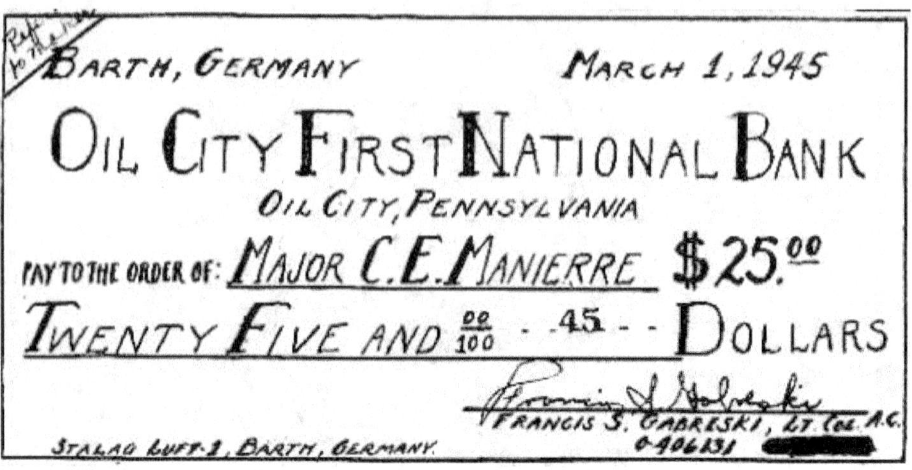

These checks have been cashed since the men returned to America. "There is usually a lot of interest at the banks when these fancy checks are presented," Manierre said, "but after checking with the men whose accounts they are drawn on, the banks did honor them."

"When the prisoners were fed adequately again in the spring, they regained their weight and vitality. The major regained 35 pounds, and his brother 20 pounds. At this time, the Americans put on boxing shows to impress the Germans, They would pick the biggest men who were in the best physical condition, and then with the Germans watching, the boxers would slug it out in bloody bouts. "We intended to refute the German myth of superiority," he said.

LIBERATED BY REDS

"The Russians overran the region about the first of May and opened the camp. For several weeks, the men waited for return to their home bases, but the Allies were busy fighting and could not get to the camp immediately. Almost 2,000 men had wandered off by foot or hitchhiked across Germany before the Americans sent planes to take away the remaining 8,000 men.

"Within 48 hours after the first American plane landed at the camp, the last prisoner was taken aboard and flown back to France, where the men were processed for the long-awaited return home. Camp Lucky Strike$_g$ on the Channel coast was the gathering spot for American prisoners of war as they were cleared and sent home.

"Maj. Manierre spent several weeks in London, reporting to his superiors, and then he too, crossed the Atlantic westward and arrived back in America.

ALLOWED FREEDOM

"For his work in managing the prison camp, Manierre was awarded the Bronze Star earlier this month. The Germans allowed the Americans and British to maintain supervision of the prisoners, and Manierre served as prison adjutant. The citation commended his great courage and daring in distributing information and plans to his fellow prisoners of war, a feat which would have meant death if it had been discovered.

"At present, the major is expecting an assignment in Washington as a member of the regular army. He intends to remain in service. His brother, the lieutenant, received his discharge this month and returned to Yale University to resume his studies where he left them in 1942 to enlist.

"Being home is as it has always been," Maj. Manierre said. "Everything else of the war years is like a bad dream."

Chapter 27
Liberation and departure from Barth
to Paris and parts further West

"We were liberated by the Russians on 2 May 1944. They tried very hard to persuade us to return to England via Odessa, but all of us were adamant in waiting for the American Army which was approaching rapidly and soon took over our camp. In the meantime we discovered a German concentration camp nearby where the prisoners were in the most frightful shape. At our camp there were stored a considerable amount of Red Cross parcels which had never been delivered to us. We took a great quantity of these to the concentration camp where they were most gratefully received.

"As things turned out we never had to move from Stalag Luft 1 until repatriated. Life in the camp slowed down considerably as we lacked the energy to do very much. I, like many others. played cards in addition to reading. I do not think that Cy ever did play cards although he did read a good bit and for a time he worked with Roger Receveau on an escape plan. I do not think that escape would have been attempted even if possible as those of us who became POWs late in the war were not to attempt escape as we had agents in the country and they did not want us to alert the Germans and have them combing the countryside. Moreover, by late fall of 1944 we all believed that the war would be over soon. It was, I think, on the 1st of May that we awakened to find that the Germans were gone. Bill Blums' book covers the events of the final days very well. As we were the new compound at the end of the line, those of us in Compound 3 were the last to leave camp. We were being evacuated by stripped down B17s that came into an airfield a few miles from the camp. The planes came in flights of six and were required to circle until cleared to land. They were allowed to land one at a time and when loaded and taken off another plane could land.

"I was on the last plane to leave and I know Bill Blum was with me but I do not recall whether Cy was on that plane or an earlier one. There were twenty of us on each plane, Bill and I managed to get in the nose where we could see everything. The pilot took us at low level and very slow down the Ruhr valley starting at Dortmund to Essen to Mulheim and then down the Rhine River to Dusseldorf to Cologne. It was a sight that I could never forget, utter total destruction. There was hardly anything left standing, just a complete pile of rubble. As you know we landed at Reims and were trucked to Camp Lucky Strike, a place with tents in every direction as far as the eye could see. I do not know for sure but there must have been close to 100,000 soldiers and ex POWs in the camp. I talked to Cy for a while. He had his new uniform and some cash from a partial pay and was heading for Paris in an effort to locate the OSS people. I did not want to go as I was very anxious to get home to my wife and daughter. I was very lucky to run into an old friend who was in charge of scheduling the ex-POWs for transport home and he managed to get me and Bill Blum on the first shipment." *(letter - George McCafferty)*

(This next portion of the story is from Mary Smith's Stalag-Luft 1 website (www.merkki.com), written by Ray Darling, one of the bomber pilots who flew to Barth to pick up the POWs)

"I was twenty three years old, had flown thirty-one missions and had just been promoted to first lieutenant when the war ended in early May 7, of 1945. When Mike Banta completed his thirty-five missions, I had taken over his crew just as the last missions of the war were being flown. We were all waiting with great anticipation for our orders to return to the States when over the intercom came this message, "All pilots and navigators report to your respective squadron orderly rooms immediately."

"Oh, boy," I thought, " the day has finally come."

"When we assembled in the Orderly Room we were told by the briefing officer that we had one more mission to fulfill. Our mission would be to fly into Northeastern Germany to rescue our POW airmen from Stalag Luft I. The Russians had liberated the camp but seemed to be hesitant about releasing the American POW airmen. They were not being at all cooperative with their Western Allies. The briefing officer told us that we were flying into an airstrip at Barth airdrome, a few miles from Stalag Luft I and just south of the Baltic Sea. Here we would load the POW's aboard our B-17's and fly them to the Bordeaux area of France where they would be put on ships and sent back to the good old U. S. A.

"The name of this operation is 'Revival,'" he said. "The Russians don't seem to want to cooperate in releasing our American airmen POW's so we're going in and getting them. If the Russian's don't like what we're doing," the briefing officer went on, "Then it's just - Tough Shit."

"That was the first time I ever heard applause at a briefing! We were told to be cautious on this mission, to stick to the flight plan and land only at the designated airfield where we would receive further orders. We would be flying singly, leaving at one or two minute intervals and would fly at an altitude under ten thousand feet so no oxygen would be required. We were told to conserve on gasoline because this would be a long trip and our twenty-eight hundred and ten gallons of gasoline had to last all the way home. Our crew would consist of five crewmen: pilot, copilot, navigator, radioman and flight engineer.

"Just so that you won't be taken by surprise," the briefing officer continued, "You will be landing at Barth

Airdrome on a narrow steel mesh runway rather than the cement runways you have been used to. But don't worry." he went on, "They have been B-17 tested."

"The B-17's had been readied with all guns and armament removed. If you can imagine a transport without any seats except for the pilot and copilot, that's what we were flying to rescue these POW airmen. I felt very comfortable as we went to full military power for take off early that May 13, 1945, morning because the crew consisted of my old crew members George Hobbs as flight engineer and Smokey Montgomery as radio man plus a good friend and navigator from Ted Santo's crew, Waldo Bowen. I'm sorry but fifty some years has erased the name of my copilot from my memory.

"Our flight started perfectly, with clear weather and a beautiful sunrise. It felt wonderful to not have to worry about assembling a group of thirty-six bombers. We took off only worrying about one B-17 and getting to Barth. It was so different and nice, no formation, no oxygen checks, no flak and no fighters. After getting to cruising altitude and trimming up the ship, the navigator gave me a heading. I set the autopilot and leaned back like an airline pilot and left the flying to it. No more six to eight hours of close formation.

"Then came the message I wanted to hear from Waldo, the navigator, "Barth straight ahead. Start your let down." Smoky, the radioman, announced he had the control tower on the radio. The control tower gave me landing instructions and reminded me of the steel mesh runway. Several B-17's had already arrived and after a smooth landing I taxied over to get into the line they had formed.

The tower advised me to look for a ground signalman with a red flashlight. "He will signal you when to stop and go," I was advised. "Don't shut down your engines and don't let any one off the airplane," the tower continued.

Barth Airdrome taken over by the Allies.
Gift in Memory of William Richard "Dick" Terrell, 2019.079

There were burned out hulks of German aircraft all around the field. But the only German aircraft I had seen in combat were 109's, 190s and 262's and there were none of those among the hulks.

"Waldo, the navigator, asked, "When we stop to load, is it OK if I jump off and get some pictures with my camera?" Knowing Waldo for a long time and trusting him I said, "Go ahead but hurry. I've got to go when they give me the signal."

"As he was leaving, the American POW airmen began to load the ship from the rear door. I sat in the pilot's seat with engines idling and brakes locked and watched through the bomb bay as the men were coming aboard. George directed six to eight of them down into the nose compartment. Most had old shabby uniforms. They were all haggard, skinny and looked and acted like they were in a trance. Their eyes appeared glazed and no one smiled. They acted as if they didn't know what was happening to them and appeared so

meek and humble. They were just following orders. I tried to comfort a few of them by assuring them, "We're going to get you the hell out of here and on your way home."

"George made his way to my side and told me, "We're all in and the waist door is secure." I told George to tell all the airmen to sit down as best they could till we were airborne. Then the "Usher" with the red flashlight motioned for me to "go, go, go." As I taxied out onto the runway, the B-17 in front of me was just getting airborne. Then it was our turn to start our takeoff roll. We started our long trip across Germany and France to an airfield near Bordeaux of which I didn't know the name nor did I know where it was located. But my navigator knew and that's all that counted.

"After climbing to altitude and trimming up the ship, I pressed the intercom button and said, "Pilot to navigator, I'm ready for my heading, over......" A few seconds later I called, "Pilot to navigator, my heading please....." Then in aggravation, I shouted. "PILOT TO NAVIGATOR! PILOT TO NAVIGATOR!"

"Then a shaky, weak voice came over the intercom saying, "Sir - uh - sir, I'm one of the POW's that just came aboard. I'm sitting in the navigator's compartment and heard your calls. There's no one up here except us guys that just came aboard.."

"I said, 'Thank you, over and out.'

"Immediately, I frantically searched the sky ahead of us, and there it was, just a speck in the sky. I could recognize that B-17 tail miles ahead. I didn't even consider going back to Barth. Waldo could catch the next plane out. I just increased my air speed to catch that dot in the sky. I told George and the copilot to keep their eyes on that B-17 ahead. I was going to follow him wherever he was going. I said a silent prayer, "God get me out of this mess I've got myself into and I'll never do it again." In no time we gained on the other B-17 until we were flying loose formation with it and we still had plenty of gasoline to make it home.

"About this time, a skinny, bedraggled, frail figure came up from the nose compartment and asked, "Sir, did you find your navigator."

"No," I said, "but it's no problem. We're following the B-17 ahead of us and we're going to the same place."

"We struck up a conversation and he commented that he had been a captain and flew B-17F's. He said he noticed that quite a few changes had been made to the B-17G. He told me what it had been like to be in Stalag I and IV. Then a thought struck me as I empathized with what he had been through. I got out of my seat and said, "Captain, get in my seat and fly the G for a while. You'll like it." He got into the left hand seat and for that brief time he looked young and vibrant again as he once again flew that magnificent machine, the B-17. He just beamed. Then after a few minutes of flying he got up and went back to the nose compartment.

"In a few moments he returned with a handful of German souvenirs he had picked up while in captivity: a box of German Matches, a swastika armband and some patches from German pilot uniforms. I still have and cherish those few small gifts he gave me.

"The rest of the flight was routine. We followed the leader to our destination, landed and watched as they loaded the rescued American POW airmen into trucks. We then parked the B-17 next to the one we had followed and had a nice tasty K ration for lunch. While eating lunch I heard a voice call out, "Ray, there you are." It was Waldo. He had caught the next plane out of Barth.

"After lunch, we flew back to Bassingbourn, no one ever mentioning what had happened. Waldo again flew with me as my navigator when I ferried a no name B-17 back to the States.

"The 91st sent forty-one B-17G's to Barth on the 13 of May 1945. If each B-17 carried thirty POW's as we did, twelve hundred and thirty American POW airmen were freed and sent on their way home that day. And Operation Revival lasted three days. *(Written and contributed by Ray Darling. All Rights Reserved.)*

"The next day, Sunday, May 13, was Mother's Day. Former POW Don Freer from the 91st Bombardment Group later reported, "I will never forget the thrill and joy of marching out of Stalag Luft I to the airfield at Barth and seeing the 91st BG aircraft waiting to take us home." The flights were extremely memorable for both the passengers and the crew.

"One of those from the evacuation crew, 91st Bombardment Group navigator George Jacobs told author John Howland, 'I consider it one of the most memorable days of my life!" Jacobs recounted, "We got outside and welcomed the group under the wing of our plane. We said, 'Guys you're on your way home.' We shook each hand as they got into the plane."

"Many of the former POWs had been airmen themselves, some from the 91st Bombardment Group, although it was perhaps years since they had been in the air. Some were reluctant to fly again, given the last time they were in the air resulted in captivity, trauma, and in many instances, death. But there was a cheer and clapping as the plane soared away from Barth and they left the prison camp behind. Former POW Oscar Richard said, "The group I was in boarded a bomber about one o'clock that afternoon. I grabbed a spot near one of the waist windows so I could see Germany once more from the air."

"Flying over former "Flak Alleys" and "Flak Valleys," crews now encountered peaceful, silent, but often devastated scenes. Many former POWs were amazed at the B-17G which became prevalent late in 1943, after many of the POWs had already been grounded. On the way to France from Barth, the "evacuation crews" conducted tours of their aircraft, showing off newer features like the GEE$_g$ box, the "automatic navigator."

"Some of the POWs were too weak to react or were in a state of disbelief that they were actually headed home. Others pointed out targets they had hit or the spots where they had been shot down.

"The next part of their waiting would commence at Camp Lucky Strike, one of the large staging areas through which most would return home. The British POWs completed the trip with the 8th Air Force fliers and were flown back to the bases in Great Britain.

(From letter - Uncle Will, 7 June 1988) "Cy and I were flown by B-17 from Barth on the last day that Stalag -1 was

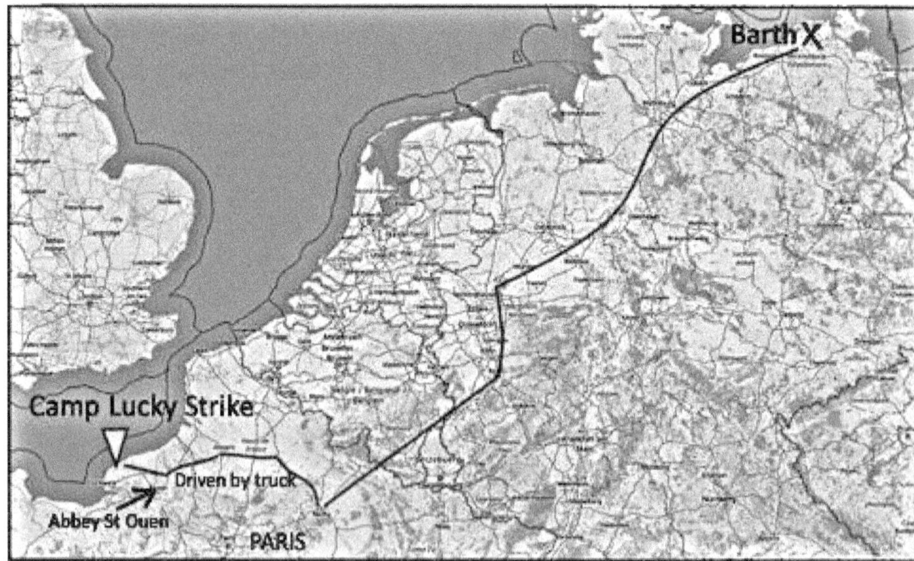

evacuated. We ended up somewhere in France. I went off by G.I. truck to a giant replacement center that went by the name of 'Camp Lucky Strike."

The former prisoners were taken to Camp Lucky Strike in trucks

"That was a dump so my bombardier and I took off without leave and hitch-hiked to Paris where we did not frequent the places where Cy was being lavishly entertained. If we had, I presume we would have been thrown into jail. Now, that would have been an ironic turnaround, No?

"Anyway, 'Russian' and I had a jolly time for several days in Paris where we entertained ourselves and were nobly wined and dined at the Jockey Club which also had a swimming pool of which we made full use.

Jockey Club, Paris

"Your father and I did not see each other again till we met at Mother's house in Lake Forest. He was dumbfounded that we two Air Force ragamuffins had not only kept from

being arrested but had made connections with members of The Jockey Club, which apparently was about as high as you can get in France - Your father was not, I sadly fear, entirely pleased at this small evidence of certain social graces on our part.

"He had gone off to Paris where he was billeted at the Hotel Francia to be de-briefed and to be entertained by Aunt Gertrude McCarthy (his god-mother) who was married to the U.S. ambassador to France."

Paraphrase of incoming Paris cable dated 18 May 1945:

"Major Cyrus E. MANIERRE, 024774, Cav., reported today to Paris, after being PW approximately 9 months. Processing for shipment to US. In good health."

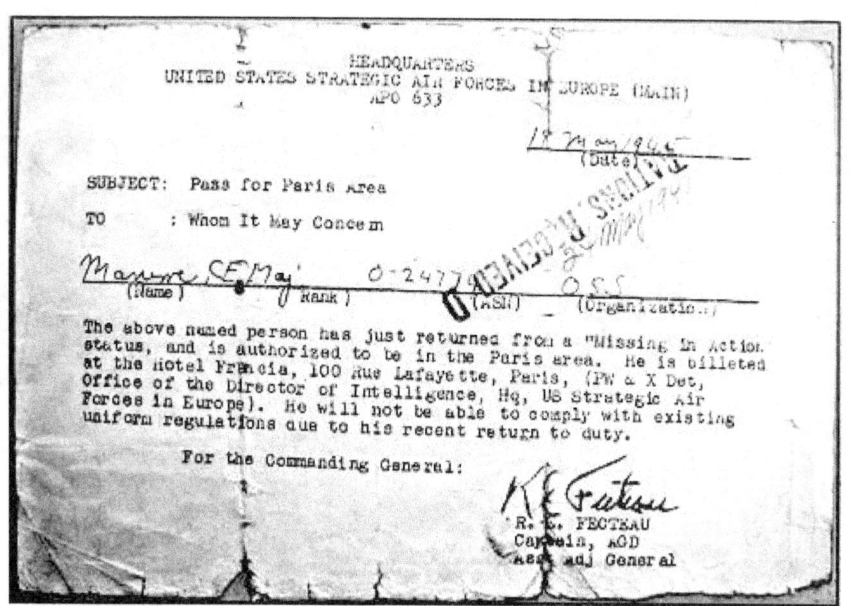

HEADQUARTERS
UNITED STATES STRATEGIC AIR FORCES IN EUROPE (MAIN)
APO 633

18 May 1945
(Date)

SUBJECT: Pass for Paris Area

TO   : Whom It May Concern

Manierre CE Maj   0-24774   220
(Name)   (Rank)   (ASN)   (Organization)

The above named person has just returned from a "Missing in Action"
status, and is authorized to be in the Paris area. He is billeted
at the Hotel Francia, 100 Rue Lafayette, Paris, (PW & X Det,
Office of the Director of Intelligence, Hq, US Strategic Air
Forces in Europe). He will not be able to comply with existing
uniform regulations due to his recent return to duty.

For the Commanding General:

R. E. FECTEAU
Captain, AGD
Asst Adj General

Hotel Francia, Rue Lafayette

While billeted in Paris, awaiting travel to London, Major Manierre took the opportunity to go sightseeing, visiting the Abbey of St. Ouen in City Hall Square, Rouen, Normandy.

(Saint-Ouen Abbey, French): is a large Gothic Catholic church and former Benedictine monastic church in Rouen. It is named for Audoin (French: Ouen, English: Owen), 7th-century bishop of Rouen in modern Normandy, France. The church's name is sometimes anglicized as St Owen's. Built on a similar scale to nearby Rouen Cathedral, the abbey is famous for both its architecture and its large, unaltered Cavaillé-Coll organ, which was described by Charles-Marie Widor as "a Michelangelo of an organ". With the cathedral and the Church of Saint-Maclou, Saint-Ouen is one of the principal French Gothic monuments of the city. *(Wikipedia)*

Full Circle

The cover picture, found by Joe deFrancesco in the US Air Force Academy Archives is paired with its mate, taken by

New York stone carver Joe Chiffriller approximately 50 years later:

Photo of front entrance to the Abbey of Saint Ouen

Leaving France and the Return to England -

From Fred McIntosh, Capt AACorps email:

"As a member of the 56th Ftr Gp. (62nd Sqdn) under the Hub before his transfer back to P-38's and P-51 Spam Cans, I am obviously aware of the circumstances involving their tour mit der Krieges. I was 500 yards behind Gabby when he tried plowing the German air field with his fine Ham Std prop and watched him run for the woods before we burned his flying machine;

"When Lucky Strike was established, Dave Schilling had me make almost daily runs with our Martin B-26 to bring the guys back. If my memory is correct Hub and Gabby were together when we brought them back. Manierre could have been with Gabby as we always filled the back end with

England-bound returnees hitching a ride. (I'm in Hub's book but only for flying through trees!!)"

Again from George McCafferty: "We left from Le Havre and after a very rough trip arrived in Boston. I had a wonderful sixty-day rest and recuperation leave. I never saw Cy again after that last meeting at Camp Lucky Strike. I did talk to him on the phone while I was in Washington DC. I suggested that we make a date for lunch and he said he would call me. I never did hear from him and I was told by some of his friends at CIA that he was not feeling well as he had experienced a very severe fall in a "Point to Point" race. This was in 1953.

I was transferred from Washington shortly after that time; you can be assured that your dad was a truly great guy. He was a wonderfully brave and dedicated member of the OSS and his experiences would equal anything that you could read in a war novel. If I think of anything else I will send it to you. I am off to Florida in a couple of days and will not be back to the computer until sometime in April.

Thanks for contacting me. George"

Appendix
(Citation below written by Major Neil Marten, whom Pop replaced in the Vercors)

S.P.O.C.   11 Oct.44.

<u>Subject:</u>   Citation

<u>MAJOR C. MANNIERE</u>. United States Army

Parachuted into France on 24 Jun 44, this officer immediately entered into his work with body and soul. Coming to a maquis of young and untrained men, he was for several weeks their instructor, a task in which he showed a very real skill, keeping his pupils always interested, and drawing out of them the
best of which they were capable, as well as gaining their affection.

He lead with outstanding successes three attacks on the railway between Valence and Grenoble, and directed an operation which destroyed vital portions of the power plant on the Basse Isere, despite the close proximity of the German detachment, thus preventing the supply of electric power to factories working for Germany.

He carried out several delicate and important reconnaissances on Route Nationale 7 and the Lyon – Marseille railway. Coming back one day from fetching explosives from a depot, his car was surprised by some milicians, and he was arrested before he had time to defend himself.

By his sang froid and the cleverness of his answers at his interrogation, he succeeded in averting suspicion from his companions in the car, so that two of them were freed, and the life of the third, who was an F.F.I. intelligence agent, was certainly saved.

N.M. Marten. Major

Northamptonshire Yeomanry.

HQ & HQ DETACHMENT
OFFICE OF STRATEGIC SERVICES
European Theater of Operations
United States Army

(Forward)

APO 887
200.6   28 June
1945

SUBJECT: Recommendation for Award of
Distinguished Service Cross

TO: Commanding General, European Theater
of Operations, United States Army, APO
887, US Army

1. a. It is recommended that CYRUS E.
MANIERRE, 0-24774, Major, Infantry, United
States Army, Office of Strategic Services
Detachment, European Theater of
Operations, APO 887, United States Army,
be awarded the DISTINGUISHED SERVICE
CROSS.

b. Major Manierre was serving as an
organizer of Resistance Groups in enemy
occupied territory at the time of the act
or service for which this award is
recommended.

c. Name and address of nearest relative:
Mother: Mrs. Edith Harrison Manierre, Rose
Terrace, Lake Forest, Illinois

d. Entered military service from: Illinois

e. Decorations previously awarded: None.

f. The entire service of Major Manierre
has been honorable since the rendition by
him of the act or service upon which this
recommendation is based,

g. A similar recommendation for this
individual has not been submitted.

2. a. The officer recommending this award
has personal knowledge of the act or
service upon which this recommendation is
based.

b. This recommendation is supported by
established records of accomplishments of
Resistance Groups during the period of the
invasion and liberation of France which
are of public knowledge.

3. a. Major Cyrus E. Manierre, 0-24774,
Infantry, while serving as a member of the
Special Operations Branch, Office of
Strategic Services Detachment, European
Theater of Operations, distinguished
himself by extraordinary heroism against
an armed enemy in enemy occupied territory
from 25 June 1944 to 5 August 1944.

b. Detailed narrative of service for which
this award is recommended:

Major Manierre (then Captain), on 22
November 1943, volunteered for the
extremely hazardous duty of entering enemy
occupied territory for the purpose of
organizing Resistance Groups, arranging
for the delivery and distribution of
supplies, supervising the activities of
the Resistance forces of the area assigned
to him in accordance with directives
received from Special Force Headquarters
to the end that the most effective
possible utilization be made of his troops
in support of the advance of the Allied
Armies, and in personally leading and
directing forays against the enemy.

After extensive training for the type
of work in which he was to engage, Major
Manierre, together with one enlisted man
who was to be his radio operator, was
parachuted into France on 25 June 1944 as
a member of Jedburgh team "DODGE", with
the mission of organizing and arming
Resistance Forces in the Drome Department.

Landing at Beaurepaire in the Isere
Department, they were directed to the
Chief of Resistance Forces in the Vercors
region who assigned Major Manierre the
mission of organizing and directing
operations of all Maquis in the Drome that

were not directly under his control in the Vercors. This was part of a plan to make the Vercors a nucleus of all resistance for that entire section of France which might be expected to play an important role in hindering German evacuation since the region straddled an important line of supply and communication running from Marseille to Germany.

Specifically, Major Manierre was to do the actual organizing of the individual Maquis into a military unit, instruct them in weapons, explosives and military procedure, and lead the individual maquis groups on whatever operations he deemed necessary to the accomplishment of the final aims already outlined.

After two and one-half weeks devoted to the organizing of smooth functioning units, Major Manierre initiated an extensive sabotage program. A high priority mission was the wiping out of all electrical power in the Drome, an operation which was planned for 25 July 1944. Major Manierre undertook to place the charges in the central power plant himself despite the fact that the building was heavily guarded inside and out.

The resulting explosion was so powerful that not only the control board was destroyed, crippling the entire system, but the roof of the building blown

off and windows in neighboring houses
shattered.

At a later date Major Manierre led a
team of seventy in another highly
successful and extremely dangerous
operation which involved the crippling of
railroad traffic along the Rhone by
knocking out a culvert while the train was
passing over. The locomotive was blown up
by the charges, and personnel and material
were destroyed by a volley of Bren and
Sten guns, grenade and anti-tank rocket
fire, the entire skirmish lasting 12
minutes and involving only slight Maquis
losses.

In addition to active participation
in major acts of sabotage Major Manierre
spent a great deal of time instructing in
weapons and explosives and in practical
application of arms, and in directing and
supervising the work of neighboring maquis
groups, one of which, the maquis of Mabou,
performed semi-weekly attacks on railroad
lines in the area.

Another part of Major Manierre's work
consisted in the search and surveying of
possible targets for aerial bombardment,
and the furnishing to Headquarters of
intelligence reports, of results of
requested bombings.

Around the beginning of August Major Manierre volunteered to work in a sector bordering on the Rhone that was extremely well patrolled by the enemy, which necessitated his adopting civilian attire in order to pass unnoticed. Their aim was to cut off completely and permanently all railroad traffic on the left bank.

Disguised as a French laborer, Major Manierre did frequent bicycle reconnaissance trips for a twenty-mile stretch of the river's length. An excellent target was discovered in the railway bridge at Serves-sur-Rhone where he barely escaped capture by a German patrol which was passing over the bridge while he was reconnoitering the framework be- low. Despite the hazard involved he resolved to destroy the bridge and the German troop train that was scheduled to pass over it. He requisitioned explosives and availed himself of a civilian truck. On 5 August 1944, while transporting this material to the scene of the intended operation, he was held up at a roadblock constructed by a group of Milicians who subsequently arrested him, interrogated him brutally, and then turned him over to the Gestapo. Despite three more days of brutal interrogation, he admitted nothing, safeguarding his Resistance contacts and the lives of the three men who were arrested with him and released shortly thereafter.

After imprisonment in solitary confinement in various French and German prisons where living conditions were indescribably bad and interrogations merciless and unending, he was sent to a prisoner of war camp where he remained until liberation by Russian Forces on 2 May 1945.

4. Proposed Citation:

"Major CYRUS E. MANIERRE, 0-24774, Infantry, for extraordinary heroism in connection with military operations against an armed enemy, in enemy occupied territory, from 25 June 1944 to 5 August 1944. After having been parachuted into France,

Major Manierre performed outstanding and heroic services in the conduct of operations which resulted in the immobilization of enemy reinforcements in the Drome Department. Working under the most perilous conditions, he continually demonstrated great personal bravery and initiative in the accomplishment of his mission. Although arrested and subjected to cruel interrogations by the Milice and the Gestapo, he disclosed nothing to compromise the Resistants with whom he had worked. The actions of Major Manierre

throughout this hazardous mission reflect
great credit upon himself and the armed
forces of the United States.

     Entered military service from
Illinois."

5. The basic document is classified
"Confidential" because of the information
contained in the detailed narrative.
However, the Proposed Citation, when
published separately need not carry the
classification of the basic document.

                    JAMES R. FORGAN
                    Colonel,
                    GSC$_G$ Commanding

CONFIDENTIAL

CITATION FOR BRONZE STAR MEDAL

Major Cyrus E. Manierre, Infantry, as Group Adjutant at Stalag-Luft I,
where he was held prisoner by the Germans from August 1944 to
May 1945, displayed great courage and daring in distributing
information and plans to fellow prisoners of war. Along with
dissemination of this important information, he carried on other
activities of value to the Allied cause, risking severe punishment
if detected by his captors.

Major Manierre's fearless and skillful achievements were
essential to maintaining the good moral of the men in
confinement and contributed materially to the war effort.

OFFICIAL COPY
THE ADJUTANT GENERAL'S
OFFICE WAR DEPARTMENT

A true copy;

Graham Campbell
GRAHAM G. CAMPBELL
Lt. Colonel, Inf.
OSS Citations Officer

Letter authority War
Department, Washington,
D.C. 24 July 1945

Gen. Vandenberg presenting the Legion of Merit

Timeline:

7/1/38   Entry in service (Arrives USMA West Point)

5/29/42   Graduates USMA, Commissioned as 2nd
                Lieutenant

5/42–11/42 Pilot training, dates unknown. Crashes a trainer.
                Washed out

11/42 – 6/4 Camp Blanding, FL
                Ft. Benning, GA Bn S-3,
                508th Parachute Infantry Camp Mackall, NC

6/15/43   Recruited for OSS - French Operational Groups
                at Camp Mackall

6/28/43   Relieved from duty 508 PIC, Assigned to OSS

7/1/43   Reported for duty Washington, DC

8/23/43   Promoted to Captain

9/17/43   Approved for overseas travel

9/22/43   Assigned to duty in London, England. Ordered to
                report for duty as directed by Col. Charles S.
                Vanderblue, Chief of SO Mission, London,

9/24/43   Leave, 9 days (Lake Forest, IL

10/4/43   Returns from Leave

10/14/43   Relieved from duty Washington DC,

Assigned duty outside continental limits US

10/30/43   Departed for England aboard SS Marina

11/26/43   Arrival in England

12/1/43   Assigned to Parachute duty

3/16/44   Assigned to Special Operations Training Branch

4/13/44   Relieved from assignment to OG_g (ET)
            Assigned to SO_g (ET)

5/31/44   Assigned to Western Europe Jedburghs

6/44   Sailed to N. Africa aboard Capetown Castle

6/22/44   Recommendation from the Field for promotion to
            next higher grade (Major)

6/25/44   Departed from North Africa, parachuted into
            department of Isere, France

7/1/44   Promotion approved by the Branch, OSS Board
            of Officers and the Acting Director

7/15/44   Promoted to Major

8/5/44   Captured by milice near Albon, France
            Taken to Milice HQ, Valence, 48 hours in cell
            Interrogation begins, Milice.

8/8/44   Transferred to Gestapo HQ, Lyon
            Taken to Montluc (Prison Militaire) in Lyon,

Interrogated by Gestapo – 6 days
OSS HQ receives report of his arrested

8/11/44   Report received OSS HQ - "Presumed shot"

8/13/44   "Passion Pit" shot down by flak.
           Uncle Bill captured

8/15/44   Gestapo Lyon liquidated by FFI, left in prison

8/16/44   Wehrmacht takes over Gestapo HQ

8/17/44   Telegram received at OSS HQ: "RUPERT
              HAS BEEN SENT TO VICHY"

9/3/44   German evacuate Lyon, prisoners loaded into
              freight cars, sent to Germany

9/12/44   Arrival at Oberusel, Germany - Dulag Luft

9/13/44   Reported "seen at Wetzler", sent to Stalag-Luft 1

10/10/44   Message received at HQ of POW status

12/20/44   Jump Pay ceases

12/24/44   Mother receives news of both son's POW status

5/02/45   Russians arrive Stalag-Luft 1

5/14/45   Liberated from Stalag Luft 1

5/17/45   Reports to Paris, France. Billeted at Hotel Francia

5/18/45	Reports to London Duty Station
6/25/45	Duty Station London to duty per Ltr O UKB
6/27/45	Departs to Temporary Duty Lake Forest, Il
6/28/45	Recommendation for DSC, downgraded to Legion of Merit
7/31/45	Temp. Duty Lake Forest to duty
7/31/45	Dy to TDY C&G Staff School Ft. Leavenworth, Kansas
9/28/45	Relieved from assignment, assigned Cav Replacement Pool Cac RTC Ft. Riley, KS report upon completion of present course
10/8/45	Temporary duty Military Intelligence Service, Washington DC
10/12/45	Transferred out of OSS (Actually departed from this orgsn 28 Sept 45.)
10/15/45	Washington, DC MID, G-2, WDGS
10/22/45	Temp duty granted
10/8/45	Extended 5 days effective 22 October 1945
2/26/46	Transferred to Cav RP Cac, Replacement Training Command, Ft Riley, Kansas

The United States Army Command and General Staff College (CGSC) educates and develops leaders for full spectrum joint, interagency and multinational operations; acts as lead agent for the Army's leader development program; and advances the art and science of the profession of arms in support of Army operational requirements. During WW II the Command and General Staff Colleges primary mission was to train large numbers of captains and majors to be staff officers in battalions, brigades, divisions, and corps Fort Belvoir

Fort Belvoir is a United States Army installation and a census-designated place (CDP) in Fairfax County, Virginia, United States. It was developed on the site of the former Belvoir plantation, seat of the prominent Fairfax family for whom Fairfax County was named. It was known as Camp A. A. Humphreys from 1917 to 1935 and Fort Belvoir afterward.

Decorations authorized to wear:

Legion of Merit for Operation Jedburgh
Bronze Star Medal for organizing prison camp escape
Parachute Badge (US), (British)
European Theater Ribbon
American Theater Ribbon
Defense Service Ribbon
Victory Ribbon
Croix de Guerre avec Etoile (France)
Invasion Arrowhead
Normandy Invasion,
S. France Star

Ball of Kirriemuir
(aka: The Gathering of the Clans)

"The Ball of Kirriemuir" (occasionally Kerrymuir and other variants), sometimes known as "The Gathering of the Clans" or "Four-and-Twenty Virgins", is a traditional song of Scottish origin. It is Roud Folk Song Index no. 4828. It consists of quatrains in which the second and fourth lines rhyme, alternating with a chorus. The words, and the number of verses (of which there are many), vary between versions, but all are strikingly bawdy. It purports to recount the goings-on at a dance party in Kirriemuir, Angus, Scotland which turned into an orgy. In many versions, there are visitors from as far away as Aviemore and Inverness in the Scottish Highlands.

The general view is that the song originated sometime around the 1880s, and is loosely based on an actual event. The tale runs, that all the men were wearing kilts, and that few women in those days wore underwear and those that were worn had an open crotch. Someone sprinkled rose hip seeds on the floor (from where they were caught up into the air as the dancing began), spiked the punchbowl with Spanish fly, and rigged the paraffin lamps to go out when the double effect of the itching powder and the aphrodisiac took hold.

Suggestions that some of the words can be attributed to Robert Burns (Scotland's national poet) or that T. S. Eliot made use of them have been refuted.

The following, in Scots, is representative of the less extreme verses:

'Twas on the first of August,
The party, it began,
Noo, ne'er shall I forget, me lads,
The gatherin' o' the clans.

[Chorus] Wha'll dae ye, lassie,
Wha'll dae ye noo?
The mon wha did ye last nicht,
Cannae dae ye noo.

Four and twenty virgins,
Cam doon frae Inverness,
And when the ball was over,
There were four and twenty less.

There was screwin' in the parlour,
An' screwin' on the stones,
Ye couldnae hear the music,
For the wheezin' and the groans.

And when the ball was over,
The opinion was expressed,
The music was exquisite, but
The screwin' was the best.

5. "The Ball o' Kirriemuir". ingeb.org. Retrieved 27 October 2021. 39 verses, in Scots.

(From Wikipedia)

(There are MANY additional verses of the a extreme variety not included in this work that can be found on various websites.)

I grew up on a diet of war stories, particularly those about the air war over Europe. My heroes were the fighter pilots of the 8th Air Force and "The Few" of the Royal Air Force. My young head visualized flak bursts, contrails, mission briefings, head-on attacks, dog fights, bailing out of burning planes, – you name it, all of which I read about in the many books I owned, and literally lived in. I had heroes - Zemke, Gabreski, Bader, Galland, Schnaufer, Hartmann, etc. I had plastic models of all the planes - Spitfires, Hurricanes, Messerschmidts, Focke Wulfs, Lancasters, B-17s, B-24s, P-51s, P-47s… I could picture POW camps – Stalag-Luft III, Colditz, and some of the great escape stories. And yet just downstairs was the one story I had never asked about, one of incredible heroism and outstanding luck – my own father's.

Every war story has a degree of commonality – there's recruitment, the training, the missions, the fear and excitement, the victories and the losses. But then … there are those stories that have an additional extra – the miraculous escape from a burning plane, the luck and/or skill of escaping the enemy, the realization that there IS a God who was watching out for one. My father's story is one of those - with remarkable, miraculous twists and "lucky escapes".

Over twenty years ago my mother received a photo from Joe DeFrancesco - a former Jed, of my father standing in front of a cathedral somewhere in France, seen on the cover of this work. This piqued my interest in my father's exploits in WW 2. I always had known that Pop was a "Jed" - whatever that was, but I had never asked him what he had done. Shortly after receiving this photo I was prowling around in the attic of the house in which I grew up, and discovered a box of old papers which turned out to be the handwritten beginnings of the book my father had started – this book. Digging further I found his "Jedburgh Activity Report" which was fascinating reading indeed. Here was the first hand account of my father's WW 2 experiences, a story of which I had heard only the briefest snippets.

I got my mother to type Pop's handwritten legal pages, and the "Jedburgh Activity Report," onto a disk which I then loaded into my computer. Having access to a decent local library, I was able to add maps and occasional sections of books in which he was mentioned, as well as pictures, plus I had photos from his scrapbook. My ability to search on the ever-expanding Internet brought me access to more photographs, better maps, and strings to pull that lead to other OSS researchers around the world. I was amazed to find photos of Pop in the Time-Life book THE RESISTANCE, part of the their series on WW 2. I later received a set of photos from a French Commando that were taken by the French photographer Andre Gamet – in France, during the war. Quelle surprise!!!

This book is a compilation of the work of many – starting with my father's writings, and his Jedburgh Activity Report; including the narratives of several other Jeds to whom I must give special posthumous thanks, the several US Army Air Corps pilots and other Officers whose narratives I found on such websites as (<www.merkki.com>), - a fabulous website – which was created by the daughter of Dick Williams jr, one of many who spent time as a "guest of the Luftwaffe" at Stalag-Luft 1, as did my father and my uncle. My grandmother had saved a three-part article by Claire Rauth that appeared in a newspaper (that I have been as yet unable to identify) which was an extensive interview, almost a debriefing, by Pop, that details much of his activities in France mid-1944. Then there is the U.S. Army Special Operations Forces website (<www.https://arsof-history.org/>) that presented the tales of other Jeds who described their experiences (which I have included as they were similar to what Pop experienced) to cover the time period of his training between the time described in his writings and the period covered in his later Jedburgh Activity Report. I had the great fortune to be able to communicate with people whom he knew and worked with – Joe deFrancesco, Dr. Henry MacIntosh, John Colemon, Francis Cammaerts, Gabby Gabreski, Irwin "Russian" Stovroff, George McCafferty (one of Pop's roommates in Stalag-Luft 1), and of course my Uncle Bill Manierre. My communications with them added immeasurably to what I found in Pop's own writings and have allowed me to add details to the story and bring this tale to life.

One example of my "string pulling" is my emails with Helga Radau, Town Historian of Barth, Germany, who suggested I read a book called **Journey to a Star**, by Col. William Blum – who turned out to be one of Pop's roommates at Stalag-Luft 1. In the back of this book were listed the names and addresses of the roommates, one of whom I was able to contact and carry on a conversation with via letters about their activities in the camp. Slowly I gathered more bits and pieces of, to me, the unknown aspects of my father's war-time exploits that I had never even imagined. I had the very great good fortune to be able to communicate with such notables as Tom Ensminger, Gerald Rix, authors Colin Beaven, Will Irwin, Roger Armstrong and others whose names I list elsewhere; listing only their names because they each rendered such assistance that to fully acknowledge each would require a chapter in itself.

Each new fact I uncovered led to new areas to search, new books to read, new locations to investigate and new people to contact and question. I saw Irwin "Russian" Stovroff's tale about my father and uncle meeting in prison camp in Gerald Astor's book THE MIGHTY EIGHTH, and found Mr. Stovroff's address listed in the back of the book, so

I called him. We eventually met. The pieces of this puzzle gradually fell into place as new avenues to investigate were revealed, until now I have a fairly complete record of his Jedburgh years. One realization I had after reading about his training under William "Dangerous Dan" Fairbairn was that, considering my capers as a teenager, I am truly amazed to still be alive. My father's self-restraint was remarkable.

In working with these pages, I have made no effort to edit Pop's words, other than to correct typos and add pieces from one set of writings to clarify another. I include the work of others in the sequence of events, filling in gaps not covered by Pop.

Additionally I've added various maps and photos that show the locations where he trained and operated, people with whom he served included correspondence from people such as one of his POW camp roommates, and various people who have websites devoted to Jedburghs and Jedburgh-related activities; essentially anything I could find that related to his activities.

MY purpose in doing this project originated from curiosity about the photo, and it developed into deeper research into my father's wartime activities. This collection is by no means a sequential narrative; rather it is a compilation of some of the common experiences written by not only my father, but by other Jeds and authors. I have attributed those paragraphs and photos to those authors, books and websites when I could find them. Because of the abundance of material, I may have inadvertently missed some of the authors whose work I have researched. I welcome any information regarding any of those authors so that I may acknowledge their contribution to the overall narrative.

In the course of research, through letters and email, I discovered many interesting new acquaintances who had known and/or worked with Pop in the OSS, and this history was greatly enhanced by their additions. I've learned quite a bit about the Jedburghs, and I am awed by their guts and determination.

Acknowledgements

The various sources I've had access to (in no particular order), and I thank each, are:

Joe deFrancesco – former Jed – Team JIM

Tony Mills - (website: (<www.jedburgh.demon.co.uk>)

Dr. Henry McIntosh – former Jed - Team CHLOROFORM

George McCafferty - Kriegie, Pop's Stalag-Luft1 roommate

Nancy Manierre – Typist, mother

Gerald Rix – OSS Researcher

Francis Cammaerets - "Roger" - letters

Colin Beaven – Author **OPERATION JEDBURGH**

Troy Sequaty – Historian ARSOF

David Harrison – Author, Historian re: SOE

Irwin "Russian" Stovroff – Passion Pit - Bombardier,

Mary Smith (website: (<http//merkki.home.att.net>), emails

Tom Ensminger – Carpetbaggers$_g$ Historian, etc.

    (<www.fortunecity.com/meltingpot/roberts/38>)

Major Ben Jones – Author -**Freeing France: The Allies, the Resistance, and the JEDBURGHs**

Jon Shafer – former-Marine, author

Lt. Col J.W. Bradbury - USAF

Helga Radau - Town Historian of Barth, GERMANY

Mike Henely – former Jed – Team JIM

Harry Cooper – Founder of Eaglehunters and Sharkhunters

Colonel Francis "Gabby" Gabreski - USAAF

Serge Blandin - French Rep. 801st/492nd B.G. Association

Denis Durocher - Son of "Oswald"

Fred McIntosh - Capt Army Air Corps

Prof. Arthur Funk – Author, University of Florida

Will Irwin – Author – **THE JEDBURGHS**

Francis Colemon – former OSS – member Operation Group
Uncle Bill Manierre – letters
Steven Kippax – Historian, Expert on SOE
Robert Kehoe - former Jed, Team FREDERICK
Joe Chiffriller (<www.newyorkcarver.com>)
Benoit Senne – French Commando
(<https://military-history.fandom.com/wiki/>)
(<https://www.vercors-resistance.fr/en/the-resistant-vercors/>)
(<https://arsof-history.org/>)
(<https://earlofcruise.blogspot.com/>)
44th Bomb Group Veterans Association - Wikipedia
Other websites found using Google.

This list of names above seems so impersonal and dry, yet
each name, and each website represents someone who gave
their valuable time and assistance to me in my "string pulling"
as I searched the completely unknown universe of Jedburgh
activities. Each of them, many of whom knew Pop, and trained
with him, shared a piece of his life and was a friend of his,
shared knowledge that I could have had first-hand but never
had the interest to ask when he was alive.

Books:
THE RESISTANCE   (Time-Life Books)
THE COMMANDOS   (Time-Life Books)
THE MIGHTY EIGHTH - Gerald Astor
THE JEDBURGHS: A SHORT HISTORY - Arthur Brown
THE BRITISH SPY MANUAL - Published by the Imperial
        War Museum
ZEMKE'S STALAG - Col. Hubert "Hub" Zemke
Les FORCES SPECIALES de la LIBERATION - Paul Gaujac
CANADIANS BEHIND ENEMY LINES - Roy Maclaren
JOURNEY TO A STAR - Col. William Blum
USA THE HARD WAY - Roger Armstrong

KRIEGIE - Kenneth W. Simmons
HIDDEN ALLY - Prof. Arthur Funk
ARMES – 1945 French magazine
VERITAS – Magazine of U.S. Army Special Operations
Forces

Newspaper article (Unknown source) by Claire Rauth

Maps courtesy of: www.OpenStreetMap.org (No ads!)
www.multimap.com
www.expedia.com
Google.com/maps
Various Atlases
Promotional foldout for "La DROME Region"
(www.drometourisme.com)

Translations using DeepL Translator (By FAR the best of any
of the other translation websites) This website very accurately
translated from French and back again to English

FREE OCR - free Optical Character Recognition Software
(<http://www.paperfile.net/>) This was incredibly useful for
scanning the many pages of decades-old reports, etc.

I have always enjoyed maps, especially when locating
scenes of action. I created a large – 2'X3' map of Pop's area
of operation which is unfortunately too large to be included
with this book. For those readers who also enjoy maps, I
recommend the website: www.Openstreetmap.com. The map
stretched from just west of the Rhone river to La Cote-Saint-
Andre, then down south to Bourg-les-Valence – all key French
locations mentioned can be found on Openstreetmap.com, all

of which are encompassed within the borders of the red box in the map of France below.

Two Key Map Locations – The following links are the Drop Zones of the missions of Jed Teams Veganin and Dodge:

Drop Zone Tarsis -
https://www.openstreetmap.org/node/12088794652#map=15/45.36915/4.97247

DZ Tanit
https://www.openstreetmap.org/note/4880015#map=15/45.35878/4.98054&layers=N

GLOSSARY

Anvil/Dragoon - Operation Anvil was the original code name for the Allied invasion of southern France in August 1944 in World War II. It was later renamed Operation Dragoon.

AGO - In the military, AGO is an abbreviation for Adjutant General's Corps.

A.P.O. - APO stands for Army Post Office, and it's used in military addresses to identify US Army and Air Force installations. The US Military Postal Service (USPS) uses APO addresses to deliver mail and packages to overseas military personnel.

AS - The Armée Secrète (AS) was a French Resistance group that combined military organizations in 1942. The AS was especially strong in the Rhône-Alpes region. The Armée secrète (AS) was formed in 1942 to combine the military organisations of the major resistance movements of Vichy France. The organisation had a particularly-strong presence in the Vercors, Lyon and Massif central départements of the Rhône-Alpes region.

AUS - In the military, "AUS" stands for "Army of the United States". It can be used to indicate that a soldier was drafted into the Army, rather than enlisting. Soldiers who enlisted served in the Regular Army (RA).

"Bosambo" - name of the character of a loyal native chief in Nigeria ("Bosambo"), played by Black actor Paul Robeson in the 1933 film **SANDERS RIVER** – in which a British District Officer in Nigeria in the 1930s rules his area strictly but justly.

He struggles with gun-runners and slavers with the aid of a loyal native chief.

Bren - The Bren gun was a licensed version of the Czechoslovak ZGB 33 light machine gun which, in turn, was a modified version of the ZB vz. 26, which British Army officials had tested during a firearms service competition in the 1930s. The later Bren gun featured a distinctive top-mounted curved box magazine, conical flash hider, and quick change barrel. The Bren gun was a series of light machine guns (LMG) made by the United Kingdom in the 1930s and used in various roles until 1992. While best known for its role as the British and Commonwealth forces' primary infantry LMG in WW II, it was also used in the Korean War and saw service throughout the latter half of the 20th century, including the 1982 Falklands War. Although fitted with a bipod, it could also be mounted on a tripod or be vehicle-mounted

British MI - "MI" in British context stands for "Military Intelligence," referring to the intelligence agencies within the UK government, most notably MI5 (domestic security) and MI6 (foreign intelligence), which both originated from the military intelligence branch during World War I.

B.W.C. - BRITISH War Cabinet

CARPETBAGGER - Operation Carpetbagger was a World War II operation to provide aerial supply of weapons and other *matériel* to resistance fighters in France, Italy and the Low Countries by the U.S. Army Air Forces that began on 4 January 1944. Two squadrons were placed under the provisional 801st Bomb Group at RAF Harrington at the beginning of 1944, and the first "Carpetbagger" missions were carried out by this unit under the control of General "Wild Bill" Donovan's Office of Strategic Services (OSS)

Chemin de Fer – A French phrase meaning "railway" or "railroad". Literally, "iron path."

Claridge's - A 5-star hotel at the corner of Brook Street and Davies Street in Mayfair, London.

COMAC - (Committee of Military Organization of Combatant Action)

Commando Order - (German: *Kommandobefehl*) was issued by the OKW, the high command of the German Armed Forces, on 18 October 1942. This order stated that all Allied commandos captured in Europe and Africa should be summarily executed without trial, even if in proper uniforms or if they attempted to surrender. Any commando or small group of commandos or a similar unit, agents, and saboteurs not in proper uniforms who fell into the hands of the German forces by some means other than direct combat (by being apprehended by the police in occupied territories, for instance), were to be handed over immediately to the *Sicherheitsdienst* (SD, or Security Service) for immediate execution.

Cordtex - Cordtex is a type of detonating cord generally used in mining. "Cordtex" and "Primacord" are two of many trademarks which have slipped into use as a generic term for detonating cord. It uses an explosive core of pentaerythritol tetranitrate (PETN) inside its plastic coating. It is commonly the thickness of electrical extension cord and has a detonation velocity of approximately 6000–7000 metres per second. It is used to "daisy-chain" a sequence of explosives together. It can also be used in short lengths in simple booby-traps and early warning devices.

Office of the Coordinator of Information (COI) was an intelligence and propaganda agency of the United States Government, founded on July 11, 1941, by President Franklin D. Roosevelt, prior to U.S. involvement in the Second World War. It was intended to overcome the lack of coordination between existing agencies which, in part, it did by duplicating some of their functions.

Roosevelt was persuaded to create the office several months before the United States entered the war by prominent New York lawyer William J. Donovan, who had been dispatched to London by the president to assess the ability of the British to continue fighting after the French capitulation to German aggression

Coup de main - (French pronunciation: [ku də mɛ̃], plural: *coups de main*, 'blow with the hand') is a swift attack that relies on speed and surprise to accomplish its objectives in a single blow.

D bar - A mixture of chocolate, sugar, powdered milk, oat flour, and vitamins provided 600 calories per serving and made a very effective survival food. The Ration D chocolate bar was designed to withstand extreme temperatures and provide substantial energy for troops.

DCA - D.C.A. - Défenses Contre Avions (or Aéronefs) - Anti-Aircraft Defence (French). French Company that manufactured the electrodes used in the carbon arc lamps that produced the intense light used in the German anti-aircraft searchlights.

DIM - 1st Army Corps, but the divisions that spent the most time with the corps were the 2nd **M**oroccan **I**nfantry **D**ivision (2e DIM)

 Donovan, William Joseph "Wild Bill" - KBE - (January 1, 1883 – February 8, 1959) was an American soldier, lawyer, intelligence officer and diplomat. He is best known for serving as the head of the Office of Strategic Services (OSS), the precursor to the Bureau of Intelligence and Research and the Central Intelligence Agency (CIA), during World War II. He is regarded as the founding father of the CIA, and a statue of him stands in the lobby of the CIA headquarters building in Langley, Virginia

Drome - A department in France that is known for its lavender fields, is the southernmost department in the Auvergne-Rhône-Alpes region of Southeastern France. Named after the river Drôme.

DSO - Distinguised Service Order, a military decoration of the United Kingdom.

Dulag Luft - Dulag Luft was a German transit camp for Allied aircrew during World War II. The camps were used to collect and interrogate captured airmen before transferring them to permanent camps. Purpose: Collect and interrogate captured airmen, Prepare airmen for transfer to permanent camps, and Gather intelligence from Allied POWs. Location: Several camps were set up in Germany and occupied countries. The main camp was at Oberursel near Frankfurt. A satellite camp was set up at Wetzlar. **Dulag** is short for Durchgangslager, which means "transit camp", **Luft** is short for Luftwaffe, which means "Airforce". The main

Dulag Luft camp in Frankfurt was the main collecting point
for intelligence from Allied POW interrogation

DWM - (Deutsche Waffen- und Munitionsfabriken
Aktiengesellschaft (German Weapons and Munitions public
limited company), known as DWM, was an arms company in
Imperial Germany created in 1896 when Ludwig Loewe &
Company united its weapons and ammunition production
facilities within one company.

Enfield - The Lee–Enfield is a bolt-action, magazine-fed
repeating rifle that served as the main firearm of the military
forces of the British Empire and Commonwealth during the
first half of the 20th century, and was the standard service rifle
of the British Armed Forces from its official adoption in 1895
until 1957

ETOUSA - European Theater of Operations, United States
Army (ETOUSA) was a theater of Operations responsible for
directing United States Army operations …

4th RTM of the 2nd DIM - 2nd Armoured Division
(**2nd** DB, former **2nd** Light Division) only for a short
time in late 1944 **2nd** Moroccan Infantry Division (**2nd DIM**)

FERRET - Allied nickname for a type of German guard.
Unlike the men in the guard towers and on the gates, they
were dressed in overalls and often carried a long metal probe.
Their job was to prevent escape attempts, discover tunnels and
concealed hiding places. They were known to try hiding
themselves in the camp or watch with binoculars and
telescopes from 'hides' outside the wire for suspicious
activities. In some camps there were permanent mobile guard

patrols in place of ferrets (although they were introduced in Schubin following the Asselin tunnel breakout)

FFI - The French Forces of the Interior were a paramilitary group of French resistance fighters during World War II. The FFI were formed after the Allied landings in Normandy and Provence. The FFI were organized into light infantry units. They were used to man less active areas of the front lines; This allowed the regular French army to concentrate their troops in more decisive areas. In October 1944, the FFI were incorporated into the French regular forces. Charles de Gaulle gave the FFI their formal name. He led the Free French forces in resisting France's capitulation to Germany during World War II.

Fil de Fer - "Fil de fer" is a French phrase that translates to "wire" in English. It can also refer to barbed wire.

Fw - "Fw" in Focke-Wulf refers to the German aircraft manufactuer Focke-Wulf Flugzeugbau AG. Focke-Wulf was a German aircraft manufacturer that produced military and civil aircraft during World War II. The Focke-Wulf Fw 190 was a German fighter aircraft that was used during World War II. It was designed by Kurt Tank in the late 1930s. The Fw 190 was the backbone of the Luftwaffe's Fighter Force, along with the Messerschmitt Bf 109.

FTP - The Francs-Tireurs et Partisans, set up in the spring of 1942, resulted from the merger of three militant communist groups: the Organisation Spéciale, formed in 1940 to protect communist leaders; the group of young communists, the first to attack German soldiers; and the fighters of the Main-d'Oeuvre Immigrée. The FTP was the military arm of the communist Front National, which decided that about 20 per cent of its members would take part in it. With the introduction of the abhorred Service du Travail Obligatoire, non-communists joined the FTP for self-protection to avoid work in Germany, as much as to fight the occupation and Vichy. The FTP claimed that in three months of 1943 it carried out 1,500 actions; among the 1,500 were 158 on train derailments, and 110 on engines and bridges. While keeping its autonomy, the FTP in 1944-02 became a part of the Forces Françaises de l'Intérieur.

Gammon grenade - also known as the No. 82 hand grenade, was a British improvised hand-thrown explosive device, primarily used by the Home Guard, Special Air Service (SAS), and Resistance groups, particularly for destroying parked aircraft or vehicles. A team under the command of Captain RS Gammon (belonging to the 1st Parachute Regiment) imagined a multi-tasking grenade that could serve both anti-personnel and anti-tank: the user can choose the explosive to use By filling a canvas bag disposed around the detonator.

Gestapo - an abbreviation for the German phrase Geheime Staatspolizei, which translates to "Secret State Police". It was the official secret police force of Nazi Germany and German-occupied Europe. The Gestapo was formed in 1933 by Hermann Göring, the Minister-President of Prussia.

GCMA - GROUPEMENT DE COMMANDOS MIXTES AÉROPORTÉS (GCMA) The history of this highly secret commando unit is complicated and its importance remains controversial. The conceptual origins of the GCMA are to be found in World War II, in Allied commando operations run against German and Japanese occupied territories - (English: Mixed Airborne Commando Group) commonly

referred as just GCMA, was the "Action Service" of
the Service de documentation extérieure et de contre-
espionnage (SDECE$_g$), the France counterintelligence service
agency, which active during the Cold War. The GCMA's
origins lay in the British - U.S - French joint Operation
Jedburgh in France in 1944.

GEE - sometimes written GEE, was a radio-navigation system
used by the Royal Air Force during World War II. It measured
the time delay between two radio signals to produce a fix, with
accuracy on the order of a few hundred metres at ranges up to
about 350 miles (560 km). It was the first hyperbolic
navigation system to be used operationally, entering service
with RAF Bomber Command in 1942.

Harrington - RAF Harrington, The first USAAF 8th Air
Force Group to use Harrington was the 1st Bombardments
Group. Arriving on 25 March 1944. The 801st Bomb Group
became best known as the **Carpetbaggers,** whose mission
was to fly Special Operations missions which entailed
delivering supplies to resistance groups in enemy-occupied
countries

Hautes Alpes - a department in southeastern France. It's
located in the heart of the French Alps, and is named after the
mountain range. The capital of Hautes-Alpes is Gap.

ISF - Internal Security Forces French: *Forces de Sécurité
Intérieure*; abbreviated ISF) are the national police
of Lebanon.

ITT - International Telephone and telegraph had a Nazi-
owned subsidiary in France.

Kriegie - Noun, *Military Slang. A*n Allied prisoner of war in a World War II German internment camp. Kriegie is what the POWs called themselves. It is short for **Kriegesgefangenen** which is the German word for prisoner of war.

Institut Le Rosey, commonly referred to as Le Rosey or simply Rosey, is a private boarding school in Rolle, Switzerland. Founded in 1880 by Paul-Émile Carnal on the site of the 14th-century Château du Rosey in the town of Rolle in the canton of Vaud, it is among the oldest boarding schools in Switzerland.

LMG - Light Machine Gun

LZ - Landing Zone, an area where aircraft can land.

M.R.D. Foot - Michael Richard Daniell Foot, CBE, TD (14 December 1919 – 18 February 2012) was a British political and military historian, and former British Army intelligence officer with the Special Operations Executive during the Second World War

Mantille bridge - Correct spelling Mantaille , a town approx 5 km east of Albon, France

Massif - The word "massif" means a block of mountains formed by this process, and surrounded by fault lines. Linear mountains like those on the western side of the Americas are usually not called massifs. a compact group of mountains, especially one that is separate from other groups. Origin: a compact group of mountains, especially one that is separate from other groups.

Massingham - The Massingham Mission operated from a base at Sidi Farruch on the coast 17 miles west of Algiers. It managed 357 all SOE operations into southern Europe and had a training element as well as conducting operations. The SOE complement were joined by Americans from the Office of Strategic Services.

MI – See British MI

Milice - Milice française, "French Militia," was a paramilitary group that fought against the French Resistance during World War II. The Vichy regime created the Milice in 1943 with German assistance. The Milice was a Franco-Nazi collaboration that persecuted Jews and committed executions.

Molotov Cocktail: *noun* - a crude incendiary device typically consisting of a bottle filled with flammable liquid and with a means of ignition. The production of similar grenades was organized by Vyacheslav Molotov during World War II. Usually a bottle filled with gasoline with a flaming rag in the neck of the bottle.

Montluc - Montluc prison (French pronunciation: [mɔ̃lyk]) is a former prison located on rue Jeanne Hachette in the 3rd arrondissement of Lyon, France. It was known for being an internment, torture and killing place by the Gestapo during the occupation of France by the Nazis. **(Also known as "Prison Militaire")**

NCO - A noncommissioned officer (NCO) is a military officer who is not commissioned, but instead earns their rank through promotion from enlisted ranks. NCOs are leaders in the military who supervise enlisted soldiers and help commissioned officers. Responsibilities: Training soldiers: NCOs prepare soldiers for military operations by providing education, training, and experience. Maintaining soldier skills: NCOs are responsible for ensuring soldiers are fit, professional, and have the skills they need. Advising commanders: NCOs are part of the command team and advise commanders on policy. Ranks: Sergeant: A common rank for NCOs. Corporal: A rank for NCOs.

N.E.T.D. - Non-Effective Transit Depot (Canadian Military abbreviation)

OGs - Operational Groups were small teams of US military commandos used by the Office of Strategic Services (OSS) during World War II. OGs were trained to fight behind enemy lines in uniform, and were often used to aid resistance groups. Purposes were to Gather information about enemy military efforts, Sabotage enemy assets, Aid resistance groups, Disrupt enemy lines of communication and supply, and Force the enemy to divert troops to protect themselves.

ORA - The Organisation de résistance de l'armée, O.R.A. (Fr: resistance organisation of the army) was a French paramilitary resistance organisation during the Second World War. It was created on 31 January 1943, following the November 1942 German invasion of the zone libre as a self-styled apolitical organisation bringing together former French military personnel in pursuit of active resistance against the German occupiers, but rejecting Charles de Gaulle.

OSS (Office of Strategic Services) was a US intelligence agency during World War II. It was established in 1942 to gather information and sabotage enemy nations. The OSS was led by William J. Donovan, a decorated World War I officer. The OSS was dissolved after the war, but its functions were later taken on by the CIA and other agencies. The OSS helped shorten the war and save lives in Europe, North Africa, and Asia.

"P" in P-51 stands for "Pursuit", which was a term used by the U.S. Army Air Service to designate fighter aircraft. The term came from the French phrase Avion de Chasse, which means "pursuit" or "hunt airplane". After World War II, the U.S. Air Force began using the term "fighter" and the designator "F"

Parabellum - The Pistole Parabellum or Parabellum-Pistole (Pistol Parabellum), commonly known as just the Luger or Luger P08, is a toggle-locked recoil-operated semi-automatic pistol. The Luger was produced in several models and by several nations from 1898 to 1949. The name *Parabellum*, which also featured in DWM's (see) telegraphic address, comes from the Latin phrase *Si vis pacem, para bellum*; "If you wish for peace, prepare for war."

Paramilitary - A paramilitary group is organized like an army but is not official and often not legal, connected with and helping the official armed forces: In some countries, police and firefighters have paramilitary training.

Petain - Henri Philippe Bénoni Omer Joseph Pétain (24 April 1856 – 23 July 1951), better known as Philippe Pétain and Marshal Pétain (French: *Maréchal Pétain*), was a French general who commanded the French Army in World War I and later became the head of the collaborationist regime of Vichy France, from 1940 to 1944, during World War II.

PLM - The Compagnie des chemins de fer de **P**aris à **L**yon et à la **M**éditerranée (French pronunciation: lit. 'Railway Company of Paris to Lyon and the Mediterranean'), also known as the Chemins de fer Paris-Lyon-Méditerranée or simply PLM The PLM operated chiefly in the Southeast of France, with a main line which connected Paris to the French Riviera by way of Dijon, Lyon and Marseille. The company, also the operator of railways in Algeria, established in 1857, was one of France's main railway companies until the nationalization of all French railways and establishment of the Société nationale des chemins de fer français (SNCF) on 1 January 1938.

rassemblement - The French word translates to "gathering" or "rally" in English. It can also mean "assembly" or "reunion".

1st RCP - The **1st** Parachute Chasseur Regiment (French: 1er Régiment de Chasseurs Parachutistes, 1er R.C.P) is the oldest and among the most decorated airborne forces…

Rosey - Sometimes referred to as Institut Le Rosey or Le Rosey, is a private boarding school in Rolle, Switzerland. Founded in 1880 by Paul-Émile Carnal on the site of the 14th-century Château du Rosey in the town of Rolle in the canton of Vaud, it is among the oldest boarding schools in Switzerland.

RPC - French paratroopers of the elite Regiment de Parachutistes Coloniaux (RPC) were extremely experienced, battle-hardened…

RN-7 - "La Nationale Sept" (the National 7), or "N7," was France's very own Route 66, a mythical road that defined summer for generations of people. The meandering path, about 600 miles long, snakes its way from Paris to Menton, a small town near the border with Italy. According to historian

Thierry Dubois, author of *C'Etait La Nationale 7* (Editions Paquet, 2012), Route 7 is often called the spine of France, as it connected the cold north to the sunny south, traversing the Loire Valley, crossing the Rhone River, working its way through Provence, and ending at the Riviera. The road has existed under one name or another since Roman times (you can still see ruins along the way), until it became Route Nationale 7 in 1871.

Route Napoleon - The Route Napoléon starts in Golfe Juan where the emperor landed on his return from the island of Elba on 1st March 1815 on his way to Grenoble via the Col Bayard. The 325 kilometre-long road goes through Castellane, Barrême, Digne-les-Bains, Malijai and Sisteron in the Alpes de Haute Provence. (See Map attached)

RTM - 4th RTM (**R**egiment de **T**irailleurs **M**arocain), In 1884, the 4th Regiment of Tirailleurs was created in Tunisia.

SAARF - Special Allied Airborne Reconnaissance Force

Sander of the River - The 1933 film **SANDERS RIVER** - A British District Officer in Nigeria in the 1930s rules his area strictly but justly. He struggles with gun-runners and slavers with the aid of a loyal native chief named "Bosambo".

SAO - Senior American (or Allied) Officer

SAS - Special Air Service. British Army airborne force for special operations. Special Air Service began life in July 1941, during the Second World War, from an unorthodox idea and plan by Lieutenant David Stirling (of the Scots Guards) who was serving with No. 8 (Guards) Commando. His idea was for small teams of parachute-trained soldiers to operate behind enemy lines to gain intelligence, destroy enemy aircraft, and attack their supply and reinforcement routes. Air Service name being a tie-in to a British disinformation campaign, trying to deceive the Axis into thinking there was a paratrooper regiment with numerous units operating in the area (the real SAS would "prove" to the Axis that the fake one existed).

SDECE - The Service de documentation extérieure et de contre-espionnage ("External Documentation and Counter-Espionage Service"), abbreviated SDECE (French: was France's external intelligence agency from 6 November 1944 to 2 April 1982, when it was replaced by the Directorate-General for External Security (DGSE). It should not be confused with the Deuxième Bureau which was intended to pursue purely military intelligence.

Sedentaires - Individuals who sympathized with the French Resistance but who did not take part in guerrilla warfare, often because of the lack of arms.

SFHQ - Special Forces Head Quarters

SHAEF - Supreme Headquarters Allied Expeditionary Force

Snafu – Military Slang – <u>S</u>ituation <u>N</u>ormal, <u>A</u>ll <u>F</u>ouled <u>U</u>p
(In other less polite circumstances the other commonly used "F word" is considered more appropriate)

SO - Special Operations

SOE - Special Operations Executive (SOE) was a British organisation formed in 1940 to conduct espionage, sabotage and reconnaissance in German-occupied Europe and to aid local resistance movements during World War II. SOE was a

British military organisation that was directed from London. It parachuted more than four hundred agents into Occupied France to establish escape routes, co-ordinate acts of sabotage, set up radio communications and supply materials and armaments for French groups. Active - 22 July 1940 – 15 January 1946.

SPOC - G-3 Special Project Operations Center, joint British-American organization in Algiers established to conduct operation in France

Stalag Luft - was a German World War II prisoner-of-war (POW) camp system that held Allied airmen. The camps were operated by the Luftwaffe. Stammlager Luft (literally "Main Camp, Air") was Luftwaffe nomenclature for a POW camp. While the camp initially held only POWs who were officers, it was not known by the usual terms for such camps – Offizier Lager or Oflag. Later camp expansions added compounds for non-commissioned officers (NCOs).

Sten - (or Sten gun) is a British submachine gun chambered in 9×19mm which was used extensively by British and Commonwealth forces throughout World War II. The Sten gun, while effective in close-quarters combat due to its high rate of fire, was generally considered not a "good" gun due to its reputation for unreliability, often jamming, and being prone to accidental discharges, primarily because of its simple design and sometimes poor build quality, particularly in earlier models; however, later versions saw improvements and were considered more reliable by some soldiers, especially when used in close-range situations.

STO - The Service du travail obligatoire (STO; lit. 'compulsory work service') was the forced enlistment and deportation of hundreds of thousands of French workers to Nazi Germany to work as forced labour for the German war effort during World War II. The STO was created under laws and regulations of Vichy France,[1] but it was used by Nazi Germany to compensate for its loss of manpower as it enlisted more and more soldiers for the Eastern Front. The German government promised that for every three French workers sent it would release one French prisoner of war (POW). Those requisitioned under the STO were accommodated in work camps on German soil.

STS - Special Training Schools The training establishments, and properties used by country sections, were designated by Arabic numbers and were widely distributed.[59] The initial training centres of SOE were at country houses such as Wanborough Manor, Guildford. Agents destined to serve in the field underwent commando training at Arisaig in Scotland, where they were taught armed and unarmed combat skills by William E. Fairbairn and Eric A. Sykes, former Inspectors in the Shanghai .

Tempo - World War II Temporary Buildings - The Main Navy and Munitions Buildings were constructed in 1918 along Constitution Avenue (then known as B Street) on Washington, D.C.'s National Mall (Potomac Park) as the largest of a set of temporary war buildings on the National Mall. Both buildings were constructed by the Navy's Bureau of Yards and Docks, with the United States Department of War occupying the Munitions Building. To make the buildings more resistant to fire, the buildings were constructed using concrete. With solid construction, the temporary buildings remained used long after the end of World War I.

Thivollet - Nom de guerre of Narcisse Geyer, leader of the
Thîvollet Maquis, which was a group of armed French
Resistance fighters during World War II. The Maquis were a
network of small groups of armed men and women who
fought in guerrilla warfare. The word "maquis" comes from
the Corsican word for dry scrub, which was the cover the
Maquis used. (One of the most beautiful wooded hills in the
Drôme des Collines area, dominated by oaks, hornbeams and
chestnut trees. Wetland providing a natural habitat of great
ecological interest.)

Tirailleurs - Skirmishers

Tireurs - Shooters

UNR - The **Union for the New Republic** (French: *L'Union
pour la nouvelle République*, pronounced UNR) was
a Gaullist political party in France, formed in support
of Charles de Gaulle in the 1958 elections.

Vichy France - (French: *Régime de Vichy*, lit. '**Vichy regime**';
10 July 1940 – 9 August 1944), officially the **French State**
(*État français*), was a French rump state headed by Marshal
Philippe Pétain during World War II, established after the
French capitulation after the defeat against Germany. It was
named after its seat of government, the city of Vichy.
Officially independent, but with half of its territory occupied
under the harsh terms of the 1940 armistice with Nazi
Germany, it adopted a policy of collaboration. Though Paris
was nominally its capital, the government established itself in
the resort town of Vichy in the unoccupied "free zone" , where
it remained responsible for the civil administration of France
as well as its colonies. The occupation of France by
Germany at first affected only the northern and western

portions of the country. In November 1942, the Allies occupied the French North Africa, and in response the Germans and Italians occupied the entire Metropolitan France, ending any pretence of independence by the Vichy government.

Vosages Mountains - (Vosges Mountains) A mountain range in eastern France, near the German border

W/T - Wireless telegraphy or telephony, an early term for radio communications. Radiotelegraphy was used for long-distance person-to-person commercial, diplomatic, and military text communication throughout the first half of the 20th century. It became a strategically important capability during the two world wars

WAC - stands for Women's Army Corps, the branch of the U.S. Army that served during World War II. The WAC was created in 1943 when Congress changed the name of the Women's Army Auxiliary Corps (WAAC).

Waffen SS - was the combat branch of the Nazi Party's paramilitary *Schutzstaffel* (SS) organisation During the Nuremberg trials, the defenders of the *Waffen-SS*, including former SS general Paul Hausser, claimed that it was a purely military organisation no different from the *Wehrmacht*. The prosecution at Nuremberg rejected that assertion and successfully argued that the *Waffen-SS* was an integral part of the SS apparatus. The tribunal found that "the units of the *Waffen-SS* were directly involved in the killings of the prisoners of war and the atrocities in the occupied countries" and judged the entire SS to be a criminal organisation.

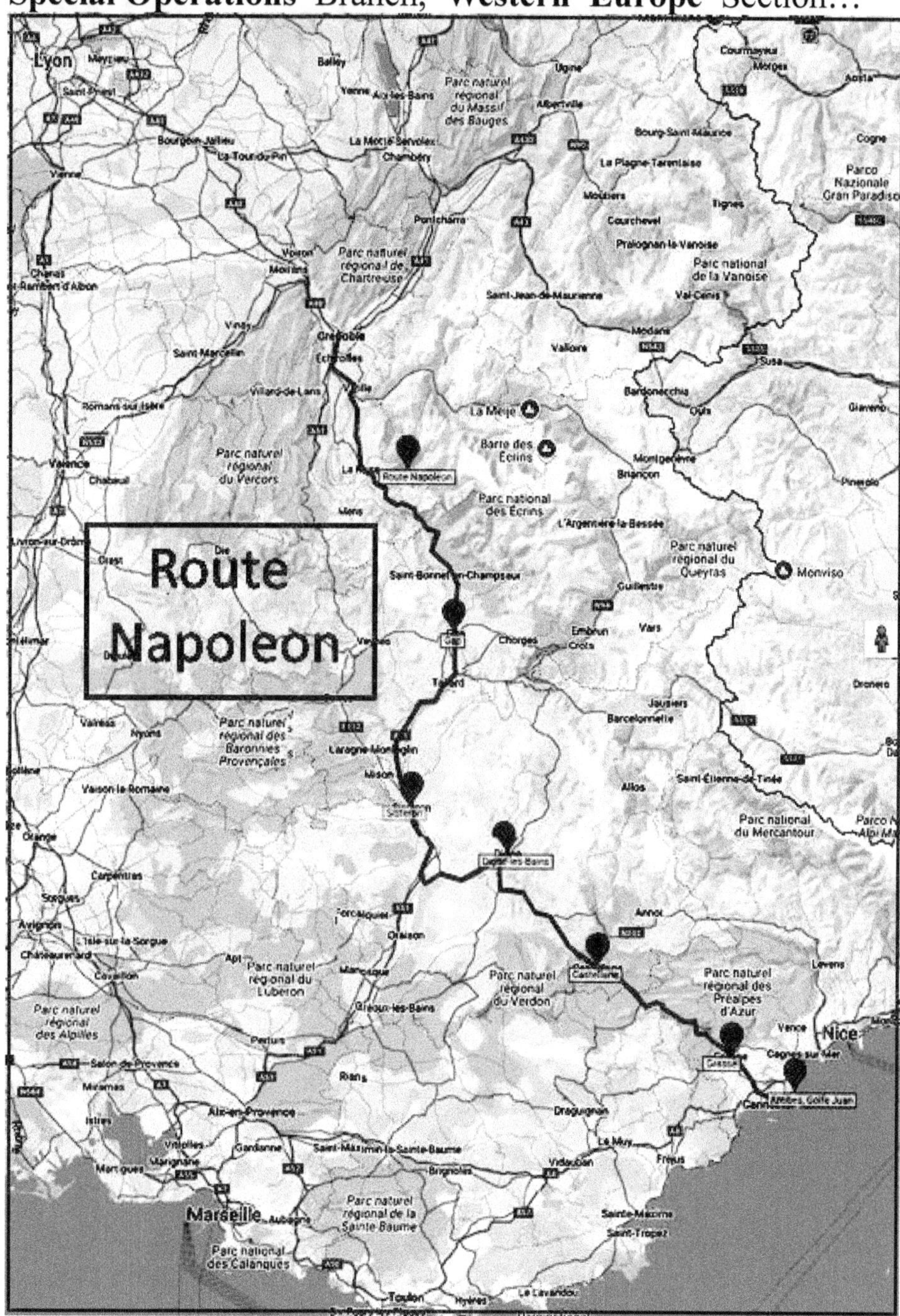

(Thanks to Google, Wikipedia, and OpenStreetMap.com)

END NOTE – Additional Video Information

Eisenhower's Guerrillas: The Jedburghs and the Liberation of France - <https://www.youtube.com/watch?v=R-JPM2QJDEQ>

CIA Declassified Files - Operation Jedburgh : WWII's Covert Allied Operations - <https://www.youtube.com/watch?v=IhmiYF9WpsI>

The Jedburghs - <https://www.youtube.com/watch?v=2mIqLElqgqE>

OSS Training at Catoctin Mountain: America's First School for Spies - <https://www.youtube.com/watch?v=QdOpjn8_8kk>

OSS Recruits at Training Area B – <https://www.youtube.com/watch?v=0ojkF0RVGbQ>

OSS "House of Horrors"Training - <https://www.youtube.com/watch?v=5Yp8ZrirsLc>

OSS Gutter Fighting Training - <https://www.youtube.com/results?search_query=oss+training>

OSS Railroad Sabotage Training - <https://www.youtube.com/watch?v=RcsorqnsbRU>

Undercover / Spy Training Film - <https://www.youtube.com/watch?v=TcPE9VyrP8s&list=PLWVp52wHfhX05ELR7JLMt-eenLCbzB4J&index=1>

OSS Final Exam at Catoctin -
<https://www.youtube.com/watch?v=KQGfWllyGZg>

Forgotten History: Vercors - the Climactic Battle of the French Resistance – <https://www.youtube.com/watch?v=dsvA0UkdRuw>

The Secret Unit They Were Afraid to Release in WW2 – (Jed Team Frederick) - <https://www.youtube.com/watch?v=d8bjYn5mPt4>

RAF Shipdham, USAAF Station 115 - The Airfield & History of the 44th Bomb Group - <https://www.youtube.com/watch?v=Z1HYlR2UTCg>

"LIBERATORS OVER EUROPE" B-24 44th BOMBARDMENT GROUP / 8TH AIR FORCE WWII COMBAT FILM XD12064 - <https://www.youtube.com/watch?v=oGo9PBlkw4Q>

44th Bomb Group Original Footage (RAF Shipdham) - <https://www.youtube.com/watch?v=8JHW8wcjoAg>

WWII Combat Footage - "The Mission" B-24s in the ETO (44th Bomb Group) - <https://www.youtube.com/watch?v=Vxwppdd4Kns>

Photo Credits

Cover - Author's collection. Found in U.S. A.F Academy
     archives by Joe deFrancesco, former Jed
Cadet Manierre - Author's collection
Graduation March – Author's collection, Herald Record
     American, courtesy of the Harry Ransom Center
Air Corps training – Author's collection
Map Camp Mackall– Openstreetmap.org
Division HQ, Camp Mackall – post card, courtesy of Owner -
     Oldtonewtreasures (ebay)
Col. Linquist – Wikipedia
Bldg K - Wikipedia, National Archives
Locations OSS Training – https://www.nps.gov/parkhistory
     online_books/oss/illustrations.pdf
Area F – Congressional CC - https://arsof-history.org/
Col. Obolensky – SOFREP National Archives (U.S. Archives)
William Fairbairn, Hans Tofte -
-https://www.nps.gov/parkhistory/online_books/oss/illustratio
ns.pdf
Trainazium – OSS Training film
Pistol training - https://www.nps.gov/parkhistory/online_
     books/oss/illustrations.pdf
Rifle Range -https://www.nps.gov/parkhistory/online_
     books/oss/illustrations.pdf
Parachute – collection of author
Cabins, Area B – OSS Records, National Archives
Map Quantico – Openstreetmap
Explosion – National Park Service (.gov)
Hotel Mayflower - Harris & Ewing, photographer (wikimedia)
Interrogation - https://www.nps.gov/parkhistory/online
SS Marina - (C1-A class Cargo ship - U.S. Navy - U.S. Navy
     photo from Navsource.org
Map Scotland - Openstreetmap
Map England - Openstreetmap

Map London - Openstreetmap
OSS HQ (today)– courtesy of Pat DiGeorge,
    LibertyLadybook.com
Glaschoille House - Jamie Lindsay -
    https://www.glaschoille.co.uk/
Map – Locations Glaschoille and Arisaig Houses –
    Openstreetmap
Map – Greenock Harbor -
    https://www.oldemaps.co.uk/greenock-map.htm
Photo - Queen Elizabeth– https://earlofcruise.blogspot.com/
Photo – Hod Fuller - Craig Robertson
    <webmaster@specialforcesroh.com> (source unknown)
Photo - Arisaig House -
    https://en.wikipedia.org/wiki/Arisaig#/
William "Dangerous Dan" Fairbairn - courtesy of Lynn Philip
    Hodgson
Railroad Sabotage Arisaig – https://arsof-history.org/
Map Arisaig House – Openstreetmap.org
Milton Hall – Courtesy of Tony Mills (National Archives)
Map Milton Hall - Openstreetmap
Milton Hall – Lecture on demolition - https://arsof-history.org/
Milton Hall Bar – source unknown
Jed Team Frederick – Jed Team Album
Capetown Castle – courtesy of Chris Isaac -
    www.bandcstaffregister.com/
Map Algiers – Openstreetmap.org
OSS Headquarters Algeria – source unknown
Photo - Pop, McIntosh, Gennerich in Algeria – collection of
    author
Blida Airbase - Le Guay, Laurence Craddock, Public Domain,
    (copyright expired)
Photo Lucien Durocher - From an Ottawa Newspaper (likely
    the Ottawa Journal - February 1945)

Photo – Lucien Durocher's armbands -
https://www.campx.ca/luciendurocher.html
Map Operation Gauntlet – Wikipedia, OpenStreetMap,
Photo Empress of Canada – wikipedia
Norwegian rescue - National Museum of the U.S. Navy
Photo - Sappers burning coal-Wikipedia - (photograph: war
correspondent Ross Munro)
Code training – OSS Training in National Parks – John
Whiteclay Chambers - National Archives
Summary of Radio Op duties – Durocher OSS file
Photo – Short Stirling - Wikipedia
Interior Stirling - permission requested 6/2/24 – pending
Jed Team Dodge – Jed Team Album
RAF Halifax - Wikipedia
Photo – "Joe Hole" -
https://www.pacaf.af.mil/Portals/6/documents/
Photo DZ Tarsis – Google Earth
Map - Drop Zone "Tarsis" - Openstreetmap.org
Jed Team Veganine – Jed Teams Album
Photo - Hermine -
https://www.ordredelaliberation.fr/fr/compagnons/jean-
drouot-lhermine
Photo - Vercors - Wikimedia
Col Joseph - https://www.vercors-resistance.fr/en/the-
resistant-vercors/
Major Noir - mussee de resistance en ligne
Photos of Pop at Les Granges – photos by Andre Gamet,
Collection of Benoit Senne
Photo - Frances Cammaerts "Roger" –
museedelaresistanceenligne.org/
Map of Jockey Area of Ops - Wikipedia
Cammaerts Letter – Collection of Author
Major Noir - museedelaresistanceenligne.org/

Photo - Cammaerts, Charles-Andre Lahmery ("Bozambo") –
     https://www.memoire-drome.com/
Photo – Marker Bozambo Maquis. Courtesy of Benoit Senne
Photo - "l'Hermine" - museedelaresistanceenligne.org/
Photo - Henri Zeller "Col. Joseph" -
     museedelaresistanceenligne.org/
"Collines-du-Nord-de-la-Drome" -
     https://museedelaresistanceenligne.org/
Cover magazine "AUX ARMES!" gift from Benoit Senne
La Legend BOZAMBO, from AUX ARMES - magazine
Photos pages 141, 142, 147, 149, 152 – AUX ARMES! -
     magazine
Map - Beaumont-Monteux Power Plant – Openstreetmap.org
Power Plant – aerial photo -
     https://museedelaresistanceenligne.org/
Power Plant Entrance – Google Maps
Turbine room -
www.flickr.com/photos/mediathequesvalenceromansagglo/34
554062842/in/dateposted/

www.flickr.com/photos/mediathequesvalenceromansagglo/
     33873500754/in/photostream/
     www.creativecommons.org/licenses/by/2.0.
B-17s dropping cannisters – Wikimedia - (This image or file is
a work of a U.S. Air Force Airman or employee, taken or
made as part of that person's official duties. As a work of
the U.S. federal government, the image or file is in the public
domain in the United States.)
Loading canisters - https://resistancefrancaise.blogspot.com
Collecting canisters - Parachute drop. (Source: Photo by
Raymond Perrillat.   https://www.cheminsdememoire.gouv.fr/
Pop demo Colt 45 – photo by Andre Gamet,
     https://www.lyoncapitale.fr/culture/expo-le-bleu-du-
     ciel-en-noir-et-blanc

Bridge near St. Vallier – Google Maps

French Rail Charge -
    http://casquerougealevres.free.fr/punbb/viewtopic.php?
    id=321

Photo - Demo RR tracks -
https://resistancefrancaise.blogspot.com/2012/12/photos-du-
    maquis-1944.html

Maquis mining tracks -

Destroyed bridge-
    https://x.com/CIA/status/1108798201144983557

Firefight – Cover Time-Life book THE RESISTANCE,

Bridge near Serves-sur-Rhone – Google Earth

Map of Bridges near Serves-sur-Rhone – Openstreetmap.org

Jed Team Veganin - Jedburgh Teams Album

Memorial to Sgt. Gardener – Gerald Rix

Map Albon – Open streetMap

Map Gestapo HQ – OpenStreetMap

Gestapo HQ - Bibliothèque nationale de France (BnF) -
    (public domain)

Prison Militaire - Lyon Capitale / Florent Deligia

RR Boxcar – National Museum of the US Air Force

Map Oberursel – OpenStreetMap

POWs Arriving Dulag-Luft – Merkki.com

POWs -Train – www.merkki.com

Map - Openstreetmap

Dulag-Luft - www.merkki.com

Dulag-Luft – Merkki.com

POWs marching through Barth - www.merkki.com

POWs arriving Stalag Luft 1 -   "

Stalag-Luft 1 – Merkki.com,

Prison ID card - collection of author

Drawing of North3 compound, Stalag-Luft 1 - merkki.com

Roll call – Merkki.com

Copy of watercolor by Col. Ross Greening, Originally published in *Not as Briefed* by Col. C. Ross Greening and Brown & Bigelow, St Paul, MN, n.d., and reprinted in *Not as Briefed: From the Doolittle Raid to a German Stalag*, by Col. C. Ross Greening, compiled and edited by Karen Morgan Driscoll, WSU Press, 2001. Used with permission.

Boxing match – ZEMKE'S STALAG

Father Charlton – Merkki.com

Certificate of Baptism – Collection of Author

Picture of check – Collection of author

Uncle Will to shower – Merkki.com

Map Shipden – Openstreetmap,

Shipden Airbase – Wikipedia

Photo - Passion Pit crew – Merkki.com

Passion Pit shot down – Collection of author

Map Missions 8/13/44 - www.americanairmuseum.com/

(Original map now in the collection of the Museum of the US
      Air Force, Dayton, Ohio.)

B-24s flying through flak bursts -
      https://www.worldwarphotos.info/

B-24 Bomb bay – Collection of author

Map of Barth, Germany – Openstreetmap.com

Roger Bushell, Guards - Copyright: Pegasus Archive

Guards - Copyright: Pegasus Archive

Oblt. Glemnitz - Copyright: Pegasus Archive

Photo – Warning wire - Copyright: Pegasus Archive

Photo - North2 compound – Merkki.com

Guard box - Merkki.com

Photo - Rollcall -
https://www.pegasusarchive.org/pow/cSL_1_History1.htm)

Drawing of North 3 compound - Merkki.com

Barracks room - Pegasus Archive

Col. Zemke - (Reprint courtesy of AIR & SPACE FORCES
      Magazine - Published April 1995.)

Col. Gabreski - Wikipedia
Gabreski Letter - Author's collection
Barth Airdrome – Dick Terrell, Merkki.com
B-17 – Merkki.com
Map route from Barth – Openstreetmap.org
Ruhr destruction - Merkki.com
B-17s landing – Dick Terrell, merkki.com
POWs arrive Camp Lucky Strike – merkki.com
Camp Lucky Strike - Photo by Jim "Pee Wee" Martin -
	G Company / 3rd Battalion / 506th PIR / 101st Airborne
	Division 1942-1945.
	(https://creativecommons.org/licenses/by/2.0/)
Jockey Club – Google maps
Pass for Paris Area – collection of author
Hotel Francia – Google maps
Abbey of St. Ouen – Google Maps
Photo of Gen. Vanndenberg presenting Bronze Star - author's
	collection
Abbey – Front - Collection of Author, Joe Chiffriller
Medals - Author's collection
Photo - Point-to-point, On Uncle Pierre – author's collection